CAPITAL IDEAS EVOLVING

Books by Peter L. Bernstein

CAPITAL IDEAS EVOLVING

PETER L. BERNSTEIN

JOHN WILEY & SONS, INC.

Published by John Wiley & Sons, Inc., Hoboken, New Jersey.
Published simultaneously in Canada.

Wiley Bicentennial Logo: Richard J. Pacifico.

For general information on our other products and services or for technical support, please
contact our Customer Care Department within the United States at (800) 762-2974,
outside the United States at (317) 572-3993 or fax (317) 572-4002.

Wiley also publishes its books in a variety of electronic formats. Some content that appears
in print may not be available in electronic books. For more information about Wiley
products, visit our web site at www.wiley.com.

Library of Congress Cataloging-in-Publication Data:

Bernstein, Peter L.
    Capital ideas evolving / Peter L. Bernstein.
        p. cm.
    Includes bibliographical references and index.
      ISBN 978-0-471-73173-3 (cloth)
  1. Finance. 2. Investments. I. Title.
      HG173.B473   2007
      658.15—dc22

                            2006102237

Printed in the United States of America.

10 9 8 7 6 5 4 3 2 1

For Barbara
With love, gratitude, and cheers

Contents

Preface

Theorists can always resist facts; for facts are hard to establish and are always changing anyway, and ceteris paribus can be made to absorb a good deal of punishment. Inevitably, at the earliest opportunity, the mind slips back into the old grooves of thought since analysis is utterly impossible without a frame of reference, a way of thinking about things, or, in short, a theory.

Paul A. Samuelson, "Lord Keynes and the General Theory,"
Economica 14 (1946), pp. 187–199

We make models to abstract reality. But there is a meta-model beyond the model that assures us that the model will eventually fail. Models fail because they fail to incorporate the inter-relationships that exist in the real world.

Myron Scholes, speech at NYU/IXIS conference
on hedge funds, New York, September 2005

The revolution in the theory and practice of investing that swept over Wall Street during the last three decades of the twentieth century had been carried out by scholars toiling in the ivory towers, far away from the heart of the financial world in New York City. Hence, the improbable origins of modern Wall Street, the subtitle of *Capital Ideas,* the book I published in 1992 and the prequel to the book you are now reading.

But the products of those improbable origins have been evolving for over three decades. Today, the concepts described in *Capital Ideas* are conventional wisdom, from Wall Street to financial centers all around the world. Beginning with the simple notion that risk is at the center of all investment decisions, that diversification is essential to successful investing, and that markets are hard to beat, the Capital Ideas—the products of the ivory towers (and also known as "neoclassical finance")—are now the intellectual core of a myriad of powerful innovations in active investing and in risk management.

These innovations involve concepts and tools no one could have conceived of in the old days. When I originally wrote *Capital Ideas* from 1989 to 1991, the fascination was with the wonders of passive management and the disturbing implications of the efficient market. Today, as we shall see in the pages that follow, even the theorists of *Capital Ideas* are at work in the capital market. Some are seeking new methods of active management and searching for alpha while others are applying their theoretical ideas to the problems of financing retirement or enhancing the fairness and efficiency of the markets.* All, in one way or another, are exploring the frontiers of risk management.

As Capital Ideas have moved down these paths from the ivory tower to the computer room, both form and function continue to undergo radical changes. This process of change is what this book, *Capital Ideas Evolving,* is about.

Consider the contrast between today's world and when I was writing *Capital Ideas* from 1989 to 1991. Much of the theory was unpalatable to an investing environment where people saw no hurdle in beating the market, never calibrated risk, and valued options on the back of an envelope. The initial response of many investors to the introduction of these uncomfortable and mathematically rooted theories in the 1970s and 1980s was to reject them as "baloney." Risk was an incidental matter. In *A Random Walk Down Wall Street,* Burt Malkiel has recalled that the reception of Efficient Market Theory "was greeted in some Wall Street quarters with as much enthusiasm as Saddam Hussein addressing a meeting of B'nai Brith." Burt informs me the ninth edition of *A Random Walk Down Wall Street* shifts the metaphor to "with as much enthusiasm as Jeff Skilling addressing the Better Business Bureau."

Nevertheless, I wanted my book to include some examples of practical applications of the Capital Ideas I was describing, in order to make

---

* "Alpha" refers to returns in excess of the returns of a benchmark such as the S&P 500, after adjustment for risk. Subsequent chapters expand upon this compressed explanation.

these theoretical advances credible to the wider audience I hoped to reach. After a good deal of scrounging around, I could come up with only three actual, hands-on cases of putting the new theoretical structure to work. There was nobody else I could find at that moment.

The first practical example was Wells Fargo Bank, where many of the creators of Capital Ideas were helping out as consultants. But Wells Fargo was struggling to find customers for its index funds and risk-controlled asset management—and it made no money at it for a matter of years. I will always remember Jim Vertin telling me about "pushin' that rock uphill." Nevertheless, as I asserted in *Capital Ideas*, "It was they who truly brought the gown to town." Chapter 10 of this book shows how well time has justified that observation.

The second case study was Barr Rosenberg. Barr, then still an academic, was developing what was probably the first viable variation on the theme of the Capital Asset Pricing Model in the form of factor analysis, but he was also carrying out hugely popular seminars at Pebble Beach to indoctrinate practitioners in the intricacies of market efficiency, mean/variance, the Capital Asset Pricing Model, and the theory of options pricing. Without Barr's powerful effort, the whole process of making Capital Ideas both comprehensible and acceptable to professional investors would surely have been more protracted. He deserves far more credit than he has received for these accomplishments.

Portfolio insurance was the third example of applying theory to practice. Hayne Leland of the University of California at Berkeley had concocted this product when he went on a search for what he boldly described to me as "the ultimate invention"—a real-life version of Merton's replicating portfolio for a put option on the market.* For a brief period, as portfolio insurance became all the rage, it looked as though Leland had achieved his dream. Then came the jumbo crash of October 19, 1987, when stock prices fell over 20 percent in one day, and portfolio insurance crashed along with the market.

But that was then. In contrast to *Capital Ideas,* this book is almost completely about the implementation of theory and only incidentally about the development of new theory.

---

*Just incidentally, in relation to how transactions costs on October 19 nearly buried portfolio insurance, Bob Merton has pointed out to me the wonderful paradox that there would be no Black-Scholes-Merton option pricing model without transactions costs. Transactions costs make the replicating portfolio impractical and options irreplaceable.

It is interesting to note that this process is not unique to finance. E. Han Kim of the Ross School of Business at the University of Michigan and two colleagues recently authored a study of papers published in major economics journals over the last thirty-five years that had received more than 500 citations as of June 2006.[1] In reviewing the content of these papers, Kim and his coauthors find that "In the early 1970s, 77 percent of the most highly cited papers were theoretical, while only 11 percent [were] empirical. At the end of the century, 60 percent are empirical and only 11 percent theoretical. . . . [The balance of] the contributions are econometric methodological contributions."

What has caused this profound change from a focus on theory to a focus on implementation? Although more subtle forces must also have been at work, the arrival of the desktop computer stands out as the most important contributor, along with the increasingly complex software it can handle. The computer provides opportunities to do handsprings with the data and to test out theories from perspectives never dreamed of in the world of slide rules and electric calculators. On the other hand, the process does not work in reverse. While scholars and practitioners can use the computer to test theories and to find new ways to put theories to use, new theories do not come out of the computer. Theory is a product of the human brain.

Over the years since *Capital Ideas* first appeared, the unquenchable vitality of these ideas has been too great to resist. Powerful forces are constantly at work in the markets to bring the resemblance between theory and reality closer with the passage of time. Indeed, the ideas have created a new world in their own image. Even the greatest skeptics of this body of knowledge now key off their opposition, both theoretical and practical, from the foundations of the improbable origins of modern Wall Street.

Bill Sharpe once said that "Markowitz came along, and there was light."[2] Before Harry Markowitz's 1952 essay on portfolio selection, there was no genuine *theory* of portfolio construction—there were just rules of thumb and folklore. It was Markowitz who first made risk the centerpiece of portfolio management by focusing on what investing is all about: *investing is a bet on an unknown future*. Before Bill Sharpe's articulation of the Capital Asset Pricing Model in 1964, there was no genuine *theory* of asset pricing in which risk plays a pivotal role—there were just rules of thumb and folklore. Before Franco Modigliani and Merton Miller's work in 1958, there was no genuine *theory* of corporate finance and no understanding of what "equilibrium" means in financial markets—there were just rules of thumb and folklore.[3] Before Eugene Fama set forth the principles of the Efficient Market Hypothesis in 1965, there was no *theory* to explain why the market is so hard to beat. There was not even a recognition that such a possibility might exist. Before Fischer Black, Myron Scholes, and Robert Merton confronted both the valuation and the essential nature of derivative securities in the early 1970s, there was no *theory* of option pricing—there were just rules of thumb and folklore.

The practice of investing that prevailed before Markowitz wrote "Portfolio Selection" in 1952 has vanished. The investors of 1952 thought the same thoughts and talked the same language as the investors of 1873, although the active topics of conversation may have changed from concerns about deflation to worries about inflation. The revolution unleashed by Capital Ideas created an entirely new way of thinking about the nature of financial markets, the theory of investing, and the role of an uncertain future in all investment decisions. Paul Samuelson has used colorful language to describe this process: "Markowitz-Sharpe-Tobin quadratic programming in terms of portfolio means and variances is a powerful approximation that has captured real-world converts the way that smallpox used to infect once-isolated aborigines."[4]

Risk was at the core of all these ideas. Markowitz's famous comment that "you have to think about risk as well as return" sounds like a homey slogan today. Yet it was a total novelty in 1952 to give risk at least equal weight with the search for reward. *Nothing more deeply divides Capital Ideas from the world before 1952.* Modigliani and Miller soon followed suit by pointing out that changing the liability structure of a corporation does not matter because the value of the corporation depends on the riskiness of its business; shuffling the liabilities only influences how the risk is parceled up among the stakeholders. The Capital Asset Pricing Model says that the expected return on assets will be a function of their risk, or beta, while the definition of the Efficient Market is a market where the predictions of CAPM are borne out. And hedging risk was one of the prime motivations for the development of the options pricing model.

Every chapter that follows, in one way or another, is about managing risks of many varieties. The protagonists in the story are smart at finding ways to make money, but, as we shall see, all of them are aware that risk management is the key to success in the search for excess returns.

Why is this point about risk so vital, at the core of everything to do with investing? Is it just because decisions in finance are always confronted by uncertainty? That is no answer. All decisions about anything are confronted by uncertainty. The true answer to this question is more illuminating.

In the old days, when most economic activity consisted of hunting, fishing, and agriculture, the weather was the only source of economic uncertainty. You cannot do anything about the weather. Consequently, people depended on prayer and incantation, in one form or another, as the only available form of risk management. What other approach could you take when everything seemed to be God's will or the will of the Fates?

As we move toward modern times, nature has declining importance. What takes its place? I would seek the answer to that question in the words of the mathematician John von Neumann, who developed the theory of games of strategy (as opposed to games of chance) during the 1920s and 1930s. The most significant insight in game theory was to recognize that men and women are not Robinson Crusoes—each individual isolated from all other individuals. Failure to keep this distinction in mind is the primary reason the techniques and concepts of the natural sciences so often lead the social scientists astray.

Before von Neumann, decision theory visualized each individual making choices that had no effect on any other individual's range of choices. They all calculated utilities in the privacy of their own room. That is an artificial concept. No man is an island. As von Neumann and his coauthor Oskar Morgenstern point out, in emphasizing the difference between a real economy and a Robinson Crusoe economy:

> Crusoe is confronted with a formal problem quite different from the one a participant in a social economy faces. . . . [Crusoe] controls all the variables exclusively . . . to obtain maximum resulting satisfac-

tion. . . . In order to bring [the rules of the game] into *the sphere of combat and competition* . . . it is necessary to consider n-person games with n ≥ 2 and thereby sacrifice the simple maximum aspect of the problem [emphasis added].[5]

All economic systems, even the most primitive, depend on production and technology, but capitalism is about combat and competition—about buying and selling even more than it is about production and technology. Capitalism is a giant von Neumann game! Buying and selling means human decisions: What will the customer decide? What will the supplier decide? What will the employee decide? What will the politicians decide? What will other investors decide? The process is intensively interactive. The enemy is us.

The decisions that each of us makes as we ask ourselves these questions will in turn have an influence on how customers, suppliers, employees, politicians, and investors will make their choices in response to ours. In the end, the value of your portfolio is not what somebody tells you is likely to happen over the long run but how much other investors out there are going to be willing to pay you for your assets.

Game theory teaches us that human beings create a complex jumble of uncertainties for one another. It is not enough to say that human nature never changes and let it go at that. Human beings learn from experience and learn from technology. Evolution, in one form or another, is always at work. Yesterday's response to a given set of circumstances is only a hint of what tomorrow's response to that set of circumstances will be—and in any case Leibniz reminds us that today's circumstances will reappear tomorrow, not precisely, but only for the most part.

So we really do not know what the future holds. Risk in our world is nothing more than uncertainty about the decisions that other human beings are going to make and how we can best respond to those decisions.

The basic concepts of Capital Ideas developed between 1952 and 1973 have survived through changes in the world of finance that have been pervasive, rapid, bewildering—and fascinating. These changes have ranged from the black years of the inflationary 1970s to the great bull market that got under way in the early 1980s, and from the small bubble that led to the crash of October 1987 to the soaring high-tech bubble that led to the crash of 2000. There have been revolutions in communication and in globalization, with new financial instruments and new players on the world scene unimaginable to investors of the 1970s or 1980s.

While all this was going on, the attacks on the body of thought in *Capital Ideas* have been fierce, brilliant, incessant, varied, significant, and immensely influential in the practice of investment management. The borders between gown and town, once so clearly drawn, have blurred to a point where the distinction between a business school professor or an engineer and a denizen of Wall Street is now often difficult to make.

When *Capital Ideas* was published in 1992, I could refer to the markets of that time as "dazzling creations," but the size, range, and impact of financial markets on all aspects of economic activity have exploded everywhere. Indeed, economic globalization would have been unthinkable without markets that led the way toward a plethora of novel and complex forms of financial instruments for the transfer of capital and the management of new exposures to risk. Market prices themselves are not shaped only by information; they convey information from informed to uninformed investors—and sometimes vice versa, just to make life more complicated.

As a consequence, the flow of information that was already rising in the early 1990s has turned into a torrent of fact and fiction assailing all of us around the clock. The computer, still a clumsy and primitive aid to most investors and business managers when I wrote the original edition of this book, is now central to the world of business and finance.* The computer has altered communication, calculations, investment portfolio decisions, and the management of risk in ways no one could have dreamed of as recently as twenty years ago.† Perhaps most important, the crazy bubble of the late 1990s and its disastrous aftermath have led many observers to raise questions about the assumptions of rationality on which the whole edifice of *Capital Ideas* was built.

---

*The manuscript was written on a DOS-based computer and is no longer available to me in that format.

†Talk about surpassing dreams. A *Wall Street Journal* article of July 27, 2006, reports that Marshall Wace, an investment advisory, has developed a computer model that received 500,000 trading ideas from 246 securities firms in 2005.

Despite all this turmoil, the applications of Capital Ideas have developed into orthodox operating procedures in the daily management of investment portfolios and trading activity in the financial markets all around the globe. The centrality of the trade-off between risk and expected return infuses all investment decisions. The notion that the market is hard to beat is conventional wisdom, even among those who declare they know how to outperform. The principles of corporate finance have undergone important changes; indeed, Modigliani–Miller's bold concepts may have had a greater impact on the bubble of the 1990s and its aftermath than many observers realize. Alpha and beta—once upon a time the unpalatable language of the Capital Asset Pricing Model—have become critical ingredients of the most sophisticated forms of portfolio management and investment performance measurement. New portfolio structures, most notably in the form of hedge funds and the increasing acceptance of short-selling, are increasingly important, but all of them have deep roots in Capital Ideas.

Finally, the proliferation of products, strategies, and innovation stemming from the options pricing model—what Eugene Fama has called "the biggest idea in economics of the century"—has been explosive, and may still have a long way to go.[6] As just one example, the total notional amount of derivatives outstanding at the end of 2006 was $370 trillion, a number to make one's head spin.[*]

The book begins by facing up front the attack on Capital Ideas by the proponents of Behavioral Finance—and especially on the idea of the Efficient Market Hypothesis. The next chapter describes the current views of Paul Samuelson, one of the great sages about market behavior and portfolio formation. Samuelson takes a dim view of efforts to outperform the returns of the market as a whole or, in a more practical sense, to outperform mutual funds indexed to some primary benchmark like the S&P 500.

Later pages offer the views of other well-known academics, all of whom, in one way or another, are involved in developing practical applications for the core ideas of finance theory in new and exciting

---

[*] Cited in International Strategy & Investment Group's publication, *ISI Reports*, December 11, 2006.

formats. We then turn to a series of chapters that relate the startling success of a few institutional investors, and we shall see how every one of those investors developed their strategies from a base composed of the principles of Capital Ideas.

That is just the beginning. It may sound ironic, but as investors increasingly draw on Capital Ideas to shape their strategies, to innovate new financial instruments, and to motivate the drive for higher returns in relation to risk, the real world itself is on a path toward an increasing resemblance to the theoretical world described in *Capital Ideas*. Subsequent pages repeat that observation on more than a few occasions. Baloney those ideas were not.

Perhaps the most remarkable feature of these ideas is the indomitable power of their influence on investment decisions, even though the theories failed to survive a battery of empirical testing. The situation is identical to what Louis Menand, the Pulitzer Prize-winning professor of English and American literature and language, had to say about Freud's *Civilization and Its Discontents*:

> The grounds have entirely eroded for whatever authority it once enjoyed as an ultimate account of the way things are, but we can no longer understand the way things are without taking it into account.[7]

The academic creators of these models were not taken by surprise by difficulties with empirical testing. The underlying assumptions are artificial in many instances, which means their straightforward application to the solution of real-time investment problems is often impossible. The academics knew as well as anyone that the real world is different from what they were defining. But they were in search of a deeper and more systematic understanding of how markets work, of how investors interact with one another, and of the dominant role of risk in the whole process of investing. They were well aware that their theories were not a finished work. They were building a jumping-off point, a beginning of exploration, and, as each step led to the next, they began the search for an integrated structure to simultaneously explain the performance of markets and to solve the investor's dilemma in trading off risk against return. That structure is still evolving.

As with all great revolutions, the passage of time has produced unanticipated variations in the basic themes, both theoretical and practical. Time has also brought periods of disillusion and efforts to mount a counterrevolution. The overarching assumption of investor rationality in every one of these Capital Ideas was admittedly an unrealistic one, but its fault lines are all too visible in markets given to high volatility, to bubbles and crashes, to concentration on short-term developments, and to shocking inconsistencies in the uses of information. We cannot examine the role of Capital Ideas in today's world without giving full consideration to the ideas of what has come to be known as Behavioral Finance—especially as here, too, Nobel Prizes have been earned by the leading thinkers.

As we shall see, the conflict has been brutal at some stages, but the impetus provided by Behavioral Finance to reexamine basic assumptions has also led to fresh perspectives of great value within the framework of the original ideas. Through it all, those Capital Ideas permeate every investment decision.

This assertion in no way minimizes the importance of the vast changes in finance since *Capital Ideas* appeared in 1992 or the incisive new ideas that have attacked the old ones from all sides. But the revolution in theory from 1952 to 1973 transformed the entire practice of investing so profoundly that the world can never go back to where it was before this revolution took place. Every new theoretical notion takes these basic ideas as its starting point.

Despite its rigid assumptions about investor rationality and the role of information, the Efficient Market Hypothesis remains the standard by which we judge market behavior and manager performance. Today, as in the past (and in some ways even more so than in the past), only a precious few investors have found strategies to beat the markets with any acceptable degree of consistency. Although Markowitz's prescription for constructing portfolios requires assumptions we cannot replicate in the real world, the risk/return trade-off is central to all investment choices. Just as essential, Markowitz's emphasis on the difference between the portfolio as a whole and its individual holdings has gained rather than lost relevance with the passage of time. The beta of the Capital Asset Pricing Model is no longer the single parameter of risk, but investors cannot afford to ignore the distinction between the risk of the expected returns of an asset class and the risk in decisions to outperform that asset class. Modigliani–Miller's perception of the stock market as the dominant determinant of whether a corporation earns its cost of capital was in many ways the intellectual driving force of the great bubble of the 1990s and the source of the scandals of corporate accounting that emerged in its wake.

Above all, the Black-Scholes-Merton insights into the valuation and the virtually unlimited applications of derivatives and into the meaning of volatility have pervaded every market for every asset all around the world. In fact, a recent study reports that 92 percent of the world's top 500 companies are using derivatives.[8] The Edinburgh professor Donald MacKenzie has described options pricing theory as "mathematics . . . performed in flesh and blood."[9]

❖

As you read on, keep in mind that the powerful body of knowledge motivating this whole story was conceived in the space of only twenty-one years, from 1952 to 1973. That is a remarkable fact.* The resulting theoretical structure had no prior existence and only a few scattered roots in the past. Few triumphs in the history of ideas can compare with this achievement. Think of the centuries from Euclid to Isaac Newton to Albert Einstein or the 160 years in the development of modern economic theory from Adam Smith in 1776 to David Ricardo, Alfred Marshall, and Karl Marx in the nineteenth century, and finally to John Maynard Keynes in 1936.

When I started work on this project early in 1989, all of my heroes were still alive, which was my prime motivation for telling the story at that moment. They were, indeed, very much alive. They were also available to me for personal interviews and correspondence, which they gave with boundless generosity. Three have since died: Merton Miller, Franco Modigliani, and Fischer Black. A significant cohort of the total—Harry Markowitz, Robert C. Merton, Merton Miller, Franco Modigliani, Myron Scholes, and William Sharpe—have won Nobel Prizes, and, if he had been alive when Scholes and Merton received

---

*In his fine book, *An Engine, Not a Camera: How Financial Models Shape Markets* (2006), MacKenzie has characterized the process as a "cascade," in which each innovator drew directly on his predecessors (p. 389).

theirs in 1997, Fischer Black would surely have been included. Jack Treynor, very much a part of the original story, should also have won a Nobel but missed out because he never published his seminal paper on the Capital Asset Pricing Model.[*]

Working on this project has been a great adventure and a rare privilege.

Peter L. Bernstein

New York, New York
March 2007

---

[*] On a personal note, I owe Jack Treynor an apology. On page 184 of *Capital Ideas*, I wrote that Treynor "left Harvard Business School in 1955 . . . ," giving the impression that Jack left without graduating. Graduate he did, with honors.

A Note on Usage

This book is a continuation of the story I told in *Capital Ideas: The Improbable Origins of Modern Wall Street,* which was published in 1992. *Capital Ideas* was primarily about theory; *Capital Ideas Evolving* tells how the theories set forth in *Capital Ideas* have become the fundamental structure of the daily business of investing money. Indeed, even the theoretical innovators of *Capital Ideas* have transformed themselves into innovators in implementation, right along with leading practitioners. While *Capital Ideas* focused on beta—the behavior of markets and how to compose and price portfolios in light of that behavior—*Capital Ideas Evolving* focuses on alpha, or the achievement of returns in excess of some benchmark. To put the case in less formal terms, *Capital Ideas Evolving* is about how the gown came to town.

The text makes frequent reference to *Capital Ideas.* In many places, I suggest referring to specific passages where the earlier text might illuminate what I have had to say here.

I also use the expression Capital Ideas, with upper-case first letters but no italics. In that format, Capital Ideas refers to the body of thought covered in *Capital Ideas,* such as the dominance of risk in decision making, the pricing of assets in competitive markets, the power of diversification, the huge hurdles involved in efforts to outperform the markets, and the giant step forward provided by the development of the options pricing model.

In short, Capital Ideas refers to Harry Markowitz's work on portfolio selection, Franco Modigliani's and Merton Miller's revolutionary views about corporate finance and the behavior of markets, the Sharpe-Treynor-Mossin-Lintner Capital Asset Pricing Model, Eugene Fama's explication of the Efficient Market Hypothesis, and the options pricing model of Fischer Black, Myron Scholes, and Robert C. Merton.

PART I
THE BEHAVIORAL ATTACK

1

Who Could Design a Brain . . .

Alfred Marshall, the great Victorian economist, opens his *Principles of Economics* with these words:

> Economics . . . examines that part of individual and social action which is most closely connected with the attainment and with the use of the material requisites of wellbeing. Thus it is on the one side a study of wealth; and, on the other, and more important side, a part of the study of man.

Marshall's *Principles* were to set the tone of economics for the next half century. In this work, despite his noble words in the quotation above, he made the study of man secondary to the study of wealth. Under all conditions, man in classical economics is an automaton capable of objective reasoning. Furthermore, disagreement about the future—a fundamental feature of the study of man—has no place in this particular study of wealth. Marshall's approach was finally dislodged, with great difficulty and after many years of dispute, by the publication in 1936 of his student John Maynard Keynes's masterwork, *The General Theory of Employment, Interest, and Money.*

The bundle of ideas, models, concepts, and systems embodied in the theoretical structure of modern finance—what I describe as Capital

Ideas—appeared between 1952 and 1973. They owe little to Keynes and almost everything to Marshall. The entire underlying structure of Capital Ideas rests on one overriding assumption: Investors have no difficulty in making optimal choices in the bewildering jumble of facts, rumors, discontinuities, vagueness, and black uncertainty that make up the real world around us.

Over time, this tension between an ideal concept of human rationality and the coarse reality of our daily lives has become an increasingly contentious issue. How much do we know about how people in the real world arrive at decisions and make choices? How great are the differences between the theoretical assumptions and the real world? And do those differences matter?

Although these questions have always been central to understanding the way investors behave and how their responses affect the performance of financial markets, no one made any systematic effort to provide the answers until the mid-1960s. The most significant and influential effort to approach these problems, a field of study that has come to be known as Behavioral Finance, began to take shape quite by accident when two junior psychology professors at Hebrew University in Jerusalem, Daniel Kahneman and Amos Tversky, happened to compare notes one day about their work and their life experiences. The hugely productive result of their friendship and subsequent collaboration has created a competing vision to the rational model of how people make choices and reach decisions under conditions of uncertainty.* The essence of this work is the study of man—of human behavior.

As Kahneman and Tversky wrote in 1992: "Theories of choice are at best approximate and incomplete. . . . Choice is a constructive and contingent process. When faced with a complex problem, people . . . use computational shortcuts and editing operations."[1] The result is a decision-making process differing in many aspects from the assumptions of Capital Ideas.

It would be a mistake to accuse Kahneman and Tversky of tarring all humanity with the black brush of irrationality. That was never the case, as Kahneman's autobiography makes clear: "The interpretation of our work as a broad attack on human rationality rather than a critique

---

*Tversky died at the age of 59 in 1996. Kahneman, now at Princeton University, was awarded the Nobel Prize in Economic Sciences in 2002.

of the rational-agent model attracted much opposition [to our efforts], some quite harsh and dismissive."[2] As Kahneman put the point to me, "The failure in the rational model is . . . in the human brain it requires. Who could design a brain that could perform in the way this model mandates? Every single one of us would have to know and *understand* everything, completely, and at once."[*] He expresses this position even more precisely in writing:

> I am now quick to reject any description of our work as demonstrating human irrationality. When the occasion arises, I carefully explain that research on heuristics and biases only refutes an unrealistic conception of rationality, which identifies it as comprehensive coherence. . . . In my current view, the study of judgment biases requires attention to the interplay between intuitive and reflective thinking, which sometimes allows biased judgments and sometimes overrides or corrects them.[3]

Kahneman's and Tversky's published papers, both individually and jointly, constitute an imposing compendium of evidence, ideas, and axioms of human behavior in the process of decision making. One of the most interesting features of Kahneman's and Tversky's work is the innovative nature of their discoveries. The patterns of human nature they discuss must have existed since the beginning of time, but no one before them had caught their vision. They unleashed a far larger flood of research from other academics and, over time, from the practitioner side as well.

In highly compressed fashion, the rest of this chapter conducts a survey of Behavioral Finance based on a small but characteristic sample of these investigations. The implications of this survey for investment are fascinating, but along the way the material also provides a mirror in which we see ourselves probably more often than we would like.

---

[*]Unless otherwise specified, all quotations come from personal interviews or personal correspondence.

The real issue is this: How much damage has this attack inflicted on the standard theories and models of finance? Do the critique of the rational-agent model and the demonstrations of its empirical failures render my book, *Capital Ideas,* useless and at best obsolete? Or, in a more practical mode, do the teachings of Behavioral Finance lead us to alpha—to an excess return on our investments after adjustment for risk?

Final judgment must await the presentation of the evidence. But final judgment will be rendered.

Before moving on, a separate point is worth making. The focus of the discussion so far has been on how the findings of Behavioral Finance relate to each of us as an investor. But a deeper issue is also involved, set forth by John Campbell of the Economics Department at Harvard in his presidential address to the American Finance Association in January 2006:

> Even if asset prices are set efficiently, investment mistakes can have large welfare costs for households. . . . They may greatly reduce the welfare gains that can be realized from the current period of financial innovation. . . . If household finance can achieve good understanding of the sources of investment mistakes, it may be possible for the field to contribute ideas to limit the costs of these mistakes.[*]

A story that Kahneman recounted in the course of his address accepting the Nobel Prize provides a typical example of the "computational shortcuts and editing operations" we use in our attempts to make choices in complex problems. Kahneman had conducted an experiment with two different audiences. Although he offered both audiences an identical set of choices, he presented these choices in different settings that led to strikingly different results.

He asked each audience to imagine a community preparing for the outbreak of a dreaded disease. The experts have predicted the disease will kill 600 people if nothing is done, but they offer two different programs to deal with the contingencies.

[*] Campbell (2006).

Under Program A, 200 people will be saved. Under Program B, there is a one-third possibility that all 600 people will be saved and a two-thirds' probability that everybody will die. Kahneman found that the audience presented with these choices overwhelmingly favored Program A, on the basis that the gamble in Program B was too risky. The certainty that 200 people would be saved was preferable to a two-thirds' chance that everybody will die.

Then Kahneman presented the identical choices to the other audience, but in a revised setting. Under Plan C, 400 people will die. Under Plan D, there is a one-third chance that nobody will die and a two-thirds' probability that 600 people will die. Now the audience's choice was for Plan D. The gamble, in its Plan D garb, now seems preferable to Plan C, in which it is certain 400 people will die.

How can we account for these opposing sets of responses to what are identical choices and probabilities? As Kahneman explains it, nobody has ever figured out a perfect technique for dealing with uncertainty. Consequently, in making choices and decisions, we tend to overweight certain outcomes relative to uncertain outcomes, even when the uncertain outcomes have a high probability. In the case of the first audience, the certainty of saving 200 out of 600 people is "disproportionately attractive." In the case of the second audience, accepting the certain death of 400 out of 600 people is "disproportionately aversive."

Kahneman and Tversky have defined these kinds of inconsistencies in decision making as "failure of invariance." The failure of invariance comes in many colors, with endless variations of the theme.* Invariance means that if A is preferred to B and B is preferred to C, rational people should prefer A to C. In the case above, if the rational decision in the first set is 200 lives saved for certain, saving 200 lives for certain should be the rational decision in the second set as well.

Kahneman and Tversky use the expression, "framing," to describe these kinds of failures of invariance, which are widely prevalent. In the example of the outbreak of the dreaded disease, the audience in the first case framed their responses around how many people would live, while the second audience framed their responses around how many people might die. Kahneman's Nobel address defines framing as "the passive

---

*See, in particular, Thaler (1991), which describes many examples of the failure of invariance and framing.

acceptance of the formulation given." And then he adds, "Invariance cannot be achieved by a finite mind."[4]

◼

Richard Thaler of the University of Chicago, one of Kahneman's and Tversky's earliest and most articulate disciples, describes an amusing example of the failure of invariance involving money. Thaler proposed to students in one of his classes that they had just won $30. Now they could choose between two outcomes: a coin flip where the individual would win $9 on heads or lose $9 on tails, or no flip of the coin at all. The coin flip was the choice of 70 percent of the students. When his next class came along, Thaler asked the students to assume that they had a starting wealth of zero. Now they could choose between these two options. The first was a coin flip where the individual wins $39 on heads and $21 on tails. The second was $30 for certain. Only 43 percent of the students chose the coin flip; the majority preferred the $30 for certain.

When you study the options offered to both classes, you will find that the payoffs are identical. Whether the starting wealth is $30 or zero, the students in both cases are going to end up with either $39 or $21 versus ending up with $30 for sure. Yet the majorities of the two classes made entirely different choices, resulting in a failure of invariance.

Thaler ascribes this inconsistency to what he calls "the house money effect." If you have money in your pocket, you will choose the gamble. If you have no money in your pocket, you would rather have the $30 for certain than take the risk of ending up with $21.[5]

In the real world, the house money effect matters. Investors who are already wealthy are willing to take significant risks because they can absorb the losses, while investors with limited means will invest conservatively because of fear they cannot afford to lose the little they have. This is precisely the opposite of how people with different wealth levels should arrive at decisions. The wealthy investor is already wealthy and does not need to take the gamble. If investors with only a small amount of savings lose it all, this would probably make little difference, but a killing on the small accumulation could change their lives.

Another investment-oriented version of the distortions caused by framing resulted in an experiment conducted in 2001 by Thaler and his frequent coauthor Shlomo Benartzi of UCLA.[6] Participants were divided into three separate groups with no contact among the groups. Each group was given a choice of two fund offerings for their retirement plans. One group was offered a fund holding just stocks and a fund holding just bonds. The second group was offered a fund holding just stocks and a balanced fund that includes stocks and bonds. The third group was offered a bond fund and a balanced fund.

Even though these choices were for retirement funds that should have had roughly the same asset allocation decisions, the three groups ended up with wide differences in portfolio structures. The differences arose because the 50–50 choice is always popular: It seems like common sense; it looks like diversification; and it avoids the complex decision about how assets should be allocated in a retirement fund. The consequences were dramatic. The first group, choosing between a stock fund and a bond fund, ended up with an average allocation of 54 percent to equities. The second group, offered a stock fund and a balanced fund, also leaned in the 50–50 direction between the two funds, but ended up with an average allocation of 73 percent to equities and only 27 percent to bonds, because half the balanced fund was already invested in equities. The third group, offered a bond fund and a balanced fund, ended up with an average of 65 percent in bonds and only 35 percent in equities.

The experiment demonstrates that framing determined the decision making among the three groups. The proper approach should have been to consider the different expected rates of return and risks of each asset class and to see through to the underlying structure of the balanced fund in making the final choice. Fifty percent to each asset class might not have been optimal, but it would have been a sensible choice for someone with no experience or no understanding of the different risk-return trade-offs between stocks and bonds. In fact, however, the design of the offering dominated. Most of the participants were unwilling to make the intellectual effort to see through the 50–50 allocation of the balanced fund and recognize that the true asset allocation was a long way from 50–50.

This experiment was not just an artificial effort to find out how people make choices where framing is likely to dominate. The 50–50 choice tends to dominate at TIAA-CREF, the huge retirement fund for university faculties. Here, at least, there is professional advice available to help participants avoid the simplifications of framing and, instead, to understand the structure that would best suit their needs. But I must also report that one of the famous developers of the theory of finance, whose current activities receive an entire chapter in this book, has confessed he has also made the 50–50 choice at TIAA-CREF.

The proponents of Behavioral Finance have drawn heavily on the writings and teachings of Kahneman and Tversky. They have made human quirks like the failure of invariance, framing, and the illusion of validity the core of their confrontation with the assumptions of the rational model that motivates and supports the structure of Capital Ideas. The issue is *why*—why does reality differ so much from the idealized world that underlies the efficient market and the Capital Asset Pricing Model? And, after we settle that matter, a more important question faces us, already suggested earlier: Can Behavioral Finance enable us to outperform the market?

Although human beings have extraordinary reasoning power compared with animals, something other than cool analysis and calculation seems to take over when we are faced with difficult choices—even though, on many occasions, we honestly believe we have made a rational decision. Nobody ever knows what the future holds, which means decision making is always a daunting challenge. The only certainty in the whole process is that more things can happen than will happen.

For example, the mean temperature on the fourth of July could be over 100 degrees or as cool as 50 degrees. But even under the unrealistic assumption that we could precisely calculate or estimate the probability of each degree of temperature in that range, and that the range is in fact the correct range, we are still in the dark about how hot or cool the day is actually going to be. And most decisions have a much wider range of possible outcomes, so wide we cannot even know all the outcomes we might have to deal with. In other words, most good forecasts should not be point forecasts or a mean of possible outcomes. Rather, it is the *range* that matters for decision making and risk measurement.

This struggle is especially intense when it comes to decisions involving our wealth. Finance and investment are bets on future outcomes—investing means we put away money today because we expect to earn a future return on it. Even in the unlikely event that everything else works out as planned, the future purchasing power of money is uncertain. As a result, these uncertain investment outcomes could range from making us rich and famous to putting us on a fast train to the poorhouse. Investing is a deadly serious process, not an enthralling game or a substitute for gambling in a casino as some people view it.

As Kahneman and Tversky put it, using psychology-speak, investors have "cognitive difficulties" in their efforts to arrive at profitable decisions.[*] Yet people who are not so smart frequently become rich. If they are lucky enough to avoid being wiped out immediately, they can survive for a long time and create all kinds of mispricings that scare away more sober investors. Keynes observes that the market could stay at crazy levels longer than most people could even imagine.[†]

Yogi Berra is reported to have said that forecasting is very difficult, especially when it comes to the future. Most of life is about making decisions whose outcome is hidden from us. Faced with what looks like an impossibly complex process, why would we not tend to look for shortcuts—or heuristics—to reach our decision more easily? Many times, and especially in investing, uncertainty comes lumped together with complexity. But the shortcuts we use to extricate ourselves from these dilemmas lead to inadequate processing of information, or avoiding the use of information entirely and relying on our gut to guide us.

An interesting slant on how we confront complexity and uncertainty comes from Barr Rosenberg of AXA Rosenberg, one of the most persuasive early proponents of Capital Ideas and a distinguished scholar on his own (see Chapter 13 of *Capital Ideas*): "I became interested in capital markets rather than other economic processes because the stock market is approximately a taste-free world; in other words, the ideal investor simply would look for superior returns. . . . Behavioral finance is the healthy antidote to that view by saying, 'No, actually, it's not a

---

[*] For a fascinating discussion of cognitive functions framed in terms of the structure and operation of the human brain, and the distinctions between so-called rational and nonrational decision making, see Cohen (2005).
[†] See De Long et al. (1991).

taste-free world.'" And then Rosenberg adds, "As you know, the discounted future dividend stream of stocks [has] such very long durations
that instinct has to play a major role in valuation."[7]

Many of the problems we encounter in this process of oversimplifi-
cation and instinctive responses stem from the limits of our imagination, although sometimes we impose limits we do not have to impose.
One of the most dangerous of these habits is to believe low-probability
events will not happen. A probability of one chance in a hundred is still
more than zero. Crossing the street can be fatal even if you are a fast
runner, and a massive earthquake could occur in San Francisco at any
moment. The chances are low that you will be hit if you run fast or that
San Francisco will crumble tomorrow, but the probabilities tell you
nothing about when such an event might occur.*

This imbalance in our imagination is just one example of how we
slice and dice our view of reality to simplify our course of action. We
focus on the short term because the long term is too vague—and anyway it is not the domain in which we live. Yet understanding the distinctions between the short run and the long run is essential. The
investor with a short-term horizon has to take what comes, for better or
for worse. The investor with a long-term horizon—which is another
way of saying the investor has a higher tolerance for volatility—has the
opportunity to hedge against unfavorable outcomes. For example, the
long-term investor can buy the U.S. Treasury's inflation-protected
bonds (TIPs), which make little difference to his fortunes over the next
year but could make a tremendous difference in what happens to his
wealth if inflation unexpectedly persists over the next twenty years.

That is not all. We extrapolate recent developments into the longer-
run future without questioning their significance for a constantly
changing world. We cling to our preconceptions even when the evidence in front of us shows they are outdated. We are content being in-
consistent because consistency may be too demanding. The possibility
of regretting a decision dilutes our ability to make a rational decision in
the first place. We often make the mistake of heeding what others say
when they agree with us, even when they may know less than we do.
We display a tendency to take greater risks when faced with losses than

---

*This point and related versions of it are elaborated skillfully in Mauboussin (2006).
Michael Mauboussin is Director of Research at Legg Mason & Co.

when faced with gains. We make judgments on the basis of small samples of information that are far from representative of the broad generalizations on which we want to base our decisions, largely because we often have nothing else available.

Yet all through the process, we display overconfidence in our own beliefs even though our better judgment should recognize the high risks in thinking we know more than the consensus of the people in the marketplace. Many of those individuals have more information and understand the situation better than we do. Kahneman describes it this way: "The central characteristic of agents is not that they reason poorly but that they often act intuitively. And the behavior of these agents is not guided by what they are able to compute, but by what they happen to see at a particular moment."[8]

The results from these kinds of heuristics can be costly. For example, Terrance Odean of the University of California, Berkeley, and Brad Barber of the University of California, Davis, studied the trading activity in a large number of investor accounts at a nationwide discount brokerage house. They found, with extraordinary frequency, that the stocks these investors sold went on to earn higher returns than the stocks these investors purchased to replace those holdings.[9]

For better or for worse, individual investors have plenty of company among sophisticated chief investment officers of pension plans, foundations, and university endowment funds. Amit Goyal and Sumil Warhal of Emory University studied some 3,700 corporate pension funds from 1994 through 2003 to determine their skill in selecting external investment managers. The 3,700 funds transferred a total of over $700 billion to external investment managers during the period covered by the study. These pension funds hired new managers showing large positive excess returns up to three years prior to hiring and fired existing managers after they had underperformed.

The result was essentially the same as for Odean and Barber's individual investors: "If plan sponsors had stayed with fired investment managers, their excess returns would be larger than those actually delivered by newly hired managers." In addition, the funds would have saved all the brokerage costs involved in management changes.[10]

In short, we are human beings. Financial theory has to take account of that incontestable fact. But how much does it matter to the Efficient Market Hypothesis and related works that the quirks of Behavioral

Finance are a good description of reality? How certain can we be that behavioral issues mean the market is inefficient? Or, to put it more bluntly, how much money can we make as investors by studying the many interesting stories Behavioral Finance has to tell us? These questions motivate the rest of this chapter.

Kahneman's and Tversky's work naturally attracted academics working in finance who were seeking new insights into how the capital markets work and how investors make decisions.* Among the earliest of their acolytes was a young graduate student named Richard Thaler, whose work on the house money effect we have already noted. Thaler is now among the leaders in the field of Behavioral Finance. Indeed, after teaching at Cornell and MIT, Thaler was appointed Robert P. Gwinn Professor of Behavioral Science and Economics at the Graduate School of Business of the University of Chicago in 1995, where Eugene Fama and his colleagues have had to put up with—and ultimately learn from—this energetic and iconoclastic man.

Thaler had been browsing in the field of psychology before he ever heard of Kahneman and Tversky. In the early 1970s, while working on his doctoral dissertation at the University of Rochester—where at the time rational theory was considered beyond dispute—he began to speculate on how to calculate the value of a human life. It occurred to him that the correct measure would be how much people are willing to pay to save a human life. And so he began asking friends and students what value they would put on their own lives.

He sought the answer to these questions. First, what would you pay to *eliminate* a one-in-a-thousand chance of immediate death? Second, turning the first question around, he asked how much you would have to be paid to *accept* a one-in-a-thousand chance of immediate death. Not knowing exactly what to expect, he was dumbfounded at the differences in the answers to the two questions.

---

*Chapter 17 of my book, *Against the Gods: The Remarkable Story of Risk,* entitled "The Theory Police," discusses the work of the people in Behavioral Finance at length. I have drawn on that discussion in what follows.

In general, most of the answers were along the lines of: "I wouldn't pay more than $200 to eliminate a small chance of immediate death, but I wouldn't accept such an extra risk for $50,000." Thaler found these huge differences between buying and selling prices "*very* interesting."

The wheels were beginning to turn. He started to compile a list of what he called "anomalous behaviors"—behaviors that went against the predictions of the standard models in finance. He discovered a variety of such violations, which he describes in a paper in 1976 that he circulated informally and "to colleagues I wanted to annoy."* A little while after he had written this paper, he met two young researchers who were familiar with Kahneman's and Tversky's notion that what the rational model would view as anomalous behavior is often normal behavior. It is the rationally reached decision that is the exception.

One of these young men sent Thaler a Kahneman and Tversky paper called "Judgment Under Uncertainty: Heuristics and Biases," later published as the introduction to a book by that name Kahneman and Tversky had edited.[11] Thaler says he could hardly contain himself after reading this article. A year later, he met Kahneman and Tversky, and he has followed in their path ever since. At latest count, he is the author or coauthor of four authoritative books on Behavioral Finance, including *The Winner's Curse: Paradoxes and Anomalies of Economic Life* and *Quasi-Rational Economics* as well as countless articles.[12]

Thaler's views on rationality are consistent with Kahneman's and Tversky's, but his language is more colorful than theirs. When Kahneman says: "I am now quick to reject any description of our work as demonstrating human irrationality. When the occasion arises, I carefully explain that research on heuristics and biases only refutes an unrealistic conception of rationality, which identifies it as comprehensive coherence," Thaler puts it this way: People are not "blithering idiots" but they are a long way from "hyperrational automatons."

In 1957, Nobel Laureate Herbert Simon proposed a calmer and more elaborate development of Thaler's distinction between blithering idiots and hyperrational automatons. Simon called his concept "bounded rationality."[13] From this perspective, people facing an uncertain future *aim* to reach rational decisions, but they often fail because the demands

---

* See note 6 to Chapter 17 of Bernstein (1996) and Thaler (1991).

of the process are too great and the variety of possible outcomes too bewildering. Rational analysis will always find a solution. In more recent
work, Kahneman has placed much emphasis on Simons's conceptual
work in this area.

Thaler has also put his money where his mouth is. He is a principal
in an investment management firm known as Fuller & Thaler, a partnership with Russell Fuller, another enthusiast for Behavioral Finance
who has been Chairman of the Finance Department at Washington
State University, author of an investment textbook, and a Wall Street
security analyst. Daniel Kahneman is an outside director of the firm.

The investment results at Fuller & Thaler are worth a careful look,
because here is Behavioral Finance in action under the guidance of the
stars of the field. The firm attempts to achieve above-market returns by
seeking opportunity where investors overreact to negative information
or underreact to positive information. They combine this basic approach with old-fashioned fundamental research and security analysis.

The firm offers a number of different strategies, ranging from large-
capitalization equities down to equities in the smallest-capitalization
group, called micro-cap, as well as international strategies investing in
companies in both large- and small-capitalization sectors. It also offers a
U.S. Large-Cap Market Neutral strategy and an international long/short
strategy. The heaviest concentration is in the small-capitalization sector
overall.

Although the firm had only $4 billion under management at the
end of 2005, its track record has been impressive. As of September 30,
2006, all but two of these strategies had outperformed their benchmarks (usually market indexes) by significant margins, and the two that
fell behind their benchmarks have been operational for a relatively short
time. Sharpe ratios (total return divided by volatility) compare favor-
ably in all cases.

The five strategies in operation for the longest periods of time (and
their dates of inception) have been Small Mid-Cap Growth Equity
(1992), Small Mid-Cap Core Equity (1996), Small-Cap Value Equity
(1996), Large-Cap Market Neutral (2000), and Micro-Cap Equity (1999).
They show the following rates of return, after all fees from inception

through the third quarter of 2006, compared to their appropriate benchmarks (which pay no fees):

| | Percent per Year | | | |
	Strategy	Benchmark	Excess Return	Years Outperformed
Small Mid-Cap Growth Equity	15.7	8.4	+7.2	10/15
Small Mid-Cap Core Equity*	14.9	11.4	+3.5	6/11
Small-Cap Value Equity	17.2	13.4	+4.5	6/11
Large-Cap Market Neutral	6.2	3.0	+3.2	6/7
Micro-Cap Equity	26.6	8.4	+18.2	6/8

* All facts and data relating to the performance of Fuller & Thaler have been graciously supplied by Russell Fuller.

Net of fees, the Micro-Cap strategy has clearly been the most spectacular, with returns of 105 percent in 1993, 94 percent in 1999, and 50 percent in 2001. The other three strategies, however, have also comfortably beaten their benchmarks, outperforming in the majority of years.

At first glance, the evidence in the table is a clear demonstration of the power of applying the principles of Behavioral Finance to the real world of the capital markets. At second glance, however, the picture here is not so clear.

Fuller & Thaler produced its most impressive results in the markets for companies with small capitalizations, those ranging from $50 million to $4 billion in market value. In contrast, the average capitalization of the 500 companies in the Standard & Poor's Index as of mid-2005 was over $20 billion; half the S&P companies have market values of more than $10 billion; the smallest company is capitalized in the market at over $500 million. This is the pool from which most large and institutional investors select their equity holdings.

There is a lot of evidence to show that the smaller-capitalization sectors are less efficient than the larger-capitalization sectors, in the sense that over- and undervaluation may be greater and can persist for a longer time in markets where most investors are relatively uninformed and untrained, and where relatively high transactions costs can cut deeply into expected returns. Furthermore, the amount of stock available in Fuller & Thaler's favorite hunting ground is much too limited for large investors to be able to trade there. Fuller & Thaler looks smart—and is smart—but the firm has minimal competition in seeking out opportunity. It has also been careful to avoid putting too much money where it could end up spoiling their efforts: Micro-Cap is closed to new investors and, as of mid-2005, the three small-cap strategies were reported as "close to their natural capacity."[14]

Fuller & Thaler has recently begun to move into the larger-capitalization sectors, international investing, and long/short strategies with encouraging results, but the time period may have been too short to reach any strong judgments about what it has been able to accomplish. As its U.S. Large-Cap Market Neutral strategy has had good success, albeit launched only recently in 2000, the experience is encouraging in both the large-cap strategies and long/short strategies.

In the end, an important question remains unanswered. Have Fuller & Thaler established this track record because of their sensitivity to behavioral anomalies? Or did their long study of behavioral anomalies give their firm a sharp eye for value, which means assets are underpriced but not necessarily as a result of the foibles of less-than-rational investors? There is no way to develop a definitive answer to these questions.

Nevertheless, the questions themselves are too important to be dismissed without further investigation and argument. We conduct that exploration in the next chapter.

2

The Strange Paradox
of Behavioral Finance

"Neoclassical Theory
Is a Theory of Sharks"

Behavioral Finance argues that most investors make decisions and choices based upon an inability, or unwillingness, to analyze situations in the cool, detached, and fully informed manner of the investors in the Capital Asset Pricing Model or the Efficient Market Hypothesis. Fuller & Thaler's sector of choice is overwhelmingly the sector of choice of these kinds of noise traders. We encountered such investors in *Capital Ideas,* on pages 124–125, in the discussion of Fischer Black's 1986 paper on noise traders.[1] As Black describes it, noise contrasts with information. Noise traders buy and sell on what they would like to believe is informed opinion and analysis, but in most instances they act on what is in fact misinformation—in the broadest sense of the word. It is surely noise when a company named Computer Literacy, Inc., changes its name to fatbrain.com and its price rises 36 percent in a day, as actually occurred on Monday, March 29, 1999.[2]

The presence of so many noise traders should lead to gross mispricings of assets, which means the cognoscenti who have read and digested the works of Kahneman and Tversky and their many followers would all get rich. But how many people are getting as rich as the clients of

Fuller & Thaler? Black himself, in characteristic style, pointed out in his 1986 paper that "noise creates opportunities to trade profitably, but at the same time makes it more difficult to trade profitably."

As a matter of luck, many investors will be beating the market at any given moment—"the market," after all, is the average result of what everybody is doing—so some people will be performing better than the market and others will be performing more poorly. This is not the same thing as outperforming after adjustment for risk, with consistency year after year. The record suggests that only a handful of investors are outperforming the markets with any degree of consistency. We will encounter a sample of these people in the chapters to follow, but it is important to recognize they warrant our attention precisely because they are part of such a tiny minority. What they do often appears to be remarkably simple, something anyone could emulate. Nevertheless, they are not emulated. What looks simple can be tricky to execute.

Consider this. From 1977 to 1990, Fidelity's Magellan Fund rose more than 2,700 percent—an annual compound return of 29 percent—under the management of the legendary Peter Lynch. Lynch is a legend precisely because nobody else has come close to his track record. Lynch always maintained that his stock-picking criteria were only common sense—"My wife was enthusiastic about the company's products"—and therefore easy for other managers to replicate. As other managers did not replicate his track record, a lot more than common sense must have been involved.

Studies of institutional investing continue to show that most active managers underperform in both equities and fixed-income markets. Mutual funds are the most visible group of institutional investors, in part because they have millions of shareholders but also because they are required to make their performance records public. Although many mutual funds show a tendency to outperform the market before fees and expenses, they then display a propensity to give that margin away in the turnover costs, taxes, and management fees that cut into the returns accruing to their shareholders.

For example, as of September 2006, the 299 mutual funds operating in the Large Growth sector as defined by Morningstar, the mutual fund survey service, had underperformed the S&P 500 Index by some 300 basis points a year over the preceding five and ten years. A shortfall of 300 basis points over ten years—5.6 percent a year for the funds versus 8.6 percent for the Index—means that $10,000 invested in the S&P 500 would have grown, with dividends, to $22,755 while the same amount invested in the large cap fund universe would have grown to $17,309, a gap of 24 percent. Expense ratios close to 1.5 percent and turnover rates over 100 percent that incurred significant transactions costs probably go a long way to account for the performance shortfall. To make matters even worse, the results do not include the impact of any load charges on purchase or capital gains taxes from realized profits.

These results, dismal as they may be, tend to understate the dismal track record, because they reflect the performance of only those funds that survived during the period under study. If we were able to include all the funds that went out of business because of bad performance during those years, the degree of underperfomance would have been even worse than the data provided here.

In 2004, Burton Malkiel of Princeton, and author of *A Random Walk Down Wall Street,* studied all the mutual funds in existence since 1970—a total of 139 funds surviving over more than thirty years.[3] He found that seventy-six of the funds underperformed the market by more than one percentage point a year; only four funds outperformed by more than two percentage points a year. On a broader perspective, Malkiel reports that more than 80 percent of the actively managed large capitalization funds covered in Lipper Analytical Services failed to match the returns of the S&P 500 over periods of longer than ten years ending in 2003. Malkiel also points out that "there's almost no persistence in excess performance. . . . In decade after decade, the top funds in one period are often the bottom funds in the next. . . . There's no way to tell in advance which funds will outperform."[4] And here, too, survivor bias understates the actual results.

Even if the evidence suggests that *most* mutual funds do underperform, are there any funds with some identifiably consistent ability to outperform—and, if so, do we have any way of identifying them in advance? Two recent studies provide some basis for both the likelihood that such skills exist and the likelihood that those skills can be identified in advance.

A paper published in December 2006 by Robert Kosowski of Imperial College in London and three coauthors studies the mutual fund industry from 1975 to 2002. Using a wide array of performance measurement models and a statistical procedure known as bootstrapping, the authors find that, "A sizable minority of managers pick stocks well enough to more than cover their costs. Moreover, the superior alphas of these managers *persist*."[5] They go on to argue that "Our bootstrap tests consistently indicate that the large positive alphas of the top 10 percent of funds, net of costs, are extremely unlikely to arise solely due to sampling variability (luck)."[6]

Even though managers with skill do exist, can we identify them in advance? A 2006 paper by W. V. Harlow of the Fidelity Research Institute in Boston and Keith Brown of the McCombs School of Business at the University of Texas in Austin—while confirming that the median manager outperforms less than half the time—does present a process of selecting managers that "improves an investor's probability of identifying a superior active manager to almost 60 percent."[7]

Harlow and Brown take the position that the question of whether most managers can outperform some benchmark is not the right question. Rather, the question should be posed this way: "Is it possible to identify in advance those active managers who offer a reasonable opportunity to produce superior risk-adjusted performance?"[8] Harlow and Brown find a number of factors explaining past superior performance, especially costs and turnover rates, but their most important finding confirms the evidence presented by Kosowski et al., namely, that the superior performance of managers with these characteristics tends to persist. Past alpha, in other words, tends to predict future alpha.

Both these papers appear to contradict the more gloomy conclusions of the vast body of research into mutual fund performance. Both papers present convincing arguments in support of the positions they have taken. Kosowski et al. provide evidence of superior performance by a segment of the fund industry—but this information has little value to investors unless they can identify such managers in advance. The Harlow and Brown paper purports to solve that problem.

It is fair to ask whether Harlow and Brown have solved the problem in real life, rather than just on paper. Harlow and Brown did their research on a database of past performance of funds, which means investors did not yet have their system available for identifying managers in advance. As a result, *we have no knowledge of how these managers would perform after they were identified by investors using the Harlow-Brown paradigm*. If identification of superior managers becomes a simple matter for investors in general, those managers will be buried under an avalanche of new money to a point where they will no longer be able to pursue the investment strategies that delivered the superior performance. There is a tipping point somewhere for every manager, regardless of skill and style, which explains why some management organizations close their funds to new money in order to prevent just such an avalanche. After that happens, identifying their past skills is of little use to the investor who is not already a stockholder in those funds.

The long history of mutual funds shows that superior performance, even in the short run, tends to attract new assets that swell the size of the portfolio under management. As assets under management increase, the costs of trading tend to follow suit, and the edge of the active manager begins to diminish.

Then there is the matter of the hedge fund industry. The hedge fund industry claims to have achieved high performance, and its generous rewards for successful management have attracted a large number of the brightest people in Wall Street. If anybody has a good chance to outperform the markets, with consistency and after adjustment for risk, the hedge funds are the most likely candidates. Many hedge funds operate under fewer constraints than conventional managers, which means the hedge funds have the opportunity to seek gain wherever they might find it instead of having to operate within a box of "large-cap" or "high-yield" or "international equity." Their ability to sell short as well as buy long also gives them the opportunity to earn profits from arbitrage—selling short what they deem is overvalued and buying a similar security that they consider undervalued. In that instance, they can accumulate a large number of small profits that may add up to a substantial return.

Yet two considerations should give us pause before accepting those facts as proof that the pricing distortions caused by cognitive errors offer widespread opportunities for these presumably smart investors.

First, calculating market-beating performance for hedge funds is not as simple as calculating it for a mutual fund or long-only active portfolio manager. There is no "market" in hedge funds as there is in stocks or bonds. What is it then that these funds are outperforming? They may outperform some arbitrary benchmark such as the Treasury bill return plus percentage points, but the result could be more the outcome of messy data and survivorship bias.

Second, calculating hedge fund risk is a controversial procedure. Volatility measures employed as risk measurements in conventional investing are not appropriate in a long/short environment. Among other things, hedge fund returns are subject to fat tails or tail risk—higher-than-normal probabilities of extreme negative returns. Hedge funds are short-sellers, and short-sellers take the risk of infinite losses (stocks can fall only to zero but can rise to infinity). They can be caught in what is known as a "short squeeze," in which they are unable to make delivery of the stock they have sold because they are unable to borrow it anywhere. Then they are forced to go into the market and buy it back at what is likely to be a higher price than the price at which they sold.

Many hedge funds own illiquid assets or assets trading only in thin markets, where the probability of large losses is much greater than in conventional investing—as the disastrous experience of Long-Term Capital Management so dramatically demonstrated.[*] All these activities become even riskier when the fund uses borrowed money, which is frequently the case.[9]

※

By definition, most investors cannot outperform the market because they are the market. On the other hand, the available evidence suggests that fewer investors are able to win out over the others than would be the case if the markets were not so competitive. What the crowd knows is already in the price, but it is not easy to think outside the crowd.

Jack Treynor, one of the pioneer developers of the Capital Asset Pricing Model and long-time editor of the *Financial Analysts Journal,* believes that systematic errors provide many opportunities to earn excess returns. His favorite approach is to tell people about the stocks that look especially attractive to him. If they agree right away that he is on to something, he figures the price of the stock already reflects this idea, and he goes on to something else. But when his friends just don't get it, he is inspired to study the matter further and, in all likelihood, invest in it.[†]

---

[*] For a more extended discussion of Long-Term Capital Management, see Chapter 6.
[†] See Mehrling (2005), pp. 253–254.

Treynor is a kind of lone wolf operator and prefers what he calls "slow ideas"—ideas that will take time to bear fruit and therefore have no attraction for most investors. In the more general case, where time horizons are much shorter, skilled investors often act so rapidly that they spoil the situation for one another as opportunities disappear almost instantly. As Paul Samuelson has put it, "No easy pickings, no sure-thing gains." That is why Fuller & Thaler seek opportunity in the smaller-capitalizations. Pickings are easier and the gains are surer, while the huge composite of large growth mutual funds can barely squeak through with something resembling outperformance before taxes and fees.

Nevertheless, there are two major interconnected qualifications to this conclusion. They warrant our most careful attention. The first concerns the matter of arbitrage in individual securities. The second, and more serious, concern is about inefficiency in the market as a whole as opposed to inefficiency in individual securities. These two matters are closely related.

Arbitrage is a critical factor in the whole debate between the doctrines of Capital Ideas and the postulates of Behavioral Finance. Arbitrage means buying one asset and simultaneously selling another asset, expecting that the price of the asset bought will rise while the price of the asset sold falls. For example, often the same security may trade in two different markets, or a security may trade as a conventional security in one market and a derivative such as a futures contract in another market. If the prices differ, convergence should take place as arbitrageurs sell the overpriced asset and buy the underpriced asset. Arbitrage in such instances is essentially a riskless transaction.

Arbitrageurs may also act in the case of two assets that closely resemble one another but are not precisely linked in the same way as a stock and a derivative based upon it. Such a case would be a convertible bond and the stock into which it is convertible. A riskier strategy is to arbitrage two securities that have similar characteristics, such as two companies in high-tech, which was a favorite activity of many hedge funds during the bubble of the 1990s. Indeed, much of the case for the Efficient Market Hypothesis assumes that arbitrage is the key explanation for why any disparities in valuation that do exist are brief and why beating the market is a high hurdle.

If in fact arbitrage opportunities are always available, and if arbitrageurs can always note the discrepancies and eliminate mispricings instantaneously without taking on any risk, then the stipulation of rationality among investors becomes a matter of secondary importance in the arguments over the Efficient Market Hypothesis. This set of conditions, under which arbitrage always prevails, has come to be known as the no-arbitrage condition because in an efficient market there will be no arbitrage opportunities remaining.

Under no-arbitrage, the debate between the doctrines of Capital Ideas and Behavioral Finance vanishes. For whatever reason, mispricings will be eliminated too rapidly for anyone to take advantage of them with any degree of consistency. That is, anomalies of Behavioral Finance may pop up, but they will disappear before any active manager can consistently make money on them.

In no uncertain words, Stephen Ross, one of the most distinguished scholars of Capital Ideas, has described the impact of no-arbitrage on this debate:

> I, for one, never thought that people—myself included—were all that rational in their behavior. To the contrary, I am always amazed at what people do. But that was never the point of financial theory. The absence of arbitrage requires that there be enough well-financed and smart investors to close arbitrage opportunities when they appear. . . . *Neoclassical theory is a theory of sharks and not a theory of rational homo economicus,* and that is the principal distinction between finance and traditional economics. . . . Well-financed arbitrageurs spot these opportunities [resulting from behavioral errors], pile on, and by their actions close aberrant price differentials [emphasis added].[10]

An attack on Ross's position on arbitrage has been mounted by Harvard economist Andrei Shleifer and by Robert Vishny, one of Thaler's colleagues at Chicago, in an influential paper titled "The Limits to Arbitrage." Shleifer and Vishny build their case on an argument describing the differences between the world in the pages of textbooks and the world where real investors are making decisions:

> Textbook arbitrage in financial markets requires no capital and entails no risk. In reality, almost all arbitrage requires capital and is typically risky. Moreover, professional arbitrage is conducted by a

relatively small number of highly specialized investors using other people's capital. Such professional arbitrage has a number of interesting implications for security pricing, including the possibility that arbitrage becomes ineffective in extreme circumstances when prices diverge far from fundamental values. The model also suggests where anomalies in financial markets are likely to appear, and why arbitrage fails to eliminate them.[11]

In short, the real world is not so simple as the Efficient Market Hypothesis or as Ross's argument describes it. As Shleifer and Vishny point out, most arbitrage is not undertaken by large numbers of investors seeking mispricings, but rather by a smaller group of more sophisticated professional investors who specialize in the strategy and manage big sums of money. Well aware of the risks involved, these arbitrageurs may stand aside or, on occasion, actually join in the fun and drive values even farther apart. Arbitrage often involves selling short, which is always risky and expensive to execute. Values that should be equal may continue to move farther apart just because noise traders take so long to recognize the errors of their ways. The greatest risk to arbitrageurs is momentum risk—when other investors start buying something simply because it has started to go up, and one upward move leads to another until a huge overvaluation has accumulated. "Don't fight the tape!" is an old saw on Wall Street that can still ring true from time to time.[*]

On the other hand, although the limits to arbitrage, and therefore to the maintenance of market efficiency, can matter, and may matter a lot, it is important to recognize that meaningful episodes of this nature are few and far between. For example, the former two pieces of Royal Dutch Petroleum—Royal Dutch trading in the United States and Shell Transport trading in London—were identical in their underlying assets. Based on their shares of those assets, the equity value of Royal Dutch should have been 1.5 times the equity value of Shell Transport, after adjustment for exchange rates. Nevertheless, Royal Dutch was undervalued relative to Shell by this metric for long periods of time, even by as much as 35 percent.

---

[*] For a vivid description of this phenomenon in the mortgage-backed securities market, see Gabaix, Krishnamurthy, and Vigneron (2005).

Another example would be the case of the well-known company MCI Communications, whose NASDAQ ticker symbol was MCIC and traded about a thousand times the daily volume of Massmutual Corporate Investors, a closed-end fund that invested mostly in corporate bonds but happened to have the ticker symbol MCI. The two companies obviously had nothing to do with each other. Nevertheless, from late 1994 to late 1997, and especially over the last twelve months when MCI was engaged in merger negotiations, the stocks tended to move together daily in terms of price and in terms of fluctuations in trading volume. The authors of the study of this example of investor confusion point out that "a large proportion of [activity in] MCI (Massmutual Corporate Investors) is . . . due to the actions of those having no intention of trading the stock [who], most likely, do not even know of its existence."[12]

Then why did arbitrageurs fail to step up and break the comovements of the two securities? These kinds of securities, with narrow markets, are difficult or costly to borrow. As a result, pricing discrepancies in special cases can persist for long periods of time, and failure of the Efficient Market Hypothesis is there for all to see.

Entertaining as these anomalies may be, that very feature reveals that violations of the no-arbitrage condition are not typical of the vast majority of situations in the market. These promising opportunities sound tempting, but we rarely encounter them.

Limits to arbitrage reappear in another guise in the second major set of evidence supporting the case for market inefficiency, namely, irrational pricing in the market as a whole in contrast to mispricing of individual securities. More familiar nomenclature for this phenomenon would be boom-and-bust. We shall return to this phenomenon from a different perspective in Chapter 6.

These widely separated but memorable demonstrations of market inefficiency are seared into memory: the 50 percent rise in stock prices from the middle of 1928 to October 1929; the subsequent plummet of 85 percent to the low of June 1932; Black Monday of October 19, 1987, when stocks lost over 20 percent of their value in one day; the Long-Term Capital Management crisis of the summer of 1998 when the imminent failure of this hedge fund nearly pulled down the whole financial system; the 140 percent boom from the end of 1995 to October 2000, and the subsequent 44 percent bust in February 2003.

Irrational pricing in the market as a whole need not take the form of boom-and-bust. In the 1970s, investors frightened by inflation and double-digit interest rates drove equity valuations down to near-record lows and dividend yields to near-record highs. As described in detail in a masterful analysis by Franco Modigliani and Richard Cohn in 1979, investors systematically ignored the positive impact of inflation on the value of corporate assets and on the dollar volume of corporate revenues, while simultaneously disregarding inflation's negative impact on the real values of corporate liabilities.[13] When Federal Reserve Chairman Paul Volcker finally won the war against inflation in 1981, investors woke up. The massive undervaluation in the equity market gave way to one of the most dramatic and extended bull markets in history.

These reminders of gross inefficiency in the market are grim enough. But what has come to be known as the "rational bubble" is another dramatic aspect of episodes that can lead to gross market inefficiency. "Rational bubble" sounds like an oxymoron, but it helps to describe conditions in which the presumably smart people—the so-called rational investors who pick off the mispricings provided for them by the noise traders—follow the crowd into a bubble on the assumption that this irrational exuberance is an opportunity to make money and that they will be so smart they will know how to get out in time.

Smart investors taking advantage of rational bubbles are by no means a new phenomenon. Peter Temin of MIT and Hans-Joachim Voth of the Universitat Pompeu Fabra in Barcelona report on a major London bank, Hoare's Bank, which rode the great South Sea bubble in 1720 and 1721.[14] Contemporary writings of the time made it clear that the South Sea Company could never earn enough to justify its bubbly price, but Hoare's Bank kept buying on the way up until August 1721, when it liquidated its position. The bubble burst in October.

A study of the recent NASDAQ bubble by Markus Brunnermeier of Princeton and Stegan Nagel of Stanford shows a similar pattern to Hoare's Bank.[15] At that time, a large sample of hedge funds was heavily tilted toward technology stocks, where the bubble of 1998–2000 was most visible. But this group of funds, on a stock-by-stock basis, reduced their holdings well before prices collapsed. As a result, these funds looked hot as they outperformed standard benchmarks. Brunnermeier and

Nagel conclude that "riding a price bubble for a while [in an irrational environment] can be the optimal strategy for rational investors."

We now return to the pivotal issue posed at the outset. Does the critique of the rational–agent model and the demonstrations of its empirical failures make the theories I set forth in *Capital Ideas* at least useless and at worst obsolete? Or can we turn instead to Merton Miller's characteristic quip about Behavioral Finance: "What can the poor kids do? The field of finance is kind of a mature field now."*[16] Eugene Fama has been almost as light-hearted as Miller in brushing off Behavioral Finance:

> Consistent with the market efficiency hypothesis that anomalies are chance results, apparent overreaction of stock prices to information is about as common as underreaction. And post-event continuation of pre-event abnormal returns is just about as frequent as post-event reversal. Most important, the long-term anomalies are fragile. . . . The evidence does not suggest that market efficiency should be abandoned.[17]

I would argue there is more to Behavioral Finance than its critics are willing to admit. As we have seen, Kahneman himself has expressed the case most emphatically: "The failure in the rational model is . . . in the human brain it requires." Valuation errors under those conditions are inevitable, and there is nothing inherent in the theory or in the no-arbitrage argument to support the notion that these errors will always offset one another.

But the issue is not whether the markets perform precisely as Capital Ideas prescribes. Rather, the issue is how well Capital Ideas have survived the attack from the behavioral side. Here the response has to be positive, not, as Fama so lightly suggests, because some of the anomalies offset one another, but for more profound reasons. The whole lesson embedded in Modern Portfolio Theory is that financial management is a risky business, and the contribution of Behavioral Finance has deep-

---

*Kahneman is no kid; he was 68 years old when he won the Nobel Prize and he is still going strong in research.

ened our understanding of how investors reach decisions and how they interact with one another under conditions of uncertainty.

There is good question, however, whether the contribution of Behavioral Finance goes farther than that. In the course of a conference call in late 2005, when I moderated a wide-ranging discussion among the five Nobel Prize winners in finance,* Kahneman observed: "I think behavioral models can be very important to institutional design, but *it isn't as clear that in the end they are going to have dramatic explanatory power for asset prices*" (emphasis added). In short, Behavioral Finance will not replace neoclassical finance until the law of supply and demand is repudiated.

As I emphasized in the Preface, the centrality of the trade-off between risk and expected return permeates all investment decisions today. Even investors confident of their ability to outperform admit the market is hard to beat—or else they would not charge such fancy fees for their efforts. Alpha and beta are essential ingredients of the complex investment strategies and an essential element of performance measurement. About a third of institutional financial assets have been indexed, even though active management is alive and well. The market and its various segments are still the primary benchmark by which clients pass judgment on their active managers. The phenomenal proliferation of derivative products needs no elaboration. Most important, we have no way of knowing whether mispricings in the marketplace are the result of behavioral anomalies or of other forces such as distorted information from managers or analysts.

An additional argument of high importance has received little attention elsewhere: Behavioral Finance has become an integral factor in this whole process. Ultimately all mispricings—all prices where expected returns and risk fail to line up systematically—arise from the heuristics investors employ in the daunting task of valuing financial assets. More precisely, behavioral anomalies are where alpha is born. Jeffrey Gould, president of the fabled hedge fund, Renaissance Investment

---

*The five Nobel Prize holders are Kahneman, Markowitz, Merton, Scholes, and Sharpe.

Management, describeds the firm's view of the process in these colorful words: "In order to protect returns, we don't show anyone else what we do or don't do. It would give people a leg up. We want them to keep doing what doesn't work, because it lets us capture more alpha."[18]

As a result, the more research the experts in Behavioral Finance provide, the greater the opportunity for active managers to identify where alpha may be lurking. In an odd way, then, Behavioral Finance plants the seeds of its own destruction, or, as Barr Rosenberg has phrased it, "By nature, such research is self-disfulfilling."[19]

The ultimate result is a market in the real world that bears a closer resemblance to the theoretical models than if Kahneman and Tversky had never encountered each other and launched their revolution in psychological research and experimentation. Exceptions and violations of efficiency will always exist. But the basic drive toward efficiency has received a great forward push from those who are teaching us so much about where the inefficiencies lurk. The normal brain will always seek a better road to riches.

At this point, our task is to see how this enriched investment process is actually taking shape in the capital markets. The most striking aspect of these changes is a total emphasis on implementation, even among the Nobel Prize winners in investment theory. The ideas are in place, but the new focus is on how the ideas can help active managers achieve alpha. As a result, a powerful mixture has developed from the deeper understanding of Capital Ideas combined with the contributions of Behavioral Finance. Both theorists and practitioners are using this blend to create ingenious applications for investment management and profound insights for understanding the whole investment process.

Sanford Grossman, chairman of the hedge fund, Quantitative Financial Strategies, Inc., and Professor of Finance Emeritus at the Wharton School, offered a more formal version of this argument thirty years ago:

> When a price system is a perfect aggregate of information it removes private incentives to collect information. If information is costly, there must be noise in the price system so that traders can

earn a return on information gathering. If there is no noise and information collection is costly, then a perfect competitive market will break down because no equilibrium exists where one collects information.[20]

A strange paradox emerges when we consider Grossman's observation in light of this review of Behavioral Finance. On the one hand, Behavioral Finance has become a primary tool for active managers seeking to earn alpha. On the other hand, and as a result of the urgent hunt for mispricing in the markets, Behavioral Finance has also become the driving force toward the Efficient Market Hypothesis that it so vigorously attacks.

Suppose that active managers ignore Behavioral Finance because they are convinced the market is dominated by too many smart traders. Then these active managers will all throw in the sponge and become indexers. If everyone becomes a passive investor, the volumes of Behavioral Finance research would lie moldering in university libraries and nobody would be seeking out the mispricings.

Thus, the team that accepts market efficiency and favors indexing would leave the behavioral anomalies in place in a market riddled with inefficiency. But the denizens of Behavioral Finance, the team fighting hardest to defeat the notion of market efficiency, are the ones who are doing the most to make market efficiency a reality.

PART II
THE THEORETICIANS

3

Paul A. Samuelson
The Worldly Philosopher

With the passage of time, the leading theorists in the field of finance have lost none of their zest, none of their fascination with innovation, none of their sense of the compelling importance of the work they are doing. Except for Paul Samuelson (who is now over ninety years old and has earned the right to observe rather than act), all these men are occupied—and on occasion obsessed—with innovations to make markets work better and protect investors from their foibles.

This ambitious goal represents a powerful idea: that forces can be unleashed to improve the functional resemblance between the markets in the real world and the markets as they are defined and described in Capital Ideas. Although reality may never duplicate the way information is disseminated and comprehended in the Efficient Market Hypothesis, the positive and systematic correlation between risk and return as defined in the Capital Asset Pricing Model is coming closer all the time.

As suggested at the end of Chapter 2 on Behavioral Finance, that is the direction the forces at work in the marketplace are heading. Indeed, the subsequent discussion of the innovations of practitioners will demonstrate how active investors in an urgent search for excess returns—or alpha—are inventing new kinds of strategies and new kinds of financial instruments that are constantly driving the markets toward equilibrium and toward the kinds of relationships and responses predicted by theory.*

◈

Paul Samuelson is the theorist with the longest perspective. To interview him for this book, I went to visit with him in the same office where he launched me, in 1989, as I was starting my research for *Capital Ideas*. When I told him about my plans for the new edition, Samuelson declared there is "no part of economics where there is greater confluence between theory and actual uses."†

Samuelson still believes there are no easy pickings in the stock market. Even when somebody's track record indicates they have outperformed the averages after adjustment for risk—they earned what finance professors call positive alpha—positive alpha is still difficult to identify beyond doubt. Benchmarks are mushy, risk measurements are arbitrary, and what we want to classify as alpha, or beating the market, is often just the return to systematic risk, or beta. Even if someone can demonstrate a manager earned alpha this year, that tells you nothing about whether they can repeat their feat the following year.

Samuelson made this point with eloquence in the first issue of *The Journal of Portfolio Management,* which appeared in the fall of 1974, which I quoted also in the original edition of *Capital Ideas:*

> They also serve who only sit and hold; but I suppose the fees to be earned by such sensible and prosaic behavior are less than from essaying to give it that old post-college try. . . . But a respect for evidence compels me to incline toward the hypothesis that most portfolio decision makers should go out of business—take up plumbing, teach Greek, or help produce the annual GNP by serving as corporate executives (*sic*). Even if this advice to drop dead is good advice, it obviously is not counsel that will be eagerly followed. Few people will commit suicide without a push.[1]

Alpha represents returns above or below what the Capital Asset Pricing Model predicts. As a practical matter, in today's world of practitioners, alpha refers to returns in excess of the returns of a benchmark such as the S&P 500, after adjustment for risk.
† All material in quotation marks is from an interview, unless otherwise indicated.

Ever the economist, Samuelson has mixed feelings about Behavioral Finance, which he wryly defined to me as "the study of people not doing the most rational thing as judged by assistant professors of finance." Nevertheless, Samuelson's connection with Behavioral Finance is far from casual. As Robert Shiller of Yale has pointed out in a recent paper, "This is a good occasion to recall that [Samuelson] was in an important sense one of the originators of the canonical intertemporal model that underlies much of the theory of neoclassical finance, but also, at the same time, anticipated a good deal of the progress of behavioral finance. This means that both maximizing finance and behavioral finance were born together, are sisters."[2] As an example, Shiller cites Samuelson's classic paper published in 1937, "A Note on Measurement of Utility," in which Samuelson argues that people are not time-consistent.[3] Aware of that weak point, they often try to control themselves with decisions designed to bind their future, such as the "behavior of men who make irrevocable trusts, in taking out life insurance as a compulsory savings measure."[*]

Samuelson admires Kahneman but considers much of the work in the area as "a lot of noise." He believes the ultimate judgment of Behavioral Finance is whether you make money out of it. In a masterful statement that reveals Samuelson's keen grasp of the real world of investing, he points out that most investors "do not even understand how to capitalize on the behavioral anomalies, even if they are skeptics about efficiency and fans of behavioral theories. Indeed, *part of their own irrationality is their unwillingness to accept the volatility and kinds of risks that do average out to be profitable*" (italics added).

As Samuelson describes it, "I realize that by the millions investors are not experts in probability and portfolio optimality. Most of them are cautious risk averters whose dislike for losses far outweighs their like for gains—although this does not rule out their betting on horse and dog racing, or buying lottery tickets, or attending bingo sessions." And

---

[*]On a personal note, I first met Paul Samuelson about the time this paper appeared. Then in his early twenties, Samuelson had already made his reputation by having published more papers than he was years old.

then he adds, "There is a separate love for the sport of gambling. But that is independent of the way they respond to the more serious business of managing their wealth. There loss aversion prevails."

◈

From Samuelson's point of view, the existence of a positive alpha somewhere is not an exception to the Efficient Market Hypothesis but a kind of vindication of the logic of it. There are rare occasions when an investor succeeds in earning positive alpha—beating the market after adjustment for risk by gaining access to information earlier than other investors or by discovering mispriced assets other investors ignored. But Samuelson believes "it is efficient for that alpha to be corrected and it is logically implied that those with better information have to make money. Although Behavioral Finance claims the vast majority of investors are shot through with systemic irrationalities, it does not follow that the market as a whole becomes irrational. You could have 98 percent of the money in the market that is irrational, and you could still have the Efficient Market Hypothesis."

Samuelson does agree that we cannot take the Efficient Market Hypothesis as dogma, but he also believes most evidence of beating the market is merely hot hands—a run of good luck. "Schumpeter taught me there are no franchises. You are king for a day." And then he adds about Schumpeter, "Schumpeter used to say the top-dollar rooms in capitalism's grand hotel are always occupied, but not by the same occupants."[4]

Yet Samuelson is not dogmatic on this vital question. He prefers to put it this way: "My twist is that modern busy bourses display what I like to call Limited Micro Efficiency. So long as a minute minority of investors, possessed of considerable assets, can seek gain by trading against willful uninformed bettors, then Limited Efficiency of Markets will be empirically observable. The temporary appearance of aberrant price profiles coaxes action from alert traders who act gleefully to wipe out the aberration." In more colorful language, he has made the same point this way: "My pitch on this occasion is not exclusively or even primarily aimed at practical men. The less of them who become sophisticated, the better for us happy few."[5]

The consequence of all this market activity is a more complex state of affairs than we would find in a truly random walk.* As Samuelson points out, "After numerous people carefully weigh new information arriving about the future, all that is pragmatically knowable is *already* in current pricing patterns. This makes speculative prices behave like what mathematicians called a 'martingale,' where in the next period prices may as likely change more than the total market index or change less." It is a paradox but nevertheless true that stock prices are so hard to predict because stock prices are themselves predictions of the future.[†]

This kind of complexity in the behavior of markets leads stock prices to have momentum in one direction in the short run but tend to reverse the momentum over the longer run as more information becomes available. Samuelson describes this phenomenon as, "Positive momentum 'blue noise' rather than purely random 'white noise' pervades in the short run, even microeconomically, [while] reversion toward the mean obtains in the long run—that is, the market emits 'red noise' rather than 'white' or 'blue.'"

This perspective has led Samuelson to agree with Shiller, who has developed an elaborate case to demonstrate how macro-*inefficiency* of markets—up bubbles and down bubbles—can happen.[††] Samuelson takes this phenomenon seriously: "Smarty-pants me dare not try to profit by timing bids aimed to bet against strong macro waves up and down in the S&P 500."

The market reverts toward the mean in the long run because investors finally begin to recognize that it is "too high" or "too low." In other words, there is always a drive toward efficiency in the market, and it becomes most potent when prices have moved far enough away from equilibrium to lure investors to change the market's direction.[†]

The crucial issue is whether you make money in the short run from recognizing these patterns. Samuelson is convinced most investors will fail because they have a fetish about smooth and growing paths for earnings per share. "Alas, knowing [these patterns] doesn't seem to garner

---

*See one of Samuelson's most influential masterpieces, "Proof That Properly Anticipated Prices Fluctuate Randomly," *Industrial Management Review*, Vol. 6 (Spring 1965), pp. 41–50.
[†] I am grateful to Frank Fabozzi for this insight.
[††] See Chapter 6.

lush trading returns. The Good Book says, 'There is a time to remember and a time to forget.' Alas, we need a better book to inform us on how and when we should switch our gears." And he concludes, "No book can make you rich; few can keep you rich; many will speed up your loss of fortune. No successful trader can teach his brother-in-law the rare art of enjoying a hard-earned living from a computer. What it boils down to is that those who manage money for billionaires can hope to learn more earlier than we run-of-the-mill investors."

Samuelson's ultimate conclusion is an old-fashioned one: He continues to believe that "wide diversification of portfolios is the canny way to sleep nights and husband one's life-cycle savings." As Harry Markowitz declared in 1952, "[A] rule of behavior which does not imply the superiority of diversification must be rejected as both a hypothesis and as a maxim."[6] Simple observation of the experiences of most investors confirms the wisdom of this simple advice. Even the humble who turn to the experts to manage their money will be disappointed in most instances. "Yes," admits Samuelson, "there are a few Babe Ruths who can outearn the crowd. There are also a few—very few—traders who do out-beat the averages in the longer run. The trouble is that you and I can't identify that special few." But suppose we can? "We can't buy their prowess cheap. Stubbornly looking for them can cost us dear."

The vigor, the freshness, and the extraordinary clarity of Samuelson's mind would be stunning to encounter in a man of any age. His research and theoretical analysis are still state-of-the art. But we can be extra thankful he has been with us so long, because he has bequeathed to posterity a remarkable collection of students who developed into great scholars. Two of his protégés, and one protégé of a protégé, appear in the next three chapters: Robert C. Merton of Harvard Business School, Andrew Lo of the Sloan School at MIT, and Robert Shiller of the Cowles Foundation at Yale.

Merton, a high-powered mathematician who started out in economics and finance as an assistant to Samuelson, helped Black and Scholes develop the options pricing model, work for which he won a Nobel Prize.

Merton, however, is no longer attempting to develop new theoretical structures. Rather, he has entered into a zealous pursuit of innovative institutional designs based on Capital Ideas to help investors overcome the behavioral anomalies we read about in Chapters 1 and 2. Here his mathematical skills are helpful but are in many ways incidental to what he is trying to achieve.

Lo was one of Merton's star students when Merton was on the MIT faculty, and Merton was the primary motivation for Lo's interest in finance (Lo took every course Merton offered). Lo is in many ways pursuing goals similar to Merton's emphasis on institutions, but his approach is different. A firm believer in the power of evolutionary forces, he is more interested in explaining institutional *change* than in creating new institutional forms. His work leads to important and original insights into the deeper meaning of such developments as pricing stocks in cents instead in quarters of a dollar and the role of hedge funds—one of the most rapidly growing institutional forms of our era.

Shiller has been fascinated for a long time in the volatility of financial markets. He has demonstrated how the volatility of these markets is far greater than the volatility of the fundamentals that theoretically determine asset prices. This field of study naturally drew Shiller's attention to patterns of boom-and-bust, ultimately giving him a reputation way beyond the academic world for his book, *Irrational Exuberance,* which appeared just as the stock market was topping out at the end of 2000. Boom-and-bust is not part of Capital Ideas, but Capital Ideas are still a part of Shiller's analytical framework.

Paul Samuelson's handiwork runs through it all.

THE
INSTITUTIONALISTS

4

Robert C. Merton

"Risk Is Not an Add-On"

R obert C. Merton, Samuelson's most famous protégé, had just moved to Harvard Business School from MIT when I interviewed him for *Capital Ideas*. Merton is still teaching at Harvard, but we met this time at the New York City office of his busy consulting firm. The shift in location from Harvard to New York defines the focus of our discussion.

Merton has in many ways left theory behind: That job is done. Now he aims to seek ways we could redesign the financial system from the busy hodge-podge it is today into a powerful and sensibly organized mechanism for risk sharing and for exploiting return opportunities.

This new goal does not mean Merton has lost his admiration for the original ideas about portfolio theory, market behavior, and the valuation of options: "The power of it is the way it cuts through to the core—asset pricing and the role of risk. Wonderful things! You can be comfortable with these abstractions because of their power. They can tell you a lot without any reference to institutional elements."*

Most important, these ideas all have risk at their core. "Risk is not an add-on," Merton observes, "it permeates the whole body of thought."[1]

Merton is gently tolerant of the critics of Capital Ideas. In a paper written as far back as 1975, he said:

---

*Unless otherwise specified, all quotations are from personal interviews.

It is not uncommon to attack our basic "mythology," particularly the "Ivory Tower" nature of our assumptions. . . . Like a Sunday morning sermon, such talks serve many useful functions. For one, they serve to deflate our professional egos. For another, they serve to remind us that the importance of a contribution as judged by our professional peers (the gold we really work for) is often not closely aligned with its operational importance in the outside world. Also, such talks serve to comfort those just entering the field, by letting them know that there is much left to do because so little has been done.[2]

Merton does find serious shortcomings with theory when we move into the real-world marketplace and seek to put what he describes as neoclassical ideas into practice. Capital Ideas were developed in a static, institution-free environment, full of faceless people, each of whom trades as an individual and who, inevitably, will hold identical portfolios of risky assets. This abstraction from the intricacies of reality is appropriate in a frictionless, perfect market environment.

Merton believes the kinds of flaws in the literature on Behavioral Finance are similar in nature to the flaws in the neoclassical theories, because so much of the behavioral material also assumes an atomistic market of individuals. Then you are left with the same unworldly model as the Efficient Market Hypothesis or the Capital Asset Pricing Model. Merton's vision of reality is closer to the reality of day-to-day financial activity. He sees a world in which institutions intermediating on behalf of individuals make for a different and more efficient market environment.

Once we introduce human beings, institutional arrangements, and transactions costs, we also introduce frictions and agency problems. Then investors are not the homogeneous crowd we met in Capital Ideas. They hold portfolios differing from one another in an almost infinite number of ways. The character of the institutions and the nature of transactions costs have an enormous impact on the variety and shape of the markets, on investor behavior, and on the development of financial instruments. A college endowment and an employee with a 401(k) plan are different investors.

Since *Capital Ideas* appeared in 1992, the institutional structure of financial markets has gone through a fundamental transformation. Investors in the early 1990s had not even a glimmer of today's flood of information by means of the computer and the Internet; the instruments being traded; the reality of computerized trading in place of exchange floors; the management of the stock exchanges themselves; the global interlocks; the size, sophistication, and orientation of the larger investors; the proliferation of money market funds, mutual funds, and hedge funds; the development of risk-sharing instruments blurring distinction between the commercial banks or insurance companies and the capital markets; or the transformation of pension funding from defined-benefit to defined-contribution. Even this extended listing of innovations is far from complete.

Merton emphasizes that form follows function. These novel institutional impulses do not change the theory of finance, but they do extend its range of applications in revolutionary fashion. These changes in both form and function are among the most powerful forces shaping the evolution of Capital Ideas. Just as Behavioral Finance exposes alpha opportunities, so the fluidity of institutional structures and functions has profound implications for how markets work, how investors behave, how investors *should* behave, and where we should look for improvements and enhancements to what we see around us today.

As we shall see, Merton, Shiller, and Lo are all finding new ways to use and even invent institutions to cushion risks and improve outcomes in a wide variety of areas.

Merton is the son of the great sociologist, Robert K. Merton, who had a profound intellectual influence on him and on his approaches to understanding problems.* Merton Senior's sociological sense has inspired Merton Junior's fascination with the essential role of institutions, because the functions of institutions can actually change the form of the whole investment process. Institutions perform functions for individual investors that individuals could never perform for themselves.

This view does not mean institutions are immune from behavioral features. Group decisions of the members of the investment committees of foundations, endowments, pension funds, and mutual funds have their own systematic behavioral quirks. While we would hope their individual behavior among a group of professionals would be more coolly

---

*Robert K. Merton died in 2003.

analytical than untrained individual investors operating on their own, that may be too much to ask.

The issue is not just that these members of committees are human beings like everyone else. Many of the mispricings and anomalies arising from group decisions will be different from the anomalies created by individuals acting alone. Agency problems are inescapable. Investment committees are always sensitive to peer pressures from other funds, especially those outperforming them. Committees have to face the judgments of the management of the company sponsoring the fund, whether it is a pension fund, an endowment, or a foundation. No committee member is likely to stay on the board for the life of the fund, because nobody is likely to live that long, but the relative brevity of their tenure naturally biases their views toward outcomes shorter in term than the expected life of the fund.

Yet Merton is sanguine about the long-run impact of institutions on the functioning of the capital markets. He is convinced that innovations developed by profit-seeking institutions, like mutual funds and insurance companies, can mitigate and even overcome the behavioral anomalies and market inefficiencies created by individual investors in the real world. In economics, it is the lowest-cost producers that determine market prices. Institutional innovation and competition are forces for the reduction of transactions costs and the allocational effects of behavioral dysfunctions. As these forces come increasingly into play, "The prediction of the neoclassical model [Capital Ideas] will be approximately valid for asset prices and resource allocation."[3]

Merton has written extensively about this vision. A paper he coauthored in 2005 with Zvi Bodie of Boston University sums up many of his ideas and proposals for bringing together the neoclassical, the institutional, and the behavioral perspectives on finance. Merton and Bodie call their goal of synthesizing these three perspectives *Functional and Structural Finance*. In their view, "This analysis has direct implications for the process of investment management and for prospective evolution of the asset management industry."[4]

But first, an important question: Why do we have the institutions we have, and why do we organize as we have organized? Merton's central argument, derived from sociological analysis, is that institutions are endogenous—developed within the system in response to needs, to anomalies, and to dysfunctional aberrations. For example, "I can design an insurance company, but can I make money? Not if it is inappropriate for the needs of the markets. That is what I mean by endogenous development."

Most individuals have too little money to achieve efficient diversification and to pay the fees demanded by high-powered investment management firms. So they pool their assets in mutual funds that enjoy the economies of scale. As a result, diversification is greater than individuals can manage on their own, and the costs in terms of fees and transactions costs are lower. In the same fashion, a defined-benefit pension plan relieves the individual employees of the tasks and risks of financing their retirement and reduces the cost of investing their retirement funds—an advantage the defined-contribution plans cannot offer.

This continuous process of institutional creativity is what leads to change and dynamics. At the forefront of those developments are the derivatives markets—the brainchildren of the Black-Scholes-Merton options pricing model, now over thirty years old. The result is a world strikingly different from the world of Capital Ideas, in which there is no change in the institutional structure: In that world, today's system looks just like yesterday's—assets get priced, portfolios get formed, risks get hedged, and then nothing happens.

Merton's case is most vivid when we turn to the problems of financing retirement. Retirement always has existed in one way or another, for all people everywhere, but how people have provided institutionally for that eventuality has varied widely over time and in different countries around the world. The tasks of taking care of retired people do not change, but the institutions to carry out those functions do change in response to advancing technology, varying cultural conditions, and a dynamic view of the future—"a rich set for us to think about."

Merton and Bodie point out that their functional perspective provides a frame to study the matter. This frame also suggests why and how institutions evolve—they are an answer to something. So now the job is to go back to the ideas, see how they work in an institutional setting, and find out how we can do it better. As Merton sees it, "You can move from the unrealistic world of theory in which everybody agrees about asset prices and risks to the real world in which everybody agrees to use institutions."

The power of innovative institutions to change markets is clear from just a few examples, which Merton and Bodie place under the heading of "the financial innovation spiral." Money market funds now compete with banks and thrifts for household savings. Securitization of auto loans and credit card receivables has intensified competition among financial institutions as sources for these purposes. High-yield bonds have liberated many companies from the icy grip of their commercial bankers. In national mortgage markets, many institutions have developed into major alternatives to thrifts as a source for residential mortgages. These institutional innovations have improved the lot of consumers and business firms by reducing the costs of the services they require.

Merton is convinced that the most fruitful source for continuing the spiral of financial innovation will develop primarily from the valuation of options, or, more precisely, of contingent claims—the contribution to the theory of finance for which he earned the Nobel Prize. Merton had joined up with Fischer Black and Myron Scholes in their search for the valuation of options in the spring of 1970, because he doubted they were on the right track in their conviction that the Capital Asset Pricing Model would produce the right answer (see *Capital Ideas*, pp. 216–219).

He unlocked the puzzle they were trying to solve by offering them the concept of a replicating portfolio—a portfolio combining the underlying asset with cash or borrowing. The replicating portfolio's holding of the underlying asset would vary depending upon the movement of the asset's price above and below the strike price of the option. Although designed to mimic changes in the valuation of the option, the replicating portfolio would perform this function with precision only when the dynamic trading it involves can be executed in a world without frictions—instant responses, no brokerage commissions, no spreads between bid and ask, no closing times for the markets, no taxes. Under those conditions, choosing between the option or the replicating portfolio would be a matter of indifference. In fact, if this frictionless environment were available to all investors, the option would be redundant.

Just two assets could create any kind of contingent contract, providing for all kinds of payoffs.[5]

The real world is something else again. Transactions costs get in the way, because the replicating portfolio is continuously trading into and out of the underlying asset, such as stocks and cash. As a result, the replicating portfolio cannot precisely mimic the value of the option as conditions change in the real world.

An effort to construct a practical application of the replicating portfolio took place in the mid-1980s, when two academics introduced a strategy they called portfolio insurance (see Chapter 14 of *Capital Ideas*). The goal of portfolio insurance was to have the portfolio perform as though the owner had bought a put option on the S&P 500. Under this strategy, the client's portfolio moved systematically from stocks to cash when the market was falling and from cash to stocks when the market was rising. But portfolio insurance came to a sad end in the shambles of the crash of October 19, 1987, when stock prices fell by over 20 percent in one day. Investors using portfolio insurance did fare better than uninsured investors, but their outcome was far from what they had been led to expect. The difficulty of executing transactions was overwhelming as panic transformed the whole market-making process into a disaster area.

Because of the practical difficulties, especially the transactions costs of managing a replicating portfolio, investors are better off trading in a derivative instrument such as an option or a futures contract, if it is available. As Merton explains, "Black-Scholes has value because of the existence of transaction costs!" If there were no transactions costs to anyone, puts and calls would be useless, portfolio insurance would have been a glorious success, and Black, Scholes, and Merton would have had to find other ways to spend their time—and would they have won a Nobel anyway?

In reality, institutions efficiently produce options and other contingent claims and sell them to investors who desire the payoff patterns of the replicating portfolio at low cost. This approach has created the virtually limitless markets for options and the myriads of derivatives we know today. To Merton, these markets are the crown jewels of the whole system, because derivative instruments have greatly expanded opportunities for risk sharing, have lowered transactions costs, and have reduced information and agency costs.

The bad news in this story is that we cannot trade without incurring the cost of producers who, in effect, do the replicating executions for us. But the good news is that competition is constantly forcing the institutions in the capital markets to seek ways of lowering transactions costs. Thus, institutional change is providing huge benefits to investors over what those investors would face without the miracles of technology and competition.

For example, the Plexus Group, specialists in the analysis of transactions costs, anticipates a dramatic reduction in the cost of trading from the mergers between purely electronic exchanges like Instinet and traditional security markets with floor brokers, like the New York Stock Exchange or NASDAQ. "Investors will be the clear winners," Plexus wrote in 2005 in a prophetic statement. "When costs come down due to enhancements in market functionality, more ideas become actionable. . . . The real gains will come from the opening up of new investment strategies. . . . Institutional investors can profit from ideas that have smaller expectations, to the benefit of investors"[6]

Merton envisions almost infinite variations along these lines. He and Bodie point to several new kinds of investment strategies designed to lower transactions costs. As one example, they foresee a major change in the role of the mutual fund "from a direct retail product to an intermediate or 'building block' product embedded in the more integrated products used to implement the consumer's financial plan. The 'fund of funds' [in the hedge fund industry] is an early, crude example."[7]

Merton and Bodie offer an assortment of institutional arrangements to deal with the kinds of "cognitive difficulties" that fill the pages of Behavioral Finance research. One of these difficulties is the influence of regret on investor decision making. Some people may be afraid to buy because the stock may fall after they buy it. Others are afraid to sell because the stock may go up after they sell it. Merton and Bodie offer a "look-back" option as "insurance" against these uncertainties. A look-back call option would give the buyer the right to buy an underlying security at the lowest price at which it traded during the term of the option. A look-back put option would give the holder the right to sell the underlying security at the highest price at which it traded during the term of the option. These options would not come for free, but the investors would have no need to fear regret under those conditions!

Merton exclaims, "That's the kind of thing that excites me. I am never going to retire!" And then he expands on the subject:

> I always wanted to implement things I believe in, such as working with the theories of finance, but now, thanks to technology, we have a whole new paradigm. No, a *richer* paradigm. The answers given by Capital Ideas are still valid—it's not like they got it wrong and now we have a revolution. My point is understanding institutions and how they make implementation of these ideas possible. . . .
>
> I look at myself as a plumber. I want to have available all the tools—government, private sector, family institutions. We need them all. The choice of tools depends on the job. . . . The beauty is in developing new theoretical concepts and then seeing them implemented to have an impact on real-world practice.

Merton is a pioneer who thinks big when it comes to implementation. Consider a country, called Country A, which has a flourishing automobile industry and no electronics firms. Country B is in the opposite situation, electronics but no automobiles. Both would like to diversify.

The traditional step would be for each to establish new industries—in which neither will have comparative advantage. A far less costly and more efficient solution to their problems is available in a simple financial instrument called a swap. Under this arrangement, Country A would pay to Country B the returns on a global portfolio of automobile stocks, while Country B would pay to Country A the returns on a world electronics portfolio. Thus, diversification is achieved, but each country will continue to benefit by producing the products in which it has comparative advantage—and all this thanks to just a few signatures on a piece of paper! As Merton describes it, "The day before the swap is done and the day after, the workers in each country go to work . . . in the same way; there are no changes required to the domestic financial system and how people practice business. Thus, this approach to potentially massive risk transfer is non-invasive of the domestic system."[8]

Direct, one-to-one swap transactions of this nature are not always available. For example, an investor may seek to swap with another investor the return on a European stock market for the return on the S&P

500, at an agreed-upon price, an arrangement that saves both sides the costs of liquidating from one market and purchasing in the other. The concept is simple, but finding somebody to do the other side of the transaction is not. At that point, the institutional traders step into the picture, because it is their business to intermediate—make markets—between two parties to a transaction. As a result, Merton observes, the swap market "has developed from bilateral dealings into a standardized, adjudicated set of instruments, where you can execute a swap at the cost of merely a few basis points. Done in a second and in the trillions of dollars." Once again, institutions make all the difference in the structure and capabilities of financial instruments.

Merton's overriding vision is right there: The process has no borders. It need not stop, and will not stop, in any area of finance. As the process advances, today's anomalies will shrink under the pressure of institutional competition, new technologies, and the inexorable decline in transactions costs. And then, as pointed out earlier, *the predictions of the neoclassical model [Capital Ideas] will be approximately valid for asset prices and resource allocation"* (emphasis added).

An interesting test of Merton's optimism is under way in, of all places, the Taiwan stock market—the world's twelfth-largest financial market. Like New York, the Taiwan market was a mighty busy place during the late 1990s, as turnover averaged more than three times the historically high rate of turnover on the New York Stock Exchange. Day trading—involving a purchase and sale of the same security on a single day—accounted for nearly one out of every four trades.

Here institutions have been the clear winners, and unsophisticated investors are the clear losers. The evidence on this remarkable story appears in a paper by Brad Barber of the University of California, Davis, and three colleagues.[9] Their analysis reports on the results from a comprehensive data set on the Taiwan market, including information on every single trade, the underlying orders for each trade, and the identity of the trade during the period 1995 through 1999.

During this period, the aggregate portfolio of corporations, dealers, foreigners, and mutual funds showed annual gains of 1.5 percent over and above the gains they would have made just from the rise or fall of the market as a whole. Individuals, on the other hand, had disastrous results. Their returns from trading were 3.8 percent a year lower than if they had just invested on a buy-and-hold basis. The absolute magnitude of that number is astonishing: It is equal to 2.2 percent of Taiwan's nominal GDP during 1995–1999, or nearly as much as total consumer spending on clothing and footwear in Taiwan.

This weird and persistent form of market behavior evokes what Daniel Kahneman has had to say on these phenomena in a more general sense: "It is quite remarkable that you have those individuals losing money, and there seems to be an endless supply of individuals, because this is not a transitory phenomenon. So the equilibrium is a very strange equilibrium that seems to exist out there."[10]

How long will this disheartening performance in Taiwan continue—and, indeed, how representative is it of markets around the world? In time, one would expect individuals to figure out what is happening to them. This paper by Barber et al., and others like it, should be a spur to action. Then these investors would give up trying to manage their own money and would transfer their funds to institutional investors to invest for them. As a result, competition among institutional investors in the Taiwan market would become more intense, and beating the market would become more difficult as the anomalies of the individual investors disappear. Merton's expectation would come true—that the institutional structure will continue to change until "the predictions of the neoclassical model [Capital Ideas] will be approximately valid for asset prices and resource allocation."

Merton is characteristically optimistic about how the process will develop. The institutional impact has powerful momentum, and that momentum will push inexorably away from the behavioral anomalies now prevailing in Taiwan and toward a market structure resembling the market structure described in standard investment theory. Function, once again, will drive the form of the investment process.

5

Andrew Lo

"The Only Part of Economics That Really Works"

Whelm Andrew Lo arrived at Yale as an undergraduate in 1977, he had every intention of going for a triple major in mathematics, physics, and biochemistry, which were the "cool" subjects at his high school, the Bronx School of Science ("the single most important educational experience of my life").[*] He also wanted to follow in the footsteps of his older brother, "a rocket scientist," and his older sister, a molecular biologist.

That is not at all what happened. Lo ended up majoring in economics at college and went on to earn a Ph.D. in economics at Harvard. Today he is Harris & Harris Group Professor of Finance and director of the Laboratory for Financial Engineering at the MIT Sloan School of Management as well as the cofounder and Chief Scientific Officer of a hedge fund. Along the way, Lo has accumulated a long list of awards and fellowships, including awards for teaching excellence at MIT.

What converted a budding scientist into a powerhouse in the world of finance? A strange book and a casual social luncheon combined to produce the Andrew Lo of today, a pioneering theorist in what financial markets are all about and, in turn, what the hurly-burly of the markets reveals about the theory of finance.

[*] Unless otherwise specified, quotations are from personal interviews or correspondence.

While he was at Bronx Science, Lo read *The Foundation Trilogy* by the science fiction writer Isaac Asimov. The story was about a mathematician who develops a theory of human behavior called "psychohistory." Psychohistory can predict the future course of human events, but only when the population reaches a certain size because the predictions are based on statistical models. Lo was hooked. He found Asimov's narrative to be plausible enough to become a reality some day, and he wanted to be the one to make it happen. Economics, especially game theory and mathematical economics, looked like the best way to get started. He made the decision in his second year at Yale to do just that.

Toward the end of the first semester of his graduate work at Harvard, Lo ran into a former classmate from Bronx Science who was studying economics at MIT. They went to lunch together. While they were chatting, she urged him to take a course in finance at MIT with a man named Robert C. Merton, as MIT and Harvard allow cross-registration between the two universities. Robert Merton? Lo had never heard of him. Finance? He knew pretty well how to balance his checkbook. But he had sufficient confidence in his friend's judgment to sign up for Merton's course.

It was a turning point. As Lo puts it, "This single course changed my life. I found that more of my intellectual thirst was slaked by Merton's lectures. This was finally what I had been searching for. Exactly 25 years later, I can still tell you exactly which lecture contained the notion of arbitrage, the idea of replicating options by dynamic trading, and the formula for Markowitz's concept of optimizing mean/variance portfolios."

Once Lo discovered finance had more to it than balancing checkbooks, the bug had bitten him. He took every single finance course the Sloan School at MIT offered, including every course Merton taught and classes with Fischer Black and Franco Modigliani.

Finance—"the only part of economics that actually works"—appealed because it combines rigorous mathematics with hard-core practical problems. At that moment, in the early 1980s, academics in the field of financial economics were still working out the full theoretical implications of Markowitz's theory of portfolio selection, the Efficient Market Hypothesis, the Capital Asset Pricing Model, the options pricing model, and Modigliani and Miller's iconoclastic ideas about corporate finance and the central role of arbitrage.

That emphasis on theory made the bait even tastier for Lo. He saw the way clear to follow Asimov's advice. By applying statistical models to the daily practice of finance in the real world, he would not only move the field of finance forward from its focus on theory, but even more enticing, he would also find the holy grail he was seeking in the first place: solutions to Asimov's psychohistory.

Progress was rapid. By 1988 he was an untenured professor at MIT, having turned down an offer of tenure to stay at Wharton. And by 1990, at the age of 29, he received a tenured professorship at MIT.

Lo looks at finance through a prism in which the theory of finance itself is just one element. He blends finance with a combination of economics, mathematics, the physical sciences, history, and evolutionary biology, as well as sociology and psychology. This perspective of markets functioning in such a broad and varied context naturally led him to an interest in institutions. But he dug deep into theory before he became aware that institutions play such a strategic role in the whole story.

From this complex perspective, he has found the Efficient Market Hypothesis an especially fruitful area for study. Prior to the development of the Efficient Market Hypothesis in the 1960s, he points out, there was no disciplined way to analyze the behavior of financial markets. By changing how people looked at markets, the Efficient Market Hypothesis has transformed the daily turmoil of the marketplace, and what seemed like an incomprehensible set of theoretical issues, into a relatively simple set of concepts. Prices in financial markets reflect the arrival of new information, but those prices reflect the new information so rapidly you cannot make money trying to be smarter than everybody else. "This is a very powerful idea—a big break with the past," Lo observes.

With all his respect for the Efficient Market Hypothesis, and the theory of rational expectations that forms the base from which it evolved, Lo laments what he sees as excessive academic emphasis on these concepts. To him, the trouble with the Efficient Market Hypothesis is less with the theory itself than with the way many academics have forgotten how these abstractions came from the real world of tumult and confusion in the capital markets. He deplores the way today's economists believe they do not have to know any history. "Economics in the real world owes more to history than to abstract theory. . . . This frustrates me to no end," Lo exclaims. "Economics is *not* a science. History matters in trying to understand and apply it."

Lo contends the Efficient Market pond has been fished out. We have to think of something else, but where do we go? The anomalies uncovered in the field of Behavioral Finance are interesting, but in the end Lo finds the behavioral approach frustrating as well. These findings are only "a collection of anomalies, not a real theory. *You need a theory to beat a theory*" (emphasis added). Indeed, you need a powerful application to beat other powerful applications. A more sophisticated view is essential, one that focuses on the nature of the individuals and groups who compose the market.

In the Efficient Market Hypothesis, all available information is reflected in market prices. But when you turn to an explanation of the dynamics and search beneath the surface of the markets, you see the resemblance to the forces of biology and evolution—intense competition among players who are constantly changing with the passage of time. "Living through a bull market, for example, can change your entire view of what the market is about, what your preferences are, your appetite for risk, the range of probabilities you see for possible outcomes. We are all creatures of our upbringing, and those preferences shape the interactions across markets—bonds, stocks, options—as well as across cultures—Chinese, Swedes, Americans."

Investors are not the automatons of the Efficient Market Hypothesis. They differ in countless ways from one another and, more important, they differ from one another and even themselves across time.

These views did not develop out of a vacuum. Lo studies with an unusual intensity and a hunger to learn. The possibility that the capital markets are not a random walk came to him quite by accident—in fact, it came to him as he was working on the opposite hypothesis that markets *are* a random walk. When the evidence fell short of supporting the random walk hypothesis, Lo just looked harder in search of an explanation.

After six years, he relates, "I finally decided that markets don't really follow random walks. The notion is a great idealization but not the real thing. And this work got me tenure at MIT!" One of the results of that extended period of study and experimentation was a book aptly titled, *A Non-Random Walk Down Wall Street,* coauthored with A. Craig MacKinlay and published in 1999.

Frustrated with the shortcomings of Behavioral Finance, but also convinced that the theoretical structure of the Efficient Market Hypothesis has profound flaws in terms of the real world, Lo returned to his original fascination with Isaac Asimov and psychohistory. Now human behavior and the impact of past experience combine with the rigors of mathematical and scientific analysis to compose the motivating forces in all of Lo's work. The central concept is the notion of change, of dynamics.

The key question is what shapes the change, what drives the dynamics. Lo's short answer is a view of history derived from Charles Darwin's theories of evolution and the biological process of natural selection. In *The Origin of Species,* Darwin demonstrates how, in order to survive, species adapt their biology as their environment shifts. The process has a trial-and-error quality about it. Those species that can adapt win out and are the survivors. Those that fail to adapt fall by the wayside and ultimately disappear from view. As a result, all the species on earth are constantly changing and will continue to change into the indefinite future.

Lo finds a parallel process of evolution and change at work in the capital markets. He calls this notion the Adaptive Market Hypothesis.[1] Although the similarity between the origin of species and the capital markets is striking, there is also a fundamental difference between evolution in nature and evolution in institutions invented by humans. Evolution has a quality of inevitability—species will change and develop as a result of forces beyond their control. But humans are a separate set among species.

Unlike natural phenomena, the development of human institutions is contingent on the goals or purposes that motivated their establishment in the first place. Many institutions are not somebody's brainstorm making an instantaneous appearance on the scene. Rather, institutions are a result of trial-and-error, where perfection is impossible, but something less-than-perfect can often suffice. Institutions change as a result of purposeful decisions by the human beings who make use of them, but institutions also change in response to the forces of evolution.*

Consider equity trading today compared with just a few years ago, merely as a result of the denominating of stock prices in pennies, or hundredths of a point, instead of in eighths, or 12½ cents. The consequence of this seemingly small modification has led to a significant modification in trading patterns. In the old days, floor brokers or other agents who knew about or held an order for execution could trade their own accounts ahead of the order by offering a more competitive price, which would cost at least 12½ cents a share. Today, they execute for only a penny! As a result, buyers and sellers trying to avoid this kind of competition from their agents tend to disclose only small parts of their total order at any one time. In addition, an increasing volume of transactions is executed in what is known as algorithmic trading, or trading carried out by computer programs that respond to changing conditions in the market. This process bypasses the marketmakers, squeezing their profits, and producing even less liquidity.

The shift from eighths of a point to hundredths of a point will work out like an ecological system that eliminates one particular species while others arise to fill that void. Only those who can continually adapt to the changing environment will make it. Only those who continually innovate can maintain an edge.† As Lo wryly points out, "These kinds of phenomena are hard to analyze from an Efficient Markets Hypothesis viewpoint, but they do lend themselves to analysis from a biological perspective."

Lo says, for example, "When you look at hedge funds, you see that the rate of innovation, evolution, competition, adaptation, births, and deaths, the whole range of evolutionary phenomena, occurs at an extraordinarily rapid clip. . . . Hedge funds are the Galapagos Islands of finance. . . . When we think about biology, we rarely think about economics, but the fact is, economic transactions . . . are essentially

---

*For an extended and illuminating explanation of the difference between natural and contingent forms of evolution, see Simon (1969).
† See Farrell (2006).

outcomes of an evolutionary process in much the same way that certain kinds of chimpanzees will use little bits of straw to 'fish' out termites from rotting wood in order to get their food."

Lo has a hands-on sense of what goes on in the hedge fund industry, as he is a managing partner of a hedge fund. He not only makes money, which is nice, but his experiences at the hedge fund also feed back into the classroom. "When I was teaching investments without actually having done it," he told me, "I felt more like a voyeur than a real professor. I really teach differently now—most of all, I teach students to be skeptical of everything. The answers they seek may be in the Efficient Market Hypothesis or portfolio theory or diversification, *but not necessarily.*"

There is a lot to learn in that final qualification. It brings to mind Gottfried von Leibniz's comment in 1703 to the Swiss scientist and mathematician, Jacob Bernoulli, that "Nature has established patterns originating in the return of events, but only for the most part." No model has an R^2 of one. Certainty in responses to questions does not exist. Leibniz's admonition—"but only for the most part"—and Lo's interjection of "but not necessarily"—explains why there is such a thing as risk in the first place. Without that qualification, everything would be predictable, and change would be impossible in a world where every event is identical to some previous event.[2]

6

Robert Shiller
The People's Risk Manager

Professor Robert Shiller of the Cowles Foundation at Yale looks much too young to have earned his Ph.D. at MIT over thirty years ago, while working with Paul Samuelson and Franco Modigliani. During those thirty years, he has managed to publish over 200 papers and five books, including the worldwide best seller, *Irrational Exuberance*. All of this mountain of material is about finance. "Finance is like the lifeblood of the economy," he points out. "Finance is what changes the way things actually happen. . . . It is full of interesting problems"* And Shiller considers real estate as much a part of finance as the stock market, the bond market, or the derivatives market.

The excitement Shiller sees in finance has kept this serious scholar from turning into a dry academic. Shiller is convinced finance is a powerful tool that could make life better for people all around the world. Despite his passionate beliefs about finance, however, Shiller has no interest in applying his wide-ranging theoretical explorations and meticulous empirical analyses into a formula that might make him rich in the stock market: "I am not one of those people reading the stock pages every day."

Shiller's view of Capital Ideas and their role in finance is an odd mixture of rebellion and orthodoxy. His intellectual curiosity prevents him from taking anything at face value. For him, analyzing and

*Unless otherwise specified, quotations are from personal interviews or correspondence.

devouring a concept is like eating a great dish of ice cream. At the same time, Shiller has profound respect for fundamental theories and the structures they provide for innovative thinking and applications. Hence, the framework of Capital Ideas "can be a workhorse for some sensible research, if it is used appropriately. More important, it can also be a starting point, a point of comparison from which to frame other theories."[1]

At the same time, Shiller is convinced people doing research must maintain a realistic perspective about human behavior. Their work will make no sense unless they are aware of the complexity of human beings and the countless elements entering into their decisions and choices. "When one does produce a model, in whatever tradition," he warns, "one should do so with a sense of the limits of the model, the reasonableness of its approximations, and the sensibility of its proposed applications."

Shiller's view of finance is a firm attachment to the basic theories of Capital Ideas blended with what he has learned about a world with more realistic kinds of assumptions about human behavior. He has shaped this combination into a launching pad for novel insights into how markets work and—most important to Shiller—into how people can use markets and financial instruments to manage all kinds of personal risks and improve their welfare as a result. Thus, despite his fascination with theory and mathematics, Shiller is ultimately in the same camp as Merton and Lo—concentrated on institutions, what they do, how they do it, and why they change.

Shiller's work in finance began while was preparing his Ph.D. dissertation under Franco Modigliani at MIT. He selected the theory of rational expectations as the topic for his dissertation, because this theory was at that time the hot but also the most controversial concept in the academic economist's toolbox. The key word here is "rational," and many economists believed it extended orthodoxy in an exciting new direction.

Rational expectations hypothesizes that individuals do not simply extrapolate past experience in forming their expectations, because that process leads them astray too often. Rather, in forming expectations they make use of *all* available information, including past experience as just one among many factors.

If individuals are taking all available information into account, and if we assume further that they also understand how to interpret that information, then average opinion is going to be as close to a correct view of the future as you can find. Average opinion will not necessarily be right all the time, because the future is full of surprises (new information), but average opinion will never be *systematically* wrong—neither too optimistic all the time nor chronically pessimistic.

If all of this sounds a lot like the Efficient Market Hypothesis, it should. It also reflects the assumptions underlying the Capital Asset Pricing Model, the Modigliani-Miller view of corporate finance, and even the Black-Scholes-Merton options pricing model. All of the Capital Ideas take the assumption of rational expectations as the foundation of their theoretical explorations. This does not mean people like Bill Sharpe or Franco Modigliani or Fischer Black believed that is how the world works. Rather, these assumptions permit a theoretician to build models that are neat, with no fuzziness around the edges, with consistency between the whole and the parts, convenient to express and manipulate mathematically. In a surprising number of cases, these assumptions turn out to be a fair description of reality.

Shiller began work on his dissertation by testing how well the rational expectations model worked in the bond market, where theory suggests that long-term interest rates at any moment reflect investor expectations of the average level of interest rates over the life of the bond. "The model seemed absurd," he concluded after studying the actual pattern of long-term rates. "Bond prices were so volatile from day to day there *had* to be more involved in bond prices than expectations of future rates over extended periods of time."

The moment was an epiphany for Shiller and has influenced everything he has done in finance since then. Volatility has been the key variable in all his work. Volatility—a fancy word for what happens when we are taken by surprise—is a vivid indicator of how ignorant of the future we are and how emotionally we respond when the future arrives and fails to conform to our expectations.

As Shiller interprets it, volatility means people are changing their minds about the future almost from moment to moment. And why? New information arrives that is different from what they had been expecting.

But there is no reason to believe the new information is necessarily correct information or readily understandable information or even the kinds of information people should be heeding. In Shiller's opinion, the so-called information on which investors base their decisions is a jumble of many factors that go beyond the cold facts of the economic fundamentals or the latest corporate earnings reports.

The rational expectations model may explain how people *should* think about the uncertain future, but the model tells us nothing about how they actually *do* think about the future as they go on about their business from day to day. The effort to figure out what the future will bring is a scary endeavor, because we can never know ahead of time what the future is going to be like. We can only guess. We never have all the available information, and even if we did many of us would be unable to correctly interpret what that information means. The whole process is so difficult, and the odds on being wrong so daunting, that we let our emotional anxieties get in the way. Often we just give up and base our decisions on what are essentially tosses of a coin. And so we often lean on the kinds of shortcuts and heuristics the researchers in Behavioral Finance describe.

Shiller adds another interesting criticism of the rational expectations model. The model not only fails to specify human behavior in decision making. It is dry in its very heart. "There is no entrepreneurial excitement. The theory does not correctly represent human emotions. People don't talk about stuff the way the theory specifies. How much to save for retirement—a critically important matter—just does not turn people on. Theory says people vary in their degrees of aversion to taking risks, but I think their appetites for risk vary in their interest in the stock market."

<hr>

The key to how volatility reveals the messy process of decision making in the capital markets is in the magnitude of the swings in security prices relative to the changes in the underlying fundamentals. Shiller describes this phenomenon as "excess volatility." And he has a nice example to demonstrate what he means:

Suppose your weatherman reports one day that he thinks that the temperature today will be 150 degrees, and the next day that he

thinks the temperature will be −50 degrees. Even if his weather report correlates with the actual temperature, we would sense that
something is wrong with the forecast. It may be that we tend to get
hot days when he says it will be 150 degrees, or cool days when he
says it will be −50 degrees, and so there may be information in his
forecast. But his forecasts should not be more volatile than the actual
temperatures he is trying to forecast. In fact, if he is really doing a
good job, his forecasts should be less volatile than the temperatures
he forecasts, for when he knows little he should just forecast something close to the historical mean. With the stock market, historically the "forecasts" have looked like the −50 to 150 degree forecasts
of our hypothetical weatherman. . . . The fundamental principle of
optimal forecasting is that the forecast must be less variable than the
variables forecasted.

Every investment decision is a bet on an unknown future, just like
a weather forecast, and price movements provide the track record of investors' forecasts. All investors are in the forecasting business, whether
they like it or not and whether or not they even recognize it.

The issue Shiller poses then revolves around the question: In the
process of making their forecasts, do investors make use of information
as in the Efficient Market Theory postulated by Eugene Fama in 1965?
"An efficient market is a market that is efficient in processing information. The prices of securities at any time are based on correct evaluation of all information available at that time. In an efficient capital
market, prices fully reflect available information."[2] An important point
deserves emphasis here, because too often people are critical of the re-
alism of theory and blame the theoretician for living in the clouds.
Fama did not assert this is the way the world works. He was explaining
how the world would work "in a market that is efficient in processing
information."

When Shiller compared the swings in stock prices to the variations
in the fundamentals, he found no evidence of market behavior in accordance with the hypothesis of an efficient market. If prices fully reflected *all available information,* as in the case of most weather
forecasting, the variability in stock prices would be less, or at the very
least not significantly greater, than the variability in the underlying
fundamentals. But Shiller's tests revealed a consistent pattern of excess
volatility.

Shiller came on strong on this matter on the next-to-last page of the first edition of his book, *Irrational Exuberance,* which, by great good luck, appeared on the eve of the great crash at the end of 2000:

> The U.S. stock market ups and downs over the past century have made virtually no sense ex post. It is curious how little known this simple fact is. Many people persist in describing productivity, profits, and prices for the aggregate stock market as if they are exactly the same thing. All these words start with the letters "pr," but that is where their actual similarity ends. The purveyors of conventional wisdom about the stock market show either lack of knowledge of the basic fact that these are all so very different, or willful disregard of it. It is just too easy, too convenient for storytellers trying to weave a plot about a new era, in which every imaginable good thing gets even better.[3]

As this quotation makes clear, Shiller's work on volatility was not just an idle piece of interesting research. The appraisal of volatility is a key indicator of market behavior, because "excess volatility" means there are times when the markets are "too high" or "too low." If we can actually identify when stock prices are too high or too low, what the market is going to do becomes predictable!

Shiller and his frequent coauthor John Campbell put it this way in a paper published in 1998: "Although one might have thought that it is easier to forecast into the near future than into the distant future . . . the data contradict such intuition."[4]

But just because something is predictable, we are not guaranteed the ability to predict it correctly. As Andrew Lo and his coauthor, A. Craig MacKinlay of Wharton, wrote in *A Non-Random Walk Down Wall Street:* "Forecasts of stock returns . . . may be subject to considerable forecast errors, so that 'excess' profit opportunities and market inefficiencies are not necessarily consequences of forecastability" (p. 115).

This observation leads to a subtle but important observation about Shiller's exploration into "excess" volatility. Excess volatility means volatility was in some sense greater than it "should" have been. But we never know how great volatility should be or even could be.

The U.S. stock market has survived through many crises, despite many episodes that would fit Shiller's definition of excess volatility, when price changes are much wilder than the changes in the underlying fundamentals. Despite these violent markets, the United States has—so far—never reached the level of volatility that would have eliminated it from the scene, as has happened in other nations. Survivorship muddies the waters of many efforts to explain market behaviors.

At best, forecasting major market moves—or market timing—is a notoriously trying activity even when you are right. Waiting for the market to correct itself takes longer than most of the bulls or the bears expect, to a point where they are constantly tempted to throw in the sponge too soon and join the other side. On the other hand, the effort to pick individual stocks can sometimes work—or wipe you out—in a day.

Shiller's answer to the question of how investors make use of information is closely related to important work by Mordecai Kurz, a mathematical economist at Stanford University.* Kurz's *Theory of Rational Beliefs* is in the spirit of Daniel Kahneman's observation to me that "The failure in the rational model is . . . in the human brain it requires. Who could design a brain that could perform in the way this model mandates? Every single one of us would have to know and *understand* everything, completely, and at once."

In a similar vein, Kurz takes the position that investors are rational because they do think about the systematic trade-offs between risk and return just as the theory of efficient markets or the Capital Asset Pricing Model describe. Yet they face an impossible task. The world never stands still, and the information on hand is too complex. We suffer from what economists call "non-stationarity." If the world were stationary, everybody would get everything right. In a non-stationary world, everybody gets it wrong—or gets it right only as a matter of luck. Error and surprise are inevitable when investors have no good way of estimating the probabilities of future events. Their beliefs may be rational, but no matter.

*For a particularly clear and user-friendly discussion of the principal ideas involved, see H.W. Brock (2006a). For the relevance of Kurz's work to "adding alpha," see Brock (2006b).

We can put the same thing another way. When many investors are using the same kinds of rules of thumb and arrive at similar kinds of beliefs about the future, asset prices are almost always wrong in the sense that the return investors anticipate is chronically too high or too low relative to the risks involved. The villain, however, is not in the intellectual and emotional structures of human beings trying to see into the future. Rather, it is in the nature of the world, and the collisions between what people expect and what actually evolves. This is a world where the notion of equilibrium will be of interest to professors but has little meaning to the turmoil of the marketplace.

Kurz's *Theory of Rational Beliefs* explains why volatility occurs, and why Shiller was able to demonstrate the prevalence of excess volatility—evidence that asset prices fluctuate in a much wider range than the economic fundamentals alone would justify. Kurz defines the volatility that arises from surprise as "endogenous volatility," which means it stems from the forecasting errors at the very heart of the investment process. Kurz fails to emphasize that volatility—large upward or downward moves—requires general agreement among investors about the future, so that sellers have difficulty finding buyers willing to take their offers near the most recent price and buyers have difficulty finding sellers willing to make offers near the most recent price. Stability in prices necessitates disagreements in outlook between buyers and sellers.

Volatility in the underlying fundamentals, such as earnings, dividends, and interest rates, is "exogenous volatility," or volatility occurring outside the marketplace. Endogenous volatility is what Shiller is talking about when he refers to excess volatility. Both Shiller and Kurz agree that endogenous volatility is about three times as great as exogenous volatility.

Shiller's studies in the area of volatility led him to another key piece of research on the Efficient Market Hypothesis, the result of which ends up in a tie: The Efficient Market Hypothesis wins half the game. The proponents of behaviorally motivated markets win the other half.

The motivation for Shiller's analysis was a view expressed by Paul Samuelson some years ago in a letter to Shiller and cited by Shiller in the second edition of his *Irrational Exuberance* (p. 243):[5]

> Modern markets show considerable micro efficiency (for the reason that the minority who spot minor aberrations from micro theory can make money from those occurrences and, in doing so, they tend to wipe out any persistent inefficiencies). In no contradiction to the previous sentence, I had hypothesized considerable macro ineffi- ciency, in the sense of long waves in the time series of aggregate in- dexes of security prices below and above various definitions of fundamental values.

In a paper published in April 2005, Shiller and a colleague named Jeeman Jung, an associate professor at Sangmyung University in Seoul, Korea, reported on a series of tests designed to test Samuelson's hypoth- esis.[6] They begin the paper explaining why they expect Samuelson's dictum (their expression) to be supported by their evidence.

In a marathon sentence, they point out that "if there is enough vari- ation in information that the market has about future fundamental growth of individual firms [some strongly positive, some strongly nega- tive], then these variations might be big enough to swamp out the effect on price of time variation in other factors, such as speculative booms and busts, making the simple efficient markets model work fairly well as an approximation for [the shares of] individual firms."[7] In studying indi- vidual companies, therefore, investors probably do tend to set prices as reliable forecasts of future cash flows from the stocks of those companies.

But the aggregate market is a different matter. It is one thing for in- vestors to study the information on individual companies and come up with a judgment about future growth. It is something else for them to perform the same task for the aggregate of all firms—the market as a whole—"because the aggregate averages out the individual stories of the firms and the reasons for changes in the aggregate are more subtle and harder for the investment public to understand, having to do with national economic growth, stabilizing economic policy, and the like." Under these circumstances, a wide range of information other than in- formation about fundamentals might influence the movement of stock prices in the market as a whole. Then, "factors such as stock market

booms and busts would swamp out the effect of information about future dividends in determining price and make the simple efficient markets model a bad approximation for the aggregate stock market."[8]

After citing related work that supports their conclusions, Jung and
Shiller then set out to study the relationship between the dividend/
price ratio—usually referred to as the dividend yield—on individual
stocks and the future growth rate of dividends on each stock. As they
wanted their results to be as robust as possible, they attempted to conduct the analysis over as long a period of time as possible. They did have
a good monthly price index for the total market from 1926 going forward, but they could find only a tiny sample of forty-nine companies in
continuous existence from 1926 through 2001. Nevertheless, the forty-
nine companies spanned a wide variety of industries, so they proceeded
with their study.

If the market is micro-efficient in Samuelson's sense, Jung and
Shiller would expect to find that the lower the dividend yield—or the
higher the stock price relative to the current dividend payment—the
more rapid the future growth of dividends should be. That is, investors
would be willing to pay a higher price for today's dividend on a given
stock if they expect the company's future growth to be rapid than if
they expected growth to be sluggish, and the market would be "efficient" if their forecast turned out to be correct. Then they would be
employing "all available information" in arriving at their judgment.

Jung and Shiller tested this hypothesis over periods of ten years and
then over longer periods. When they analyzed the results for the forty-
nine companies considered separately to examine the hypothesis of
micro-efficiency, their investigation confirmed a negative relation between the dividend yield on the individual stocks and subsequent rates
of dividend growth, with reliable statistical significance. The results
were stronger for the ten-year periods than for the longer periods, but
the inverse relation between dividend yield and future dividend growth
held for all but seven of the forty-nine companies. As the results showed
"that [the dividend yield] substantially correctly forecasts the future
growth rate of dividends . . . [it also proves] that *variations of price relative to dividends are largely justified in terms of market efficiency*."[9]
Half the prize goes to the Efficient Market Hypothesis.

Then Jung and Shiller pooled the forty-nine companies to create an
equal-weighted index of stock prices, and tested the aggregate dividend

on the index (as a proxy for "the market") against the future growth in dividends. Now the relation between the dividend yield and future dividend growth turned out to be *positive*—dividend growth was faster after stock prices were depressed and the starting yield was high than after periods when the yield was low and stock prices were booming. The statistical significance of even that finding was weak. Jung and Shiller concluded there is no indication of any reliability between the dividend yield on the market as a whole and subsequent dividend growth for the market as a whole.

Summing it all up, including the strong support for their case from the work of others they cite in this paper (and from Shiller's earlier work itself), Jung and Shiller interpret their results as "confirming the Samuelson dictum. . . . There is no evidence of macro-efficiency." In simpler words, the Jung-Shiller study proves Shiller's case for the prevalence of excess volatility in the market as a whole. *But the case for micro-efficiency—the Efficient Market Hypothesis—emerges unscathed.*[*]

Although this is an impressive study with clear results, it does have three shortcomings. First, the forty-nine companies represent only a small sample (one might even say a "micro-sample") of the total number of listed companies. Second, the sample omits companies that disappeared from the scene, which gives a distorted view of what actually happened. Finally, the Efficient Market Hypothesis is there to observe every minute the markets are open and investors are trading, while the number of big macro swings to which Samuelson refers can be counted on the fingers of one hand. Nevertheless, the case is a strong one as far as it can go.

One of the ironies of this investigation appears in a little table near the end of the second edition of *Irrational Exuberance,* published in the spring of 2005, five years after the first edition. Here Shiller reports on his questionnaire survey of individual investors made in 1996 when he asked about their confidence level in investing. When he asked his respondents to finish the phrase: "Trying to time the market to get out

---

[*] For another persuasive case in support of Samuelson's dictum, see Lamont and Stein (2006). See, also, the case of the failure of market efficiency during the NASDAQ bubble at the end of the 1990s, when the short interest (the volume of shares sold short) declined as the NASDAQ Index approached its peak. The Efficient Market Hypothesis predicts precisely the opposite sequence of events.

before it goes down and to get in before it goes up is . . . ," only 11 percent chose: "a smart thing to try to do; I can reasonably expect to be a success at it." Yet when he asked them to complete this phrase: "Trying to pick individual stocks, trying to predict, for example, if and when Ford Motor stock will go up or IBM stock will go up is . . . ," 40 percent of the respondents chose "a smart thing to do, I can reasonably expect to be a success at it." Stock picking to this group beats timing the market any day. This view of the market is the opposite of Samuelson's dictum that the market is macro-inefficient but probably micro-efficient.

We now digress briefly to discuss an important instance of high macro volatility in August 1998, when stock prices fell by over 14 percent, the largest one-month decline since the famous crash of October 1987. A monetary crisis had been moving across Asia for some months, but on August 17, without warning, the Russians abruptly defaulted on their government bonds, devalued the ruble by 25 percent, and declared a three-month moratorium on foreign obligations of Russian banks. The Russians had issued $3.5 billion of euro-denominated debt as recently as July 24. The most shocking feature of this debacle was in the default on bonds denominated in rubles as well as in foreign currencies; defaults on bonds denominated in foreign currencies have been all too frequent in financial history, but defaults on obligations in a country's own currency have been rare. Financial markets worldwide responded to the shock with steep drops in prices.

The events of 1998 have special interest for the story in this book, because the crisis was brought to a head in the financial markets by the imminent failure of a hedge fund called Long-Term Capital Management, or LTCM, which had opened for business in February 1994. Nobel Prize winners Robert C. Merton and Myron Scholes were partners in LTCM, and the managing partner was John Meriwether, the legendary bond trader from Salomon Brothers. The repercussions of a possible LTCM default were viewed as so serious in financial markets around the world, especially in view of the participation of Merton and Scholes, that the Federal Reserve Bank of New York had to organize a bailout to prevent this disaster from becoming a reality. The bailout instantly reversed the sharp market decline then under way.

There is a case that arrogance and hubris brought down LTCM. There is also a case that the fund was the victim of circumstances beyond its control.

The most persuasive argument in support of the former view appears in a lively book by the financial writer Roger Lowenstein, *When Genius Failed: The Rise and Fall of Long-Term Capital Management.* Lowenstein's argument is summed up in just a few words on the back of the book's dust jacket: "Lowenstein explains not just how the fund made and lost its money, but also how the personalities of Long-Term's partners, the arrogance of their mathematical certainties, and the culture of Wall Street in the late nineties contributed to both their rise and fall."

Other observers, such as Donald MacKenzie of the University of Edinburgh, argue that LTCM was a victim of widespread imitation by other players in the market, and that: "Gambling—conscious reckless risk-taking—does not explain LTCM's 1998 disaster. Nor [was it] blind faith in mathematical models. Models were much less critical to LTCM's trading than commonly thought. . . . All those involved knew that models were an approximation to reality and a guide to strategy rather than a determinant of it."[*][10]

LTCM's primary activity had been bond market arbitrage—selling one security and buying a related or similar security in the expectation that the market would in time narrow any pricing discrepancy between the two assets. Arbitrage is a time-honored activity in finance, and these kinds of strategies were nothing new. LTCM's investors expected the firm to be an outstanding performer at this game because of the experience and brainpower the firm would bring to the task. Until disaster struck, this expectation was more than fulfilled. After three and a half years, the firm's capital had risen from $1.1 billion to $6.7 billion, with returns of over 40 percent in 1995 and 1996, achieved at volatility below the volatility of the S&P 500. There were only eight months of negative performance over that period of time. On December 31, 1997, the fund returned $2.7 billion out of a total of $7.5 billion of capital to its partners, declaring that the fund was so successful it had "excess capital."

---

[*]See, in Chapter 4, pages 47–48, for Merton's view of the models of Capital Ideas.

The $2.7 billion distribution was funded by borrowing against LTCM's assets, raising the ratio of borrowings to equity from 18.3 percent to 27.7 percent. Over the course of succeeding months, LTCM would raise its borrowings to 31 percent of equity. The motivation was to raise the rate of return from individual transactions, each of whose profit—when earned—was tiny.

By July 1998, however, the capital had shrunk to $4.1 billion from $4.7 billion immediately after the distribution, even though, for at least half of July, there was no indication of anything unusual at work in the markets in which LTCM concentrated most of its activity. Trouble was brewing nevertheless. On the single day of August 21, 1998, LTCM lost $550 million, about 15 percent of its remaining capital.

Trading to get out of positions had become virtually impossible, as traders in the market were unwilling to take the other side of LTCM's offers, especially in view of the large size of those positions. Indeed, in a copycat kind of process over the previous months, many other bond houses and funds were looking to achieve the same kinds of returns as LTCM, and were taking on positions identical to, or almost identical to, LTCM's. MacKenzie describes this situation as a "superportfolio" in the market, with just about all owners now eager to exchange their holdings for cash.

As one might expect from a fund with Merton and Scholes as partners, LTCM had in place an elaborate set of risk management controls. In fact, the highly sophisticated and diversified structure of risk management systematically erred on the side of extra caution. Events make clear, however, that the principals never anticipated the superportfolio, with so many other traders taking the same kinds of positions as LTCM would take. Nor could anyone have predicted the Russian fiasco following on the financial crisis in Asia. Unwinding the fund in the crisis became impossible for the managers of LTCM, especially as asking their banks for credit to tide them over would only reveal to everyone how fragile the fund's condition had become.

This summary of the LTCM crisis is much too brief to suggest an answer to the question as to whether LTCM was the victim of circumstances or a blazing example of hubris by individuals who were considered geniuses by everyone, including themselves. That question is in any case not the question to ask here.

The issue is whether LTCM reveals a failure of Capital Ideas. On this score, Capital Ideas do not appear to be vulnerable. Theory never excludes the possibility of a financial crisis and recognizes that markets will move to reflect unexpected changes in the underlying fundamentals. Although Behavioral Finance does predict the kind of herding that attracted other firms to copy what LTCM was doing, there is no doubt the sharp drops in stock prices in July and August 1998 were related to treacherous economic fundamentals giving many signs of a cumulative and systemic impact. Then the markets turned around and started back up the instant the Federal Reserve resolved this emergency, with stock prices rising in September and making new highs by November.

In short, developments come as close as one could ask to Fama's definition of an efficient market, quoted earlier, that "An efficient capital market is a market that is efficient in processing information. The prices of securities at any time are based on correct evaluation of all information available at that time. In an efficient capital market, prices fully reflect available information."

In a famous paper published in 1981, Shiller set forth for the first time his goal of demonstrating and defining his concept of "excess volatility." He computed, for each year since 1871, the present value subsequent to that year of the real dividends on the Standard & Poor's Composite Index of common stock prices, discounted by a constant real discount rate equal to the geometric average real return since 1871. The result of this calculation was a stable upward trend in the discounted present value of the future stream of dividends, while the stock price index "gyrates wildly up and down around this trend."[11]

In subsequent work, Shiller performed a similar analysis on stock prices relative to changes in interest rates and personal consumption expenditures, with identical results. Shiller wrote an entire book on market volatility, first published in 1986, which presents the results of this line of analysis of bond markets and even real estate markets. Investors, whether in the markets or in pricing their own homes, are like a weatherman who predicts tomorrow's weather will range between 100 degrees and −50 degrees.

To Shiller, excess volatility implies "that changes occur for no fundamental reason at all."[12] The swings in stock prices seem to reflect investors' attention to many factors other than the present value of the future stream of dividend payments: fads and fashions, fears and hopes, rumors and restlessness, recent stock price performance, or old saws about how in the long run everything comes out rosy in the stock market.

None of this diversion of attention from prices reflecting only Fama's "relevant information" should be taken to mean investors are "irrational." As Shiller argues this point, "The broadly based failures in thinking are not wholly attributable to . . . capriciousness of investors. Instead, these failures reflect lack of systematic attention and automatic reliance on popular or intuitive models."[13] Shiller insists that the views people express, even under panic conditions, are usually "not palpably unreasonable. One would make the criticism that they are vague, impressionistic, and cliché ridden."[14] As Daniel Kahneman had also suggested, this view is a long way from "irrational." But it does relate to the sheer impossibility of knowing what future events are in store to make stock prices go one direction or the other.

John Maynard Keynes observed way back in the mid-1930s that the complexity of arriving at a rational forecast—even if "all the available information" is in fact available—is so complex that many investors make their judgments on the basis of what they think other investors' judgments are likely to be. For Keynes, this explains why true long-term investors are so scarce. The volatility of stock prices can try the soul of even the coolest investor. When you know only a little, and you know you know only a little, it is tempting to believe others may know more, especially when markets are moving strongly in one direction or another.

* * *

As his study of Samuelson's dictum indicates, Shiller does not minimize the contribution of financial theory to the practice of financial management and investing. On the other hand, his research has led him to be critical of how many of his academic colleagues in finance use the theory. The Capital Ideas are powerful, with exciting kinds of applications in a wide set of areas: "But people who do theoretical work in finance don't think of those applications. In carrying the theory too far, they miss the broader picture. The world they have constructed is not the world we live in. They either do not know the limitations of the theory or they are not interested in trying to fix those limitations. I am." He takes the critique a step further (knowing that he is exaggerating): "They write Efficient Markets Hypothesis finance, but in their spare time they are trying to beat the market. They don't integrate the two activities. Over beer, they are transformed into entirely different people from who they are in the classroom."

Shiller's view of finance starts from a different foundation. He focuses on how the economics and finance of the classroom interact with the economics and finance of the real world. The interaction is critical. He agrees with Merton that only by understanding how far theory explains reality, and how reality illuminates theory, can we devise financial institutions and financial instruments to help people manage their lives. "Ultimately, people matter," he asserts. "Corporations matter only insofar as they help people. People think about investing in very conventional ways. The right financial instruments will help them overcome that narrow view."

He finds it a frustrating process. The very people he and his colleagues are trying to help are most resistant to thinking about the nature of the risks they are exposed to. In his book *Macro Markets: Creating Institutions for Managing Society's Largest Economic Risks,* and again in his more recent book, *The New Financial Order,* designed for a wider audience, Shiller argues that the progress of risk management has been hindered over the centuries by thought processes that just don't fit, by assumptions that inhibit people from doing risk management.* This disheartening view is the inspiration for much of the work Shiller is doing in the area of financial innovation.

"The models everybody is rationally optimizing are so misleading," he complains: "The puzzle is why it takes so long to design proper institutions to accomplish these purposes. The government has done a lot such as Social Security, disability insurance, and Medicare. But the huge private sector often seems to miss some of the most creative ideas and most significant innovations." Why does the private sector lag in innovation in risk management? "The problem is not so much with the managers of private sector enterprises," he observes, "as with the public nature of financial innovations. As financial innovations are not generally

---

* *The New Financial Order* won the first Paul A. Samuelson Award from TIAA-CREF in 1996.

patentable, financial innovators are reluctant to spend large sums developing new products that others can use. Hence, it is difficult for private sector companies to get important new things started along the lines we suggested in *Macro Markets* and *New Financial Order*."

"Why doesn't everybody who is retired have an annuity indexed to inflation?" Shiller asks. "The need is so *obvious*. The public has not demanded annuities, but that is no reason against trying to offer them. After the terrible inflationary years of the 1970s, why did it take until 1997 before the U.S. government began to offer inflation-indexed Treasury securities? The U.K. launched this instrument back in 1985." Shiller shakes his head. "Amazing," he concludes.

If Robert Merton can describe himself as a plumber, Robert Shiller is a roofer. His interest in volatility and all it means in terms of risk and uncertainty has led him far afield from conventional asset markets like stocks and bonds. He expects derivatives to be a bigger and bigger part of our lives, because of how effectively they serve as hedging instruments and how easy it is to create markets for them. The most basic function of derivatives is to create markets in volatility. One of Shiller's primary goals has been to develop instruments that enable people to insure or hedge against the huge risks they have to take just in the process of living from day to day—risks such as volatility in the prices of their own homes.

As we have seen, Shiller's interest in the nature of volatility began with the bond market and then led him with increased attention into the behavior of the stock market. From there, the progression to the market for real estate seemed a natural step: "Real estate is a huge market with booms and busts just like in the capital markets." He and his associates Karl Case and Allan Weiss are now among the nation's leading experts in the history of real estate prices and in the impact of changing real estate prices, not just on the economy as a whole, but on the financial welfare of individual families. Here is where Shiller is most eager to be a pioneer.

Except for the very rich, most people have the largest share of their wealth invested in their homes. In the simplest sense of the word, they are undiversified. Events that would reduce the resale value of their homes—a general decline in home prices, a radical change in the character of their neighborhood, or the loss of a local industry—could suddenly threaten what equity they have left in their homes or affect their ability to keep up their mortgage payments. If they cannot meet the monthly payments on their mortgages, the bank could foreclose and take their homes away from them. Their whole way of life could be damaged.

This imbalance in their family balance sheet does not concern many home owners, because they simply do not think about such matters as diversification and management of risk, at least where their houses are concerned. They tend to employ what has come to be known as "mental accounting," which means they maintain a separate basket in their heads for their home and its mortgage, another basket for their 401(k) accounts, still another for their savings accounts, one for their consumer credit, and another to store their concerns about the cost of their children's education. No basket has a relation to any of the other baskets. As a result, they seldom—if ever—take the time to develop an overview of the total amount of the assets and liabilities in all the baskets considered together. And if they did, they would have no idea of what to do about it anyway. So they focus their attention elsewhere.

But the concentration of risk in their real estate means they might have to sell their homes if they were in trouble, and probably under unfavorable circumstances. That should not have to happen. Shiller, along with Sam Masucci, Allan Weiss, and colleagues at the firm MacroMarkets, LLC, are trying to devise risk management vehicles to protect people from that dreadful imperative.* The trick, in one form or another, is to create liquid markets of some kind for the equities individual families have in their homes or for vehicles to help them hedge the great undiversified risk their homes represent to them.

The first step along that road is to have good indexes of home prices for as many areas as possible, although even a national index would serve a purpose. When Shiller first investigated what kinds of home

---

*Sam Masucci is CEO and Allan Weiss is Chairman of the Board of MacroMarkets, LLC.

price indexes might be available, he found there was nothing of any kind for prices prior to 1960. He immediately set to work and constructed a national index of home prices reaching all the way back to the 1890s.

Once you have a broadly accepted index, it is possible to create a market in futures on that index, just as there are highly active global markets for futures on interest rates, stock market indexes, exchange rates, and on many commodities like corn and copper. In futures markets on financial instruments, settlements are made in cash. When the price of the underlying instrument rises, the accounts of the investors with long positions—those who have bought futures on the instrument—will increase; their accounts will be debited when the price of the underlying instrument falls. Precisely the opposite occurs with investors who sell the futures short to protect themselves against a decline in the index. Their accounts will be credited when the index falls but will be debited when the index rises. At the clearinghouse, debits and credits will precisely offset each other as the underlying price fluctuates, much in the spirit of Merton's Country A and Country B industry swap.

At this point, Shiller reverts to Capital Ideas and brings up the underlying logic to which the Capital Asset Pricing Model (CAPM) leads— that all investors should own "the market portfolio." "We make do with limited replications of the market portfolio like the S&P 500 or a basket of stocks tracking the Wilshire 5000 or a basket of bonds tracking the Shearson-Lehman bond index." But the market portfolio is much more than any of these. It is global in its scope and covers all financial assets— and, for Shiller, real estate is as much a financial asset as a share in General Motors, a Treasury bond, or a futures contract on the euro.

In reality, nobody is likely to own the entire market portfolio mandated by CAPM. But nobody even comes close to owning the entire market portfolio today, because there are no index funds or other kinds of serviceable instruments representing that one huge asset class known as real estate. There are REITs—equities in real estate investment trusts—but they are a pinprick in the market and would serve little purpose to home owners whose personal balance sheet is top-heavy with the value of their homes.

Nor are home owners likely to venture into a futures markets to hedge the current value on their homes. The process is too complicated and the minimum amounts for trading would be out of reach for most people. But Shiller has a solution for this problem, too, which is once again philosophically close to Merton's kinds of solutions.

Taking his lead from the basic notion of contingent claims underlying the Black–Scholes–Merton options pricing model, Shiller has been working on a design for an insurance policy to guarantee home owners the preset price on their home, regardless of what happens in their local residential real estate market. Settlement of insurance claims could be based on an index of home prices for individual neighborhoods or small geographic areas. While the insurance companies will be exposed to home price risk if they write such policies, they could use the new futures market to lay off the risk. Thus, Shiller's different ideas feed on each other.

This idea is now a reality. MacroMarkets, LLC, has entered into a contract with the Chicago Mercantile Exchange to produce futures and options markets on home prices. Trading in the contract was launched in March 2006. Trading initially covers ten U.S. cities as well as a national index. These markets are already a success, with frequent references in the press to the predictions for housing prices incorporated in the futures instruments. Now everyone with a stake in home real estate has minute-by-minute data on home price expectations by city, for various horizons. These data will indicate what the market thinks of the real estate booms and depressions, and we will have price signals to help builders avoid the boom–and–bust cycles that have always plagued the construction industry.

Shiller futures and his insurance policy would protect not only an individual home owner, but could also protect values in an entire neighborhood. Consider a family in fear of some neighborhood change threatening to reduce home values. They might well decide to dump their home on the market at a sacrifice price and flee to some other and probably more expensive neighborhood. Yet with home equity insurance in place, or an ability to protect their home value against price declines by selling futures short, this family and its neighbors would be more likely to hold on and monitor developments before taking off, thereby reducing the probability that home prices would decline at all.

If prices do decline, and the insurance company is stuck paying off the home equity policyholders, how does the insurance company avoid going bankrupt under such circumstances? An insurance company is a large and sophisticated investor. As it writes these kinds of policies, it can also go short the home price index futures market in the amounts of insurance it has issued.

Shiller's fertile mind has also come up with more unconventional schemes to do something about helping home owners reduce their over-exposure to the value of their homes. He proposes an instrument allowing home owners to swap fluctuations in the value of their homes with the returns earned by investors in the stock market who are top-heavy with stocks and want to diversify out of the market but are reluctant to sell because of their capital gains liability. That would give home own-ers a stake in the equity market at the same time that it would reduce the exposure for investors locked in by capital gains tax liabilities.

"We would like to do that," Shiller says, "but it's so hard to make progress on institutions. That's why I wrote two books and a string of articles about these ideas. There is such public resistance, such a narrow mind-set about what kinds of securities should exist. People mouth al-legiance to diversification in the abstract, 'but not on my block!' Diver-sification just does not provoke enough excitement for people to be curious about more efficient ways of achieving it."

Shiller's boldest proposal is the creation of macro markets—mar-kets where people could buy and sell securities based, among other things, on the gross domestic product. Gross domestic product, or GDP, is the broadest measure of the value of the total output of goods and services in entire nations. The GDP of the United States, for exam-ple, is around $12 trillion as of this writing, compared with about $2.5 trillion for China and approaching $800 billion for Brazil. The prof-itability of most companies and the job security of many people in the workforce are correlated with swings in the growth rate of GDP. Al-though the volatility of the economy as a whole is a lot milder than volatility in the capital markets, even small declines in the growth rate of GDP can cause unemployment to rise and profits to cave in.

As Shiller sees these risks, "In the real world, most people are de-pendent on labor income or some kind of income they are stuck with. They are at risk if the economy falls into recession but now have no way of protecting themselves against that idiosyncratic risk. They need to get out of that risk and go into something really diversified like the market portfolio—a portfolio of paper representing the GDP of all other countries around the world. The security they sell representing the GDP of their own country would be bought by portfolio investors who would own the whole market portfolio, just as the Capital Asset Pricing Model specifies and mandates."

There may be a simpler way to diversify excessive dependence of one's livelihood on the prosperity of the country you work in: Buy the equities of other countries, and sell the home equities short. Over the long run, equity markets do reflect the fortunes of the countries in which they are located and could, therefore, serve the purpose in a simpler fashion than the one Shiller has devised.

Nevertheless, although Shiller comes from different directions, he clearly shares Merton's vision of finance as the tool to make the financial side of life safer for people everywhere in many different dimension. Nor does the process have any borders for Shiller. He is, in a sense, the people's Risk Manager. His ingenious and restless mind seems never to come to a stop.

THE ENGINEERS

7

Bill Sharpe

"It's Dangerous to Think of Risk as a Number"

W hen Bill Sharpe received the Nobel Prize in Economics in 1990, the primary achievement that won him the award was a paper he had published a long twenty-six years earlier, in 1964. The original article appeared in the *Journal of Finance* carrying the unwieldy title, "Capital Asset Prices: A Theory of Market Equilibrium Under Conditions of Risk" (see pp. 188–193 of *Capital Ideas*). Here Sharpe set forth the case for the Capital Asset Pricing Model, or what has come to be known as CAPM, pronounced by the cognoscenti in effort-saving fashion as "CAP-EM."

What does Bill Sharpe think about CAPM today—its meaning, its role in the marketplace, and the controversies about its empirical weaknesses that have grown up around it over the years? Sharpe now sees CAPM from a different perspective. As this chapter demonstrates, he has transformed himself from a Nobel Laureate theoretician into a pioneering financial engineer. Like an engineer who looks across a river and begins to design in his mind a method to cross that river, Sharpe is looking for ways to help individual investors get from here to there, from a miasma of self-defeating decisions into an environment where they know how to analyze the investment problem and where to seek solutions to it.

His views on CAPM follow, but first, a brief review of what the model is all about.

◩

In essence, the model builds up from Harry Markowitz's key notion of diversification: The risk of a portfolio is less than the risk of all the assets of which it is composed. Even a portfolio composed of highly risky assets would not be a risky portfolio if the returns on the individual assets in the portfolio had low levels of correlation with one another. On the other hand, the expected return of the portfolio as a whole *will* be the weighted average of the individual risky assets held. A carefully composed portfolio, therefore, is a kind of free lunch in which the investor can reduce risk without reducing expected return. But it also means the investor must evaluate any asset under consideration to be added to the portfolio in terms of both its expected return and its contribution to the portfolio's overall level of risk.

CAPM says the expected return on an asset will be equal to the expected return on the market (in excess of the return on a riskless asset) multiplied by how much the asset in question fluctuates in sympathy with the market. This latter measurement, which has come to be known as "beta," reflects the contribution of the asset to the portfolio's overall level of risk. Thus, beta is a measure of the asset's *systematic* risk, or the riskiness of the asset relative to the overall risk the investor takes from being in the market in the first place.*

At the same time, the returns on most individual assets are not always precisely aligned with the return of the market as a whole, giving rise to non-market or *unsystematic* risk. Alpha is what we call the expected difference between the actual return and the return that would be consistent with its beta.† CAPM then determines how assets would be priced in the market in equilibrium on the assumption that all in-

---

*Mathematically, beta is equal to the covariance of the asset's returns with the market returns divided by the market's variance of returns (or the correlation of the asset's returns with the market's return times the ratio of the standard deviation of the asset return divided by the standard deviation of the market's return).

†In a more technical sense, CAPM is usually estimated by performing a regression of the asset's historical returns on the market's returns. Beta is then the ratio of the individual asset's return to the market's return. Alpha is the residual that falls out from the regression calculations.

vestors use this particular procedure in valuing individual assets and composing the optimal portfolio.*

Although slow to gain general acceptance, CAPM has become a standard for the valuation of risky assets and for calibrating investment performance, both in the whole and in part. Beta is a popular indicator of investment risk, and, as we shall see in considerable detail in later chapters, alpha and beta are the starting points for many portfolio strategies, both complex and simple. Quite aside from its role in the investment world, CAPM is also an integral step for calculating the cost of capital in operating corporations—where, prior to the development of CAPM, the little matter of risk had not figured at all in the calculations.

CAPM's vitality among practitioners is remarkable, in view of how frequently it has failed in a wide variety and a great number of statistical tests. As a practical matter, nobody today considers the estimates derived from the model as anywhere near the last word in evaluating assets or making judgments about the performance of a portfolio. Nevertheless, beta serves widely as a measure of systematic risk, and alpha has become the holy grail of investment management—the excess return after adjustment for risk that can be earned over and above what the market returns.

When Sharpe looks back at CAPM, he admits, "Yes, I still think it is good to assume that you have to take higher risks if you are seeking higher returns. If you take risks other than the risk of being in the market itself, you probably will not be rewarded, because stock picking seldom pays off. So why do it?"† Consequently, Sharpe is not surprised that the concepts and, to an even greater extent, the vocabulary of CAPM are the favorite topics of conversation and guideposts in the world of investment practitioners.

Nevertheless, Sharpe himself has been moving away from his brainchild. "That whole brand of research," as he characterizes Capital Ideas in general and CAPM in particular, may have permeated the investment industry and the business schools, but he is seeking a richer set of assumptions in considering how assets are priced and how to optimize the trade-off between risk and return. He responds emphatically:

---

*For a full and elegant description of the model, its history, and its significance, see Perold (2004).

† Unless otherwise specified, all quotations are from personal interviews or correspondence.

Yes, Gene Fama would say "Yes, Virginia, there is a premium for holding stocks instead of putting money in the bank." On the other hand, that premium averages 5% to 6% after inflation, with a standard deviation of 15% to 20%. Under those conditions, you can have a 25- to 50-year period in which your return will be less than zero, and who wants that? So if we can't expect to get empirical proof of the equity risk premium in an experimental setting, I don't think fiduciaries should keep throwing that basic premise of stocks as a sure thing over the long run at their clients.

Sharpe is concerned that too many practitioners—and a large number of the business school professors from whom they learned their trade—tend to forget that all asset pricing models are about expectations. And how in the world can you measure expectations, which are a look forward, not backward? You cannot just look at history and deduce much about what expectations have been—or will be. The whole matter revolves around the future. Therefore, the historical data on which we all depend so heavily may be useless for asset pricing: As we never know with certainty what the future holds, all we have to rely on is a sense of the probabilities of future events.

"You are just reduced to a religious statement," Sharpe concludes. "I have been around long enough to see empirical results that seem to be really solid until you try a different country or different statistical method or different time period. Maybe that's why Fischer Black said you should put your trust only in logic and theory and forget about statistical empirical results."

The alternative approach Sharpe now favors is state-preference theory, another unwieldy name, developed some thirty years ago by Kenneth Arrow of Stanford and Gérard Debreu of the University of California, who won the Nobel Prize in Economics together in 1972. The essence of Arrow's theory is that the same asset can change in character as we look forward to the range of outcomes the future might hold.

As Sharpe describes it:

The basic premise is really quite straightforward. Imagine a world in which you could contract to receive $1 in purchasing power if there is a depression next year. This would cost $pd now. A contract to receive $1 in purchasing power if there is a boom would cost $pb. If the two contracts cost the same, people would choose to have as many of one as of the other. But this wouldn't work since there are many fewer real dollars available in a depression. Hence pd would have to be higher than pb in order to clear the markets.

We don't have simple securities of this type, but a stock market portfolio can be thought of as a bundle of claims with higher payoffs in good times than in bad times. A riskless security has the same payoffs in good and bad times. The prices of the two must adjust until people are willing to hold the stocks. One can think of the price of either one as that of a portfolio of claims to receive payment in different future states of the world. The principle holds here as well. Payoffs in bad times are more expensive. Put another way, investing to receive a payment in bad times must have a lower expected return than investing to receive a payment in good times.*

Using state-preference theory may be more complicated than calculating betas, but Sharpe believes Arrow points the way to a better method for thinking about risk and for making optimal investment choices. In contrast, "CAPM is *really* a special case." CAPM derives from mean/variance estimates for only one time period; there is only one asset to worry about and value; being in the market is the only risk that is rewarded; the investor takes no risks other than the risk of being in the market; and expected return and risk are always positively correlated. "These are really extreme assumptions," Sharpe adds.

Once unshackled from CAPM's stylized view of the real world, the investor can employ a more varied and realistic setting when making choices. State-preference theory enables us to price assets and optimize the risk/return trade-off under a wide range of possible outcomes, taking into consideration the probabilities that each outcome may occur. As a consequence, this approach could include situations where the distribution of returns differs from the bell-shaped normal distribution. As Sharpe describes this approach, it also allows investors to consider "at least a limited range of more complex preferences of the sort Danny Kahneman has talked about [or] the implications of a world in which people have disagreements about

---

*A more complete and extended version of Sharpe's views on these matters appears in Sharpe (2006). For recent papers covering this subject, see also http://www.stanford.edu /~wfsharpe/wp/index.html.

how likely . . . certain outcomes are in the future. . . . Certainly in the real world we know all of those things take place."[1]

Sharpe sums it up, "It's dangerous, at least in general, to think of risk as a number. . . . The problem we all face is that there are many scenarios that can unfold in the future. . . . The issue is: Do you have similar outcomes in the scenarios, or do you have diverse outcomes? Ultimately, that depends on your preferences or, as economists would term them, your utility function. So there is a lot more that can be done."[2]

And Sharpe the engineer is hard at work to accomplish what remains to be done, such as revising CAPM and Markowitz's mean/variance approach so that investors can use them under the varying conditions of state-preference theory. And Sharpe is using a simulator similar in function to Harry Markowitz's simulator described in Chapter 8 instead of working off a formal theory to test out his ideas.

⬛

As I have already suggested, Sharpe made his reputation as a theorist, but he has always been fascinated by practical applications of theoretical ideas. Over the years since the 1960s, he has been engaged in a series of business enterprises related to his theoretical work. Now he is concentrating on the theoretical and practical problems of a new field in finance he calls Retirement Economics, which addresses the problems of a new retiree aged somewhere between sixty-five and seventy. He is employing everything from basic theory to the institutional setting to figure out how people in all walks of life can best reach optimal decisions to the daunting problem of having enough money when retirement inevitably arrives. "It's absolutely frightening!" he asserts, "Our kids will be fine if we just die soon—and I have five grandsons."

Sharpe sees a great irony in the field of retirement today:

> In the old days, the default decision was that the government and your employer saved for your retirement, and when the day came they provided you with an annuity. That was all there was to it. Now the default decision is to decide how much you should save, how much and how to invest, and whether to take an annuity at retirement—but few people do save enough to fund their retirement, or know anything about how much and how to invest, and too many

of them end up taking lump sums instead of annuities. We were really wrong before, or we are really wrong now.

Retirement Economics is nothing new for Sharpe. In 1998, he was cofounder of Financial Engines, a successful Silicon Valley business venture to help individuals make the kinds of choices they confront as potential retirees—especially asset allocation and strategies to manage the risks they face. Financial Engines uses a computerized program, based on Sharpe's contributions to portfolio theory and asset pricing. The output provides individuals with the same kind of sophisticated advice long available to institutional investors, high-ranking corporate officers, and wealthy people. Financial Engines is available, for example, at E*Trade, and for Vanguard investors with Admiral accounts, but many corporations and financial advisers also provide it for the benefit of their employees.

The software begins by asking you to provide your age, sex, current asset holdings and distribution, your salary, the state in which you pay taxes, your expected Social Security income, and, finally, the age at which you expect or wish to retire. The program proceeds to forecast—after adjustment for inflation—your retirement income, your total income, and the value of your investment portfolio. All the data are entered into what is known as a Monte Carlo simulation, in which your data and a wide range of many different future rates of return on financial assets, interest rates, and inflation are combined in thousands of calculations, each representing a different scenario for the asset classes, interest rates, and inflation. The resulting forecasts are summarized in three pieces: the 5 percent of the outcomes that would be most favorable, the median outcome, and the 5 percent of the outcomes under the worst expected conditions.

The program will also predict the probability of your meeting your goals as well as how the outcomes would vary if you want to change the underlying assumptions, which is why it has come to be known as "outcome-investing." Deeply rooted in Capital Ideas, outcome-investing is just plain English for what institutional investors describe as mean/variance analysis—a mathematical system for finding the highest expected return for any given level of risk exposure. Unlike widely advertised programs of financial advisers and brokerage houses, Financial Engines does not provide a definitive answer as to whether the individual will have enough money to provide for the needs of retirement. Rather,

Financial Engines furnishes the individual with the probable consequences of individual decisions based on a range of outcomes with
which a person would be comfortable.

The program is sophisticated, exciting, and crystal clear in the information it provides, and it is constantly being revised and improved
by a skilled staff. As a financial adviser, the company has none of the
usual conflicts of interest because it is beholden to no one—indeed, it is
a popular tool among professional financial planners as well as among
individuals who have access to it.*

Employers originally retained Financial Engines to make available
the expertise of more sophisticated investors to employees struggling
with the complexities of a 401(k) plan and the myriad of investment
products offered to them. Under these arrangements, and in addition
to an online service, employees receive a complete personalized pro-
jection once a year showing how their plan is doing, not just in terms
of the year's investment results, but also in achieving their ultimate retirement goals.

Even with the kinds of help the Financial Engines model can provide, most people today find these kinds of problems too complicated
and lose interest. Their loss of interest would not matter under other
circumstances, but the future of the employees and their families is at
stake in these decisions. Anybody who is not an investment professional—and probably many professionals as well—needs all the help he
can get. As a result, Financial Engines has recently gone into the business of managing instead of just providing advice on these individual
portfolios; Financial Engines charges a company's employees a direct fee
for choosing and maintaining the appropriate mix of mutual funds the
program recommends.

This development has led Sharpe and his partners to change the company, as Sharpe describes it, "from a hot software group of propeller-
heads to a more staid and cautious group—we want to be sure we don't
make a mistake!" And he adds, "People really need help, and we must be
certain they do the right thing."

Sharpe's observation is interesting in its own right, but it also reveals a more important aspect of his goals. He is in effect an engineer,

---

* Vanguard customers in the Admiral category have free access to the facilities of Financial Engines. For others, the fee for using the program is $300.

as I pointed out earlier, but he is attempting to do more than building bridges to get people from here to there. In the process, as with Behavioral Finance and institutionalism, financial engineers like Sharpe, Markowitz, and Shiller improve neoclassical finance by toughening it and by improving the business payoffs with new and better techniques.

8

Harry Markowitz

"You Have a Little World"

"**Y**ou will be completely surprised if I tell you about my latest research," declared Harry Markowitz at the outset of our interview. He was correct in his forecast.*

Markowitz has come a long way from the Harry Markowitz who launched Capital Ideas in 1952 with his theory of portfolio selection, in which he specified a process for optimizing the trade-off between risk and return and composing the result into a diversified investment portfolio. He is no longer the same Harry Markowitz whose view of these matters first put Bill Sharpe to work on the relation between individual stocks and the market as a whole—a step that led to the Single-Index Model and then the Capital Asset Pricing Model. Markowitz has lost faith in what he terms the traditional neoclassical "equilibrium models." These models, he claims, "make unrealistic—absurd—assumptions about the actors. For example, they can borrow all they want at the risk-free rate. Or they can revise their portfolios continuously. It would be nice to think through systems in which there would be more recognizable economic agents."[1]

Furthermore, at a time when the world changes so rapidly and the markets are so dynamic, the equilibrium at the foundation of Capital Ideas will never come about or will stand still for too short a time to matter.

---

*Unless otherwise specified, all quotations are from personal interviews or correspondence.

Today's Harry Markowitz has no preconceived notions about how "recognizable economic agents" actually make decisions and act, even though he has strong convictions on how they *should* act. After all, as he points out, you can look at stock prices swinging up and down every day, but what you observe reveals nothing about what is going on under the surface, such as the degree to which investors are succumbing to the over-confidence and loss aversion featured in Behavioral Finance. Markowitz has wanted to explore in detail how stock prices would behave in a market where some investors have behavioral quirks while others are coolly rational. He is also interested in studying the consequences for stock prices when some investors take on risks that differ from the risks other investors are taking.

Markowitz believes none of this can be accomplished by modeling. Nor can you accomplish it by just looking at stock prices and trying to figure out what drives them. Like Sharpe, he has become a financial engineer who believes you need a laboratory where you can reverse the process: You begin with a set of assumptions about "recognizable economic agents," and then see how stock prices behave and how the dynamics play out when those recognizable economic agents begin to trade in the market. After that, you change the assumptions and run the simulation all over again, as many times as you want. By combining rational investors with irrational investors and with a set of additional realistic assumptions, Markowitz hopes to use these micro-scenes to derive implications for the market as a whole, including responses to regulatory changes.

To this end, Markowitz has collaborated with Bruce Jacobs and Kenneth Levy, partners in a leading portfolio management firm and well-known in their own right for their quantitative research. Together, Markowitz, Jacobs, and Levy have built and run a computer program they call JLMSim, using their initials.[2] The tool they are employing, an asynchronous discrete event simulator, is less forbidding than its title. It is also simpler to explain than to create.

Simulation is a procedure for generating possible future outcomes by drawing random numbers from a distribution with predefined parameters. In asynchronous simulation, processes change sporadically or at irregular intervals over time, which fits the pattern of equity markets well. Individual markets do not function twenty-four hours a day—not yet, at least—nor are they open every day. Even during trading hours, there are times nothing is happening with any given stock, and the time between trades can vary widely. There are also times an investor places an order but a delay occurs until the execution takes place. Meanwhile, a series of other trades may be occurring in response to orders from other investors.

The type of computer simulation Markowitz and his colleagues are using has mind-boggling power, and they are carrying out elaborate experiments with this device. The simulator they employ is not a model of a market as such but a tool to allow researchers to create a model of a market using their inputs of choice. Investors are not the only actors in the dramas who compose the input to the simulations. These imaginary participants also include security analysts and statisticians, portfolio managers, and traders. Markowitz and his colleagues define the decision rules for each of these players, such as some of the patterns of Behavioral Finance, the frequency of trading, and the dependence of investors on traders and statisticians. The simulation also includes order slips and the individual securities to be traded or to be arranged into portfolios.

One nice feature concerns the investors. They have all read Markowitz's 1952 paper on portfolio selection. As a result, none of them makes a move without going through the process of mean/variance analysis—or optimizing the trade-offs between expected return and risk. Each investor picks an ideal portfolio on the basis of individual risk aversion.

After investors decide how to move their current portfolios toward this ideal portfolio, they send their orders to traders. The traders execute these orders if there are matching orders; otherwise the order is included on the books of the traders awaiting a buyer or seller wishing to transact at the specified price—just as in the real world.

The process results in securities moving from investors with one kind of risk aversion to investors with different kinds of risk aversion, all based on mean/variance analysis. The frequency with which each investor goes through this exercise and the speed of moving from an old portfolio to a new portfolio will govern how often an investor places orders with the traders to execute transactions.

The program allows the user to specify how many groups and classifications of investors will function in any particular run. Markowitz and his associates divide the investors into eight groups of 1,000 each, depending on how often they optimize, their risk parameters, and their dependence on traders and statisticians in selecting and executing their transactions. Traders are equally sophisticated in portfolio theory, employing various rules to set limit prices for orders.

As Markowitz told me about this complex computer game in which he was engaged, I could not begin to imagine what kind of computer output these complex sets of inputs can produce. Markowitz assured me the outputs involve overwhelming detail, but he and his friends are having lots of fun at their task.

The computer produces different kinds of output, in which, Markowitz told me, "What you get looks very pretty." One particular simulation, for example, assumed there were sixteen individual securities in the market. One set of outputs from this example provides high-low-close and volume data for any individual security or for the market of these sixteen securities as a whole. The computer also provides a printout with a summary of 1,000 individual transactions per day in each of these securities.

One part of this voluminous printout is a daily Excel file showing the closing price of each security as well as a capitalization-weighted index of all sixteen individual securities, the total volume for the market, and a picture of how each of the eight groups of investors is doing—"how many have gone bankrupt and how many have growing wealth." The simulation also produces a "market impact printout" that provides the twenty-five largest orders each of the eight investor groups attempted to execute, what time they started, the bid and ask on each order, and how much of their order they were able to complete.

When I expressed wonder that anybody could design something as complex as this, Markowitz reminded me of his experience in writing computer programming languages during some of the years after the publication of "Portfolio Selection" in 1952. Then he added, as though it were just that simple, "You think about a market—the types of entities there and their attributes; you think about order slips for buys and sells; and then you think about the kinds of events—reoptimizing, placing orders, reviewing orders, and end of the day events. You think about margin requirements, and what happens when an investor on margin fails to meet the requirements. By the time you are through, you have a little world."

One of the more interesting developments that appears in these simulations is the feedback process at work. In one run, all the investors engage in mean/variance analysis but form their expected returns from historical average returns. The system turned out to be explosive. Markowitz describes the outcome: "You would start out with sixteen simulated stocks, all priced about 100, and in a few years you would find some stock had gone up to $20 million. Suppose that were the world!"

The system was explosive because of positive feedback. Everybody looked at history for an average return. If some stock did particularly well, everybody said, "We have to increase the expected return on this stock." Everybody went out and tried to buy it. That raised the price, which amplified the average return, which raised investors' expectations of future returns, and so on.

So a different kind of investor was added to the market, one who had an estimate of the value of the stock per share without regard to past price movements. Then, as prices went up, this investor perceived the stock as less attractive, because she would have to pay more for the same ultimate result. As a result, Markowitz and his colleagues found that if there were a proper balance between different kinds of investors, they would have markets fluctuating in a realistic manner. But, "the markets did continue to fluctuate, and we could see the dynamics of the situation as distinguished from just purely the equilibrium condition."[3]

A little world indeed!

Markowitz is still involved in a larger world as well. In the September/October 2005 issue of the *Financial Analysts Journal,* Markowitz takes aim at two of the underlying assumptions of the Capital Asset Pricing Model as stock prices and portfolios move toward overall equilibrium.[4] First, CAPM assumes investors can borrow infinite amounts of money at the risk-free rate—and without any regard to their current resources, which are obviously a matter of high importance to any lender. Second, investors can sell short without limit and use the proceeds to take on long positions—which means any investor can deposit $1,000 with a broker, sell short $1 million worth of one security, and buy long $1,001,000 of another security.

Neither of these assumptions is realistic. No lender parts with cash without some indication the borrower has the capacity to repay. No one can borrow money at a rate as low as what the U.S. government pays. Furthermore, Federal Reserve Regulation T prevents an investor with only $1,000 from selling short more than $2,000 in securities, or from taking on $1,000 long and $1,000 short. That is a far cry from $1,001,000.*

According to Markowitz, the result of making these two assumptions more realistic is a shocker: "*[T]he market portfolio need not be an efficient portfolio*"[†] (emphasis added). Indeed, "This departure from efficiency can be quite substantial. The market portfolio can have almost *maximum* variability among feasible portfolios with the same expected value" (italics in the original).

The consequences for investment strategy are stunning. If the market portfolio is not an efficient portfolio, then indexing makes no sense, and perhaps no strategy of broad diversification makes sense.

In order to explain why these counter-intuitive deductions occur, a brief digression is necessary. In 1958, James Tobin had demonstrated that portfolio selection was a remarkably simple matter. The process begins with the efficient frontier, as suggested by Markowitz's 1952 selection model.[††] As with Markowitz, the riskiest portfolio on the frontier—the one at the top—is not diversified; it includes only one security. As you come down the efficient frontier, the portfolios become

---

*A variant of this view had been reflected earlier at Wells Fargo Bank, as we shall see in Chapter 10.

Jacobs, Levy, and Markowitz have also worked out a technique for optimizing portfolios with both long and short positions and subject to Regulation T type constraints. See Jacobs, Levy, and Markowitz (2003) and (2006).

[†] An efficient portfolio is the portfolio an investor expects to provide the highest expected return for a given level of risk, or the lowest risk for a given level of expected return (see *Capital Ideas,* pp. 192–193).

[††] The efficient frontier is the range of efficient portfolios from lowest to highest risk, or from lowest to highest expected return (see *Capital Ideas,* pp. 58–60).

increasingly diversified. That is, the portfolios hold an increasing number of securities.

Markowitz had allowed for cash or for riskless lending at the risk-free rate in this process, and so did Tobin. But Tobin saw something extra. Once riskless lending comes into the picture, as the asset with the least risk out of all those available, that is the end of what you can add to the portfolios on the frontier. So the frontier beyond that point is composed only of portfolios with increasing amounts of cash.

Bill Sharpe's 1964 paper on the Capital Asset Pricing Model adds one more assumption to what Markowitz and Tobin had developed: that you can borrow as well as lend at the risk-free rate—all you want, in either direction. Under these conditions, the investor selects only one risky portfolio—the market portfolio—which is then mixed with lending or borrowing at the risk-free rate in order to create the frontier.

These are the conditions in which Markowitz, Tobin, and Sharpe had worked out the structure of the efficient frontier. But now Markowitz declares the market portfolio is not an efficient portfolio! Why should this be so? These traditional calculations of the efficient frontier undergo profound change when we apply real-world constraints to borrowing or short-selling. Now portfolios at the riskier end of the efficient frontier will hold only a small number of volatile securities. At the low end of the frontier, portfolios are likely to be more diversified, but with an extra dollop of less volatile securities. These distorted results can have a powerful impact on portfolio selection based on mean/variance calculations.

In a more recent and illuminating exploration into the nature of the left, or least risky, end of the efficient frontier, Roger Clarke of Analytic Investors and two colleagues point out that security weights at that point are independent of expected security returns.[5] This means the investor need be concerned only with the covariance matrix of the securities under consideration, with reference to expected returns. This curious set of circumstances can lead to portfolios with less risk than the market portfolio but also with higher expected returns, a kind of free lunch enabling investors to increase their allocation to equities without increasing the amount of risk in the total portfolio.

Under Tobin's original reasoning—whether investors are risk-averse or whether they have a big appetite for taking on risk—every single investor should hold risky assets only in the form of the market portfolio, or something like an index fund with broad diversification like the Standard & Poor's 500. Depending on how they feel about risk, investors should adjust their portfolios by investing a larger or smaller proportion of their total resources in the market portfolio. Risk-averse investors would place the balance into riskless assets like U.S. Treasury bills; investors with an appetite for risk would put more than 100 percent of their resources into the market portfolio, borrowing the money to make up the difference (see pp. 72–74 of *Capital Ideas*).

This prescription ran headlong into conventional wisdoms of the time, for Tobin concluded that "interior decorating"—such as conservative equity portfolios for widows and orphans and aggressive portfolios for business executives—would lead to suboptimal results.

But when we make more realistic assumptions about borrowing and short-selling, Markowitz now demonstrates that Tobin's prescription fails to hold. Under those conditions, "The high end of the frontier will indeed tend to be dominated by businessman-risk securities, whereas the low end . . . will typically have more than its proportionate share of widow-and-orphan securities." Interior decorating is in, not out! Conventional wisdom, for once, turns out to be on the right track.

All is not lost for CAPM, however. "CAPM is a thing of beauty," Markowitz declares near the end of his *FAJ* article. We cannot afford to ignore its lessons or dump it in the ashcan:

> CAPM should be taught. It is like studying the motion of objects on Earth under the assumption that the Earth has no air. The calculations and results are much simpler if this assumption is made. But at some point, the obvious fact that on Earth, cannonballs and feathers do not fall at the same rate should be noted and explained. . . . Similarly, at some point, the finance student should be shown the effect of replacing [unlimited borrowing and short-selling] with more realistic constraints and the "so what" should be explained.

Despite his ventures into new ways to consider how markets behave and how investors should invest for optimal outcomes, Markowitz remains an enthusiast for quantitative techniques in investment analysis. *Pensions & Investments,* a trade paper, reported in October 2005 that, "In the investment risk category, Mr. Markowitz . . . noted that plan sponsors now regularly use mathematical techniques to analyze their managers' portfolios. . . . 'That's something really great to see,' Mr. Markowitz said."[6]

◈

An odd twist to the Markowitz story came to light in 2006 when an American financial journal published in English part of an article that had first appeared in Italy in 1940. The author of this article was a distinguished Italian mathematician and academic, Bruno de Finetti. Nearly ninety pages long in the original, de Finetti's paper proposed mean/variance analysis as the method to optimize the trade-offs between risk and return.[7]

De Finetti's line of analysis bears a remarkable resemblance to what Markowitz would develop completely on his own twelve years later, and for which Markowitz won the Nobel Prize. De Finetti includes the efficient frontier and the importance of correlations among returns in determining the riskiness of a portfolio of assets.* The process of mean/variance optimization, as we shall see in subsequent chapters, plays a major role today in asset allocation decisions in institutional investment management.

A chapter of de Finetti's full text in English appeared in the Fall 2006 issue of *The Journal of Investment Management,* along with background commentary by Mark Rubinstein of the University of California at Berkeley and by Markowitz himself. Markowitz's contribution carries the catchy title of "De Finetti Scoops Markowitz" and goes into extended detail in discussing the resemblances and differences between de Finetti's work and his own.

Rubinstein, who first learned about this paper from a friend in 2005, appears to be the first English-speaking financial economist to be aware of its existence. Rubinstein offers several reasons to explain why de Finetti's work has been unknown for so long among English-speaking economists and, most notably, by Harry Markowitz. As Rubinstein points out, de Finetti's primary interest was in probability and in the world of insurance (he had been an actuary); the problem he was at-

---

*A.D. Roy, an English academic, also published an article along similar lines later in 1952 than Markowitz's, but Roy's paper attracted little attention at the time and he never pursued the matter any further. See *Capital Ideas,* pp. 55–56.

tempting to solve in this paper relates to reinsurance, not investment portfolio selection. This difference in focus probably explains why de Finetti never pursued the insights of his 1940 paper in any of his later works. He was sufficiently well-known, however, to have been invited to the United States in 1950 by the eminent American mathematician, Leonard Savage, to deliver a paper on probability at a conference at Berkeley.

Rubinstein also speculates that, "With the intellectual separation of academics in actuarial science and economics/finance, and since his paper was only available in Italian (and a high-style Italian at that), those who knew of de Finetti's work did not communicate with financial economists, even in Italy. By the time Markowitz's work appeared, de Finetti's was largely forgotten." Rubinstein also reports de Finetti's daughter's view of her father as someone who, "as a general attitude of his character [was] not interested to claim merits for himself, but just to fight for the triumph of the idea he thought to be correct against the wrong paradigm."

What would have transpired if someone had brought de Finetti's 1940 paper to Markowitz's attention around 1950, while he was still working out his own version of mean/variance analysis as applied to the selection of assets for an investment portfolio? Although Markowitz had earned his undergraduate degree in economics at the University of Chicago, he came upon the notion of mean/variance for portfolio selection around 1950 quite by chance as he was searching for a topic for his Ph.D. thesis (see *Capital Ideas,* pp. 44–47). Finance in general and the selection of assets for an investment portfolio in particular, were only examples for Markowitz at that time, useful not in themselves but as a means of illustrating what his methodology could achieve. As we know from subsequent events over the past fifty-odd years, finance soon fascinated Markowitz and has remained his primary interest ever since.

When I asked Markowitz what he would have done if someone had shown him the de Finetti paper while he was working on his thesis, his response was unqualified: "I would have seen at once that de Finetti was related to my portfolio selection work, but by no means identical to it. I guess I would have given him a footnote in my paper."

This answer was a great relief to me, as it should be to all who appreciate the value of Capital Ideas to the world of investing. Markowitz's work on portfolio selection was the foundation of all that followed in the theory of finance, and of the Capital Asset Pricing Model in particular.

9

Myron Scholes
"Omega Has a Nice Ring to It"

W hen Myron Scholes graduated from McMaster University in Hamilton, Ontario, in 1962, his family wanted him to join their book publishing business. Scholes was not interested in going into business at that time. Instead, he went to the Graduate School of Business at the University of Chicago, where he launched what would turn out to be a spectacular career as an academic, including a Nobel Prize in Economic Science for his contribution to the Black-Scholes-Merton option pricing model.

Although Scholes clearly has more than the credential to qualify as one of the theoreticians in this story, the route he is following today is distinctly different from the route taken by his fellow theoreticians. Each of the others, with the exception of Samuelson, is dabbling in some kind of business operation, but they are also engaged in a variety of activities unrelated to their business interests—including teaching. Scholes's primary activity is business. He may travel around the world to give talks on his research interests or give advice, and he still explores many aspects of theory, but, as co-managing partner of a $2.6 billion hedge fund called Platinum Grove Asset Management, his priority is the hedge fund. "This has been a great experience," he told me. "It involves a lot of good economic thinking and yet I am still engaged in a business."

The fund is serious business. Scholes organized Platinum Grove in 1999 following the abrupt demise of Long-Term Capital Management, of which he had been a principal, because he wanted to see whether he could manage risk, preserve capital, and make enough money for the project to be worthwhile. Scholes was joined by a former student and colleague, Chi-fu Huang, who had been a student at Stanford and then became a professor at MIT. Chi-fu Huang brought along one of *his* former students at MIT, Ayman Hindy. "Thus," said Scholes, "we have the academic grandfather, son, and grandson all under one roof."

So far so good. With sixty-five employees on the job today, the fund since inception has generated returns of 9.6 percent a year after fees, and 6.5 percent a year over the popular cash-equivalent benchmark of LIBOR (the London Interbank Offered Rate). Annual volatility has been only 4.5 percent, or a little less than half the rate of return. The fund has almost zero correlation with bond markets or stock markets.

Although Platinum Grove does hold short positions, its resemblance to most hedge funds ends there. Platinum Grove makes no forecasts of systematic factors—such as betas or alphas—and has no intention of doing so. Scholes and his associates trade in the capital markets to make money by providing what Scholes describes as "liquidity and risk transfer services," which involve taking on risks that a wide variety of investors and business firms do not wish to carry and are willing to pay others to assume for them.

These are not face-to-face transactions, such as the risk transfer that takes place when a young man buys a life insurance policy to protect his family in case he dies before his life expectancy. Rather, Platinum Grove tends to invest in financial instruments that other investors or business firms employ for hedging risks they do not want to take. The sellers of these kinds of instruments are not interested in nickel-and-diming the transaction price—they are interested in balancing the risks in their businesses or in their investment portfolios. That is where Platinum Grove can step in and make a profit by taking on the risks others want to shed.

Scholes uses the word "omega"—the last letter in the Greek alphabet—to describe the opportunity to make money by carrying risks for other parties. Providing these services does not require predictions of macro forces or cash flows, which is what beta and alpha predictions are all about—and alpha and beta are the first two letters of the Greek alphabet. As Scholes describes it, "Omega has a nice ring to it. Best of all, omega is not a zero-sum game, like the search for alpha. We are providing a service, not seeking an edge in processing information. Simply put, people at our end of these transactions are paid for taking risks others do not want to carry."

Scholes likes the contrast of the last letter with the first two letters of the Greek alphabet, but his reasons for choosing omega were more serious. He was thinking in terms of Ohm's Law, which says that voltage equals current times resistance ($V = I \times R$). The Greek letter for resistance is omega. When agents are seeking to transfer risks to others in the financial markets, speculators will resist taking the flow, or the current, unless they receive adequate compensation in lower prices. To Scholes, then, omega symbolizes the role his firm takes in seeking out opportunities where assets are underpriced because someone, somewhere, is attempting to transfer a risk to the market.

Although Scholes explicitly excludes considerations of alpha and beta in the management of his hedge fund, and although he claims the search for omega is not a zero-sum game, the roots of his strategies are still deeply imbedded in the basic structures of Capital Ideas. Risk, in all its manifestations, is the central consideration in everything his fund undertakes, and the risk/return trade-off is basic to all decisions. He makes little use of the Capital Asset Pricing Model, but assumptions of market efficiency explain why he insists the investments in his fund are not based on "mispricings" but, rather, on value created by investors seeking to shed risks by making it profitable for others to assume those risks for them. His fund's generous use of the options pricing model throughout speaks for itself.

Scholes's words sound like plain English, larded with a little Greek for spice, but what he is saying has a more profound meaning than he indicates. By trading in the markets without regard to alpha and beta, he is functioning in a world that is not only fundamentally different from active investors like the Yale University endowment or Goldman Sachs—whose activities we will analyze in future chapters—but his world is in many ways more closely related than they are to what financial markets are all about.

Most people are aware financial markets play an important role in our economy—indeed, in our society—because financial markets are reputedly the grease in our economy that keeps the wheels of enterprise turning. Yet few of us stop to consider what is actually playing out in the frenzied activity in these markets or how and why financial markets fulfill so many important roles in the economic process.

Most obvious, but also most significant, financial markets are *markets,* where exchanges take place between two parties offering to buy or sell bits and pieces of corporate ownership, private and public debts, and derivative instruments, all of which appear in countless varieties. Each party is seeking a different objective from the other side, but the market enables the parties to settle on a price that is satisfactory to both of them. *Indeed, if the two parties did not have different views, buyers could never find sellers, and vice versa.* Boom and bust are what occurs when everybody agrees about what the future holds.*

The prices set in markets are perhaps the single most important piece of information in the economy. They are actual numbers, not estimates by some government agency. They tell us how people with opposing views agree on the value of some product, service, or asset. With this information, we can plan; we can forecast; we can move or stand still; we can allocate resources.

That does not mean the price is always "right" or the "best price." That outcome would occur only when both sides have all the available information relating to the transaction. It is a paradox, but prices that are always and everywhere right would discourage anyone from seeking better information about what is going on—and gathering information is costly. But people do spend much time, effort, and money gathering information, which reveals that prices are never quite right, that they do not yet reflect all available information. And a good thing, too, because those efforts to gather information are what tend to push prices toward their equilibrium levels.†

We instinctively think of financial markets as centers where buyers are looking for undervalued assets and sellers are shedding what they perceive as overvalued assets—in other words, where the price is seldom "right." But the search for value, or for alpha, is only a part of what goes

---

* I am grateful to Robert Prasch (1992) for his critique of my failure to include this important point in *Capital Ideas.*
† For a brilliant exploration of this paradox, see Grossman and Stiglitz (1980).

on in financial markets, and often only a small part. Transactions in these markets can vary widely in their objectives, because financial markets are a place where owners of outstanding assets can convert those assets into cash, or where owners of cash can find longer-term uses for their money. In this role, investors who use their cash to buy assets with future cash flows are giving the sellers of those assets the option of realizing in the present the discounted value of those future cash flows.

But something more profound is going on. In this kind of role, financial markets are a time machine that allows selling investors to compress the future into the present and buying investors to stretch the present into the future. Without financial markets, all assets would be buy-and-hold, and the cost of capital would be an order of magnitude higher than it is today. Some of these kinds of transactions arise because one side or the other sees an opportunity to buy a bargain or to sell an overpriced asset. Either way, the seller is compressing the future into the present by raising cash, while the buyer is stretching the present into the future by committing cash.

Bringing buyers and sellers together, financial markets do more than create the time machine swapping money today for money tomorrow. Many other activities are under way at the same time. These markets create liquidity; they provide an opportunity for corporations to finance their activities, and they reveal at every instant the market's appraisal of the value of a corporation or any of the many other instruments constantly being priced. While each of these functions explains why financial markets are so active, we should recognize that the markets could not function as they do *if they were not all these different things at the same time.*

Buyers and sellers are also attracted to financial markets as a place to hedge bets—or to transfer risks from one party to another. Financial markets were always a place to hedge bets, but the development of the market for derivative instruments over the past thirty years or more has extended and significantly amplified those opportunities.

Sanford Grossman of Quantitative Investment Strategies and the Wharton School has sensed this character of the markets more clearly than many. As far back as 1989, he put it this way:

If the only reason people trade is that they believe they know more than the next person—e.g., have better information—there would be no gains from trade. . . . There have to be other reasons for trade. Although some price moves occur because of changes in information, other price changes take place because of changes in the risk tolerance or liquidity preferences of certain investors.[1]

Grossman cites two examples of price changes taking place because of changes in risk tolerance or liquidity preferences. The first example involves a pension fund aiming to improve the match between its assets and liabilities by shifting out of stocks into an immunized bond portfolio. The second example involves investors who desire immediacy of execution. To carry out their objectives, these investors must accept adverse equity prices to persuade other investors to cooperate by taking the equities off their hands. Grossman describes precisely the kind of environment in which Scholes and his hedge fund can flourish by making it possible for other investors to transfer risks.

The oldest known example of risk transfer in the markets relates to the miller who buys the farmer's wheat crop to store and later to process and sell as flour. The miller faces two primary sources of risk.

The first source is idiosyncratic, or risks that are typical of the milling business and unavoidable if you choose to make your living at that activity. For example, will there be local demand for flour? Will some competitor open up a new mill in the neighborhood? Will a favored customer run into financial difficulty? These kinds of risks are inescapable in the business the miller has chosen.

The second source of risk for the miller is macro or generalized risk, which is risk outside the miller's particular business—risks faced by everybody dealing in any way with agricultural commodities. Macro risk begins the instant the miller buys the farmer's crop and puts it into storage. What happens if the price of grain drops between the time the newly purchased wheat goes into storage and the time it goes on the market in the form of flour? The miller can sustain a serious loss if the price falls. If the decline is steep enough, the impact could even force the miller into bankruptcy.

The miller can protect himself against this dire eventuality by holding a large extra margin of equity in his business. Would that be a wise decision? He is not in the business of speculating on the future price of grain in the commodities markets, and holding that much extra equity is expensive if it does not earn a good return relative to the risks involved. Rather, he expects to make his money by converting grain into flour and selling the flour. Consequently, he would seek a way to hedge the *price risk*—to transfer the risk of price fluctuation to someone else whose business it is to take such risks.

The financial markets provide the medium by which the miller can transfer the price risk. At the time he puts the grain into storage, the miller also sells a futures contract committing him to deliver the grain at a future date and *at a price fixed at the time of the transaction.* Note, once again, how the transfer of time is an inherent element of financial transactions, and how time defines the nature of the risks being assumed to be transferred out.

The miller is now insured against a fall in the price, because that loss will be borne by the speculator who buys the futures contract. The miller would fail to gain if the price rises in the interim, but, he will tell himself, speculating on price is not his business. His business is storing grain, later converting it into flour, and selling the flour to his customers. The miller converts risk to basis risk, or residual risk, the risk that remains as the price of wheat in his locale might not change in lockstep with the price of wheat generally. This is an extremely small risk relatively, however, given the high correlation of local and general price movements. Hedging contracts must have a high degree of association to survive and to be useful as hedging instruments.

But what motivates the speculator who buys the futures contract the miller wants to sell? Speculators will step in and buy only when the price of the contract is low enough so they can expect a return in excess of the interest they could have earned on their money if they had not bought the contract. Meanwhile, the speculators might reduce their risk as well by hedging in other markets or diversifying across strategies. The miller is fully aware the price he is receiving reflects a compensation to the speculator for accepting the transfer of the risk of price fluctuation. Like any service, the service of risk transfer has to earn a return, or nobody would provide it.

Scholes has a keen sense of the essential meaning of risk transfer. As he explained it to me:

> Risk transfer is a *time series* of asset holdings, moving assets or securities or risks from now into the future. That is, excess inventory must be moved forward in time until new demanders enter the market. Speculators bring current time to future time to meet demands. Indeed, bringing current time to future time is a fundamental function of the broker/dealer community or banks or hedge funds, because these investors earn their keep by holding inventories of specific securities awaiting future demanders. In my view, similar to the hedgers in the commodity markets, the sellers of excess inventory know the price they are receiving includes a return to the speculators as compensation for taking the risk during the inventory holding period.

From Scholes's perspective, risk transfer is just as important to the investment process and risk management as diversification and optimizing the risk/return trade-off. Perhaps it is even more important to the economy as a whole.

Every business must concentrate its product lines and other activities to make money for owners. And every business faces a critical choice. On the one hand, it could carry sufficient equity capital to absorb all the risks its business requires, even risks with no expected excess return or no net present value to the business. On the other hand, the firm can reduce the amount of equity it has to carry by hedging the zero present value risks. Equity and hedging both involve costs, but hedging is a much more efficient method. The corporation knows it is paying the speculators for hedging services and does so willingly because hedging almost always works out to be less expensive than holding additional equity.

As Scholes put it to me, "The big idea for the firm is to determine how it makes money. Then the firm must decide on which risks it needs to take and which risks it should transfer when—as is most often the case—hedging is less expensive than carrying additional equity. Generalized risks, like price or interest rate movements, are far less costly to transfer than idiosyncratic risks peculiar to the firm itself. 'Separation' is the key: Make business decisions first, and then change the nature of the risks faced by the business."

The business of Platinum Grove is to take on risks—at a favorable price—that others want to lay off. As Scholes describes it, Platinum Grove's business has nothing to do with forecasting asset prices. Rather, Platinum Grove's business is to shape its strategies based on questions of a fundamentally different character. For example, why are risk transfer opportunities available? Why is the price of transferring money payments from today to tomorrow varying? For how long will Platinum Grove have to carry or provide inventory to the market? Which macro factors might change the duration of its holding period? Does the opportunity offer a high enough expected return on the risk and working capital needed to support the inventory risks, and, once the answer to that question has been determined, how large should the position be, given the current expected return?

Risk transfer is similar to providing liquidity, but the two are not the same thing. Liquidity means people will accept lower rates of return for immediacy; a liquidity premium is the higher return available to those who are willing to sacrifice immediacy. Renting versus owning, for example, is ultimately a matter of how you feel about liquidity. Providing liquidity to those who seek it is can be profitable and, like risk transfer, is not a zero-sum game. "Providing liquidity also earns omega," says Scholes.

Scholes believes these are matters of the highest importance. "When we observe asset pricing in general," he told me, "we are missing a big component of market price behavior if we ignore questions such as how and when changes occur in the price of liquidity or the price of risk transfer. When investors are demanding more liquidity or seeking to transfer more risks to others, correlations of asset returns tend to increase—in the extreme, multiple asset classes that generally exhibit low correlations begin moving together in the same direction."

I asked Scholes how Platinum Grove actually functions on a day-to-day basis. "We are in a reactive business; we wait for opportunities to arise," he responded. "We are the classic speculator. We are one group among myriad teams making markets more efficient by compressing time. In part, we try to rely on negative feedback systems—we seek to buy when relative prices are too low and to sell when relative prices are too high—on the assumption that prices out of line will return to equilibrium levels. As you know from my papers, substitution is a powerful force in markets; that is, assets with similar risk characteristics will be priced to provide similar expected returns."

To illustrate this point, Scholes gave an actual example of a Platinum Grove transaction involving CTAs—Commodity Trading Advisors who trade in the futures markets and are registered with the Commodity Futures Trading Commission. In 2006, the Bank of Japan appeared close to ending its long-held practice of a continuously easing monetary policy and maintaining interest rates close to zero. Many CTAs saw this development as an opportunity to sell—to go short—futures contracts on Japanese bonds maturing ten years out. If a policy shift by the Bank of Japan would cause yields on those bonds to rise in the market, the price of the bonds would fall, and the price of the futures contract would follow suit. Then the CTAs could repurchase the futures contracts at prices below the prices at which they had sold the contracts short.

In effect, the CTAs sold long-term bonds through selling futures contracts, where a market maker made a bid and purchased the futures from them. The CTAs understood that all market makers offer to buy securities at a lower price than the price at which they would offer to sell. They make their living out of that spread, but, if the CTAs had made a correct forecast, they would be expecting to make a lot more than the fraction they had to pay the market maker for executing their transaction.

Now the market maker is holding a futures contract that might well lose value if the Bank of Japan were to shift its policy as expected. To hedge this risk, the market maker, in turn, sold short a seven-year Japanese government bond, choosing seven instead of ten years because the seven-year bond happened to be cheaper to deliver to the buyer. Thus, the market maker ends up earning an income on the bid-offer spreads and has transferred the interest rate risk to the market with the short sale of the seven-year bond.

With CTAs selling long-bond futures and market makers selling the seven-year maturity as a hedge, both the futures and the cheapest-to-deliver bonds fall in price. Scholes's hedge fund senses an opportunity. Its models indicate that the seven-year bond is cheap relative to both the ten-year and, in the other direction, to the five-year government bond as well. Platinum Grove proceeds to buy the seven-year and to sell the five- and ten-year bonds in the correct proportions to hedge against any general interest rate changes, but it stands to gain if the seven-year bond outperforms the other two.

What has all this to do with risk transfer? The CTAs expressed a view on the future of the market by selling the bond future to the market maker. The market maker sold the seven-year bond to hedge the risk he took on by buying the ten-year from the CTAs. Platinum Grove took on the market maker's risk at a price the market maker was satisfied to receive because he no longer carried the risk of an increase in interest rates. The CTAs have made their bet; the market maker expects a profit on the bid-ask spread, and has shifted the risk in the transaction to Platinum Grove. In a sense, the CTAs are like the farmer who sells his crop to a miller for storage and conversion into flour; the market maker plays the role of the miller, while Platinum is like the speculator who buys the futures contract from the miller who is hedging against an unfavorable movement in the price of grain while he is storing the farmer's crop.

Scholes then offered another example involving the bond market. Elements of this example are hypothetical, but it does provide an additional insight into the nature of Platinum Grove's activities in the business of risk transfer services to the market.

During the fall of 2004, a group of investment banks designed and sold their clients a large volume of structured notes. Structured notes appear to be conventional fixed-income instruments at first glance—debt paper with a maturity date and an interest rate—but they also contain additional features that justify a yield above what they would be worth as plain-vanilla debt instruments. Many structured notes have highly complex options embedded in them, but even in their simplest forms can involve puts and calls on assets that may have nothing to do with the issuer of the notes, or may include options to either reduce or extend the maturity of the notes.

Investors can also use structured notes to protect against the risks of a systemic shock to a portfolio. Suppose, for example, there were concerns that Quebec Separatists in Canada might win in a referendum on sovereignty, an event that would trigger a sharp drop in the Canadian dollar in foreign exchange markets. There could be a structured note with an embedded put on the Canadian dollar that could be exercised if the Separatists won or left alone under other conditions.*

The structured notes in Scholes's example paid coupons of 7 percent, a generous yield indeed. They matured in thirty years if interest rates remained above specified levels; otherwise the investment banks could call the notes and pay them off prior to maturity. At a time when U.S. government bonds of similar maturity offered only 4.25 percent, these notes turned out to be very popular among high net-worth individuals and some institutions, particularly in Asia, the Middle East, and Europe. These investors had a lot of cash at this time, thanks to oil money and money earned from exports. They also tend to seek high yields and to worry less about embedded options and risks.

Do these notes sound too good to be true? They were not as good as they sound. The noteholder received the 7 percent coupon *only if* the thirty-year government bond yield were above the ten-year yield at the time a coupon payment was due. Otherwise the coupon was zero—no interest paid to the holders. The notes in fact had two embedded options. The investment banks had sold an option, a so-called digital option, to pay a 7 percent coupon to the noteholders if and only if the long end of the term structure of interest rates were upward-sloping. The noteholders received payoffs on their series of options if, and only if, the thirty-year/ten-year yield spread were positive on the coupon date and the bond had not been called. Simultaneously, the noteholders had sold an option to the issuing banks, in which the payoff to the noteholders was zero if the thirty-year bond yield were equal to or less than the yield on ten-year bonds.

The investment banks were taking the risk that longer-term bond yields would remain above shorter-term bond yields, but they had no

---

* A put is an option to sell the underlying asset at a specified price no later than a specified date.

intention of losing money on the notes they provided to these yield-hungry investors. As the banks issued these notes on their own account, they could either keep the risk that they might have to pay 7 percent to the holder, or they could transfer that risk to the marketplace. The investment banks decided to hedge their risks and lock in the profits they earned from selling the notes. They did so by dynamically selling longer-dated instruments and buying shorter-dated instruments as the spread increased and reversing these hedges dynamically as the spread narrowed.

The investment banks had the same point of view about risk as the farmer or the miller in our earlier example. They chose which risks they must take to make money and hedged out the risks with zero present value. The business of the investment banks was to design and sell new securities, not to speculate on the ups and downs of the bond market, and they were perfectly willing to pay speculators to carry their risks forward for them by accepting prices that favored the other side. As in other examples, the speculators here were carrying out a risk transfer service and getting paid by transacting at prices favorable to themselves.

If the yield on the thirty-year bonds were to rise relative to the yield on the ten-year bonds, the value of the noteholder's option would increase as the investment banks would most likely need to pay more 7 percent coupons. At the same time, however, the price of the thirty-year bonds would be falling relative to the price of the ten-year bonds, so the banks would simultaneously show a profit on their hedge. If the relative movements were in the opposite direction, the banks would gain on the decline in the value of the option but have an offsetting loss on their hedge.

As the story played out, it led to an interesting sequence of events. The banks were hedging by selling thirty-year instruments and buying ten-year instruments every time they found new buyers for their 7 percent notes. Over time, these transactions were exerting constant downward pressure on the price of the thirty-year instruments and upward pressure on the price of the ten-years. The result was a steadily widening spread between the thirty-year yield, which was rising, and the ten-year yield, which was falling. As prospective customers for the 7 percent notes surveyed the developing situation, they concluded there was a shrinking probability of a further relative rise in longer-term bond yields relative to the ten-year yields from that point forward. Demand for the 7 percent notes fell off rapidly.

End of story.

▧

After Scholes had explained at length the nature of Platinum Grove's business, and after he had supplied even more examples than those set forth here, I was still left wondering how he could differentiate between a transaction in which Platinum Grove performed a risk transfer service and one in which a group of exceptionally talented investors just made a good forecast or discovered a good value in the markets.

When I put the question to him directly, he took the time to respond in detail:

> Other investors do express their forecasts in combination with "good values." At times, however, they will be required to express their forecasts in combination with "bad values." This is when we step in. They are demanding our services by their willingness to pay for our acumen.
>
> When we are providing risk transfer and providing liquidity, we don't forecast cash flows or whether interest rates will rise or fall in finding opportunities. That is for the people playing the alpha and beta game. Our game is different, even though we do need technology to identify opportunities and we also have to arrive at value judgments to assess why and for how long our risk transfer services are needed and how much capital is necessary to support the positions.
>
> In our case, we buy cheap and we sell expensive inventory of securities mostly in G-7 debt markets, based on our valuation models. We do forecast changes in monetary policy and as a result, at times, we do change the sizing of our positions to enhance our returns. We also need to turn over the inventory to earn returns. When we can forecast faster turnover, the annualized return on our capital will increase. Under those conditions, we assume larger positions.
>
> Every speculator must have technology to identify opportunities, to structure inventory positions, to hedge exogenous risks, to scale positions, to optimize among competing alternatives, and to plan for shocks. Technology must be supported and augmented by

know-how, contacts, and economic understanding to forecast when the inventory investment period will end. Nevertheless, our forecasting is far different from the forecasts that others need to generate returns.

Finally, Scholes reviewed what Platinum Grove is all about. "We continually need to upgrade our technology and conduct research to enhance our models. With better technology, we can identify opportunities and monitor activities more efficiently. With new research, we not only enhance our current technology, but also we will intermediate in different markets and grow the business. In addition to helping with our scaling, discussions with contacts allow us to gain keener insights into the functioning of the capital markets and where we should conduct research and add to our technology to intermediate."

Scholes ended the discussion by expressing his enthusiasm for what he is doing. "This is a great business," he pointed out. "We can teach the next generation that follows us on how to conduct the business, an opportunity few other investment organizations enjoy because they draw on intuition more heavily than we do. And, as we learn more, we can systematize and coordinate the business more efficiently. We believe models are incomplete without intuition, but intuition is incomplete without models. They complement each other.

"This combination excites me. Although we are in business, hoping to end up with a profit, we replicate the university setting. We conduct research; we discuss it and improve it; and we build models and empirically test them. And, in some sense we publish them and verify them when we test them in the market."

PART III
THE PRACTITIONERS

10

Barclays Global Investors

"It Was an Evangelical Undertaking"

> The momentum that McQuown, Vertin, and Fouse created . . . was robust enough to continue in force despite subsequent changes in leadership and even in credo. Considering how early in the game they fired their first shots, how little was known, understood, or appreciated about the theories they advanced, their achievement was indeed extraordinary. It was they who truly brought the gown to town.
>
> —*Capital Ideas*, p. 252

This chapter tells the story of a revolutionary time in converting theoretical ideas into commercial fulfillment and how, in search of that goal, an academically brilliant but economically *deficient* group transformed itself into an academically brilliant and economically *profitable* group. Along the way, we shall see how hard-nosed leadership ultimately revealed the vitality of financial theory in the most challenging arena of all—the rough-and-tumble of the business marketplace. Indeed, the intense focus on profitability created opportunities for combining all these ideas as a base for innovating new kinds of products.

The narrative of how Wells Fargo Investment Advisors became today's powerhouse of investment management dates back to July 1971, when the group—then known as the Wells Fargo Trust Department—confidently launched the world's first index fund. This step was just the beginning (see Chapter 12 of *Capital Ideas,* "The Constellation").* In 1977, the trust department went on to develop the first computer-driven methodology for tactical asset allocation. Two years later it offered a variation on the index fund theme that blended the index fund structure with a risk–controlled active management strategy. Soon after, the trust department was promoting a full-fledged active strategy based on expected returns derived from the dividend discount model. In 1979, Wells Fargo launched the "Yield-Tilt Fund," a quasi-index fund favoring stocks with higher yields. In 1981, it started the first international equity index fund and then the first bond index fund in 1983.

By that time, Wells Fargo was already managing money for non-U.S. clients, having also marketed a mutual fund called the Stagecoach Fund, designed by none other than Fischer Black and Myron Scholes (see *Capital Ideas,* p. 250). All these innovations were rooted in the basic underpinnings of financial theory: diversification, optimizing the risk/return trade-off, market efficiency, and the Capital Asset Pricing Model.

Given these achievements, can you guess how much this whole operation was earning by 1983, when assets under management had risen to the impressive sum of $11 billion? Wrong! From a business viewpoint, the Wells Fargo asset management operation was a cripple. The unit had never earned a penny. Assets in the index fund and related products were never sufficient to produce a profit. The Stagecoach Fund had attracted only a dribble of money and then ran afoul of the mutual fund trade association, which succeeded at that time in banning commercial banks from offering mutual funds to the public. Finally, Bill Fouse, the prime motivator of product development, defected in 1983 to the Mellon Bank with a group of key colleagues.

For a time, it seemed as though this was the end of a dream, the failure of Jim Vertin's promise to me in the 1970s that as director of Wells Fargo Investment Advisors (WFIA), he would keep "pushin' that rock uphill" (see *Capital Ideas,* p. 247). All the powerful academic and theoretical accomplishments, all the ingenious efforts to convert these ideas into commercially marketable products, and all the grim determi-

---

*This group was part of the old Wells Fargo Bank in San Francisco, whose traditions reached back to 1852 and the Pony Express. As we shall see, the trust department ultimately became a separate entity. The old Wells Fargo Bank was acquired in 1998 by the Minneapolis-based Norwest Bank, which adopted the Wells Fargo name but has an entirely different background and business plan.

nation of the leadership group consisting of Mac McQuown, Jim Vertin, and Bill Fouse—for as long as Fouse held out at Wells Fargo—began to look like a waste of effort in a world where the final test of value was the bottom line.

▣

Yet this single-minded group never gave up in its determination to push that rock uphill. The commercial frustrations turned out to be only the birth pangs of a great enterprise offering products directly linked to the innovations and theoretical insights of the 1970s and early 1980s. Today, marching under the name of Barclays Global Investors, or BGI, the organization is the largest portfolio manager of institutional assets in the world and the largest manager of both index funds and exchange-traded funds.

BGI manages a total of some $1.6 trillion in assets, including $400 billion in Europe and $160 billion in Asia. This is almost double the pre-crash stock market peak in 2000, with over 2,000 employees globally and close to 3,000 clients in forty-nine countries, many of whom are using at least five different BGI products. BGI manages over $10 billion each for nineteen clients and over $1 billion each for 199 clients. The client list—featuring an imposing group of marquee names like Exxon, Sony, and the London Business School—includes over 50 percent of the world's 300 largest pension funds and 76 percent of the top fifty U.S. pension funds. The twenty largest global clients have averaged fourteen years with BGI; the overall average is seven years in a business where rapid client turnover is a familiar event.

As of mid-2006, BGI is the largest index fund manager in the world, with some $1.3 trillion in indexed assets.[1] This side of the business accounts for nearly 80 percent of the total of $1.6 trillion, which includes $230 billion in exchange-traded funds (ETF)—making BGI the world's leading ETF manager after starting with only $2 billion in 2000.* But BGI is also one of the largest active investment managers, with responsibility for over $300 billion in assets. The hedge fund segment alone amounts to over $127 billion in mid-2006, all managed

---

*According to the Investment Company Institute, the trade association for mutual funds, total assets of exchange-traded funds as of March 2006 came to $321 billion.

in-house, which makes BGI the sixth-largest single hedge fund manager in the world.[2] All other index fund managers of that size or larger are funds of funds, where individual funds are grouped together in one master fund managed by outsiders.

BGI now claims a remarkable track record, justifying all the dreams of the original leaders of the Wells Fargo Trust Department. According to Blake Grossman, current CEO of the firm, "Virtually every single active strategy—across equity, fixed-income, asset allocation, and currencies—has delivered positive alpha since inception. That is, the strategies have consistently outperformed their benchmarks after adjustment for risk, and we tend to keep our strategies around for a long time. I can think of only a few strategies that we've closed down in the past ten years, and in most instances we closed one down because we were converting it to another strategy. For example, the original Yield Tilt fund was eventually closed down as most of those assets—and certainly our focus—shifted to Alpha Tilts. Nevertheless, Yield Tilt had a great record when we shuttered it. In a few exceptional cases, we didn't think the alpha opportunity was likely to remain and liquidated the strategy."[*]

And finally, the bottom line now shines through. Despite a research budget of $100 million, total revenues on the order of $2.4 billion are producing operating profits of $1.0 billion, nearly 10 percent of the pretax profits of BGI's parent company, Barclays Bank of London, which alone has total assets of close to a trillion dollars.

❖

The first important step into profitability came in September 1983, when at Bill Sharpe's recommendation Wells Fargo recruited Fred Grauer as CEO of WFIA to replace Bill Fouse and Bill Jahnke, who were veterans of WFIA and active as innovators of new strategies. Grauer interpreted his mission as stabilizing WFIA employees and clients, while converting the business into an enterprise of growth and profitability. In return, he wanted compensation consistent with independent advisory firms, including profit sharing. Grauer was already known to some of the Wells Fargo people involved, because he had

[*]Unless otherwise specified, all quotations are from personal interviews or correspondence.

worked there earlier, and he had also been a professor of finance at both Columbia and MIT (where he had known Fischer Black). Subsequently, Grauer had moved out of academia and into Merrill Lynch Capital Markets, but he felt underutilized and isolated there.

Nevertheless, the time at Merrill Lynch, as Grauer described it to me, was "a transformational experience." He had learned two important principles at Merrill Lynch: First, making money matters, and, second, "You don't make money if people don't buy your story." Grauer assured me, however, he was still "a cerebral kind of guy." As proof, he was able to make up with Fouse and the others with whom relations had been less than cordial during his earlier days at Wells Fargo.

In 1985, the trust department and the senior management of Wells Fargo Bank decided the vanguard of the department might act more like a business firm if it looked more like a business firm. Accordingly, they changed the name to Wells Fargo Investment Advisors (WFIA), making it a wholly autonomous subsidiary and profit center of Wells Fargo Bank. This move meant independence for the group, and independence meant freedom to set compensation without regard to bank standards. Freedom to set compensation, however, was a constant reminder that the objective of this spin-off was to maximize profitability.

Profitability and growth are impossible without clients, and the staff at Wells Fargo was a long way from sales-oriented. When the current CEO, Blake Grossman, joined the organization in 1985 right out of Stanford Business School (where he had worked as Bill Sharpe's research assistant), the WFIA sales staff were hard at work presenting the unique strategies derived from the index fund structure to prospective clients—but losing the business to a traditional manager with active strategies. "It happened all the time," Grossman recalls. "We were too caught up in the theory and academic underpinnings. We emphasized theory and statistical testing, and the approach just did not resonate. It took us a while to learn how to market, and only then did our excellent track record become the key selling point."

The big problem, as Grauer saw it, when he first took up his responsibilities at Wells Fargo, was the leadership, who were in love with their big ideas and relished doing battle with the traditionalists in the field of portfolio management. In fact, they relished doing battle more than they relished a profitable return for their efforts. Meanwhile, the battlefield failed to provide any meaningful gains in market share or black figures on the bottom line. Grauer's goal was different: Save the business, and then build the business, which meant profitability combined with "best in class" performance and no blowups.

Grauer pointed to the experience with the Stagecoach Fund as an example of what he had to confront. Fischer Black, Myron Scholes, and Michael Jensen noted in empirical tests of CAPM that stocks with low betas realized higher returns than CAPM predicted, while high-beta stocks had lower returns than predicted. There were two possible explanations: Either CAPM was simply wrong, or CAPM was correct but the market was inefficient and low-beta stocks were underpriced. John Lintner, one of the original creators of CAPM (*Capital Ideas,* pp. 198–199), had argued in favor of the model as the villain of the piece, but Black, Scholes, and Jensen were convinced the explanation was market inefficiency.

They began searching for a reason investors did not correct this bias, as efficient market theory suggested should happen. The answer, they decided, was that investors could not borrow enough money to drive the underpriced low-beta stock prices up to a point where the CAPM-derived expected return would match the beta. Nor could they sell enough overpriced high-beta shares short to bring the prices of high-beta stocks down to where the CAPM-derived expected return would be raised to match the beta.[*]

This discrepancy offered an opportunity to earn some alpha or excess return. Compared with a typical individual investor, Wells Fargo Bank could borrow larger sums, at lower interest rates, with fewer emotional inhibitions. Tests based on past performance of various forms of this strategy were encouraging. Black and Scholes also suggested an early version of today's hedge funds, by proposing that the Stagecoach Fund should not only buy low-beta stocks but should also sell high-beta stocks short at the same time.

---

[*] See Markowitz's comments about this problem for CAPM in Markowitz (2005) as well as comments quoted on pp. 104–108 above.

The actual fund, designed in a muted and more conservative version than Black and Scholes had wanted, came to market in January 1972. The controversy within the group about the structure of the fund resulted in a bitter controversy between Black and Fouse, when Fouse expressed concerns that a big position in low-beta stocks would be badly diversified and therefore riskier than it appeared. The dispute grew so noisy and intense that Black became furious—a rare event—and walked out of the room. With a less-than-optimal resolution of these disruptions, the legal tangles, and a lack of enthusiasm by risk-averse clients, the Stagecoach Fund came to an early demise in August 1973.*

Although the Stagecoach Fund was a commercial disaster, it would turn out to be a powerful innovation to set the scene for significant developments in the future. First, valuations of stocks were managed by computer, not human judgments as to stock values. Second, this fund, acting as a trader on computer instructions rather than on some kind of information advantage, was able to trade at lower expense than a fund where brokers were concerned about taking orders from investors who might have more knowledge or information about the stock. Finally, when WFIA negotiated the leveraging loans for the fund on the basis of the daily rate for federal funds—or the rate banks charge one another for overnight money—these novel credit arrangements turned out to be a crude precursor of today's repurchase agreements.[†] In a rough kind of way, Wells Fargo was beginning to make its mark as an innovator in financial markets.

Grauer's reaction to this sequence of events with the Stagecoach Fund was, "Thank God, it never got off the ground!" He was convinced the fund would have cost more to operate than Black's projections had indicated and would have produced a large tracking error against a passive benchmark. To Grauer, the Stagecoach Fund was just one more example of how the zest for big theoretical battles diverted resources from more profitable projects.

▣

---

[*] For a detailed discussion of this episode, see Mehrling (2005), pp. 103–109.
[†] Ibid., p. 111.

After Grauer's arrival in 1983, the road to growth and profitability began to open up. This happened to be the moment indexing was finally going to take off after years of being perceived as a worthless strategy capable of producing only average returns. The stock market had hit the low point of a long and agonizing bear market in July 1982, with stock prices down 20 percent from the 1980 high and still 9 percent below the January 1973 peak, over nine years earlier. Measured on an inflation-adjusted basis, the damage was much worse. But beginning in August 1982, stock prices took off like a shot out of a cannon. Just a year later, prices were up 53 percent. By the end of 1985, a year and a half after Grauer's arrival, stock prices were 70 percent above the 1982 low and almost double the old high in January 1973. WFIA was stabilized, clients recommitted, processes rebuilt, and many nonstrategic activities closed down. The trust and continuing relationships with major clients like Exxon, New York City Teachers, and Yale University provided confidence that all would ultimately work out for the best.

This was also the moment institutional demand to get into the market was exploding. Everybody seemed to be in a belated rush for equity exposure and to dump what now appeared to be an excessive hoard of low-risk investments. Active managers could not handle the flood of money coming their way, but the Wells Fargo S&P 500 Index Fund could take everything thrown at it and immediately invest the money. At the end of 1985, Wells Fargo had $33 billion under management and ranked eighteenth in *Institutional Investor*'s listing of the 300 largest managers in America; by the end of 1986, assets under management had jumped to $55 billion, and the ranking had soared to 9th.[3]

In the process, Wells Fargo discovered that the tipping point for profitability in running an index fund—given the very low fees charged—was around $25 billion. This was not a business for small managers. Scale mattered. Growth was easy to handle when all clients held the same portfolio and sophisticated trading strategies could minimize transactions costs. True, fees charged by active managers were a multiple of index fund fees, so the break-even point in active management was far around $100 million. But growth for active managers can soon become an obstacle to performance by raising transactions costs and by messing up the basic process of managing portfolios while trying to maintain communication with a large and increasing number of clients. Having once been in that position in my own career as a portfolio manager, I know well how an abrupt and crowded inflow of new clients can disrupt both performance and relationships.

In the wake of the surge of business into its index funds, Wells Fargo henceforth centered its product line on the notion of the Science of Investing, a slogan and a concept its salespeople would consistently emphasize in communicating with institutional clients. Nothing was haphazard. The computer in many ways ran the show. No strategy was accepted without the most thorough objective testing from every possible perspective. All the pieces had to fit and join together. Three elements were the focus of all this work: low transactions costs, control of risk, and strategies derived from the index fund platform where scale was a plus instead of a drawback and source of weakness. Scale was where Wells Fargo's products could develop their comparative advantage and run ahead of the competition, especially for managers whose business was in stock picking and market timing.

Wells Fargo did not emphasize low transactions costs just because they were something nice for clients. Low transactions costs meant Wells Fargo could pursue strategies that were out of the ranges of typical active management firms. Cutting the cost threshold for execution by 50 percent, and sometimes by even more than 50 percent, created monopoly opportunities for Wells Fargo to create alpha–producing products no other manager could afford to take on. Grauer describes this bonanza as "gold on the street—El Dorado!"

None of the low-cost Wells Fargo strategies were designed to shoot the moon. Nevertheless, alpha measured in nickels and dimes does add up when earned on a large number of positions and when the sums of money involved are so large they would be unwieldy in any other environment. Moreover, the probability of earning alphas in nickels and dimes was much higher than in the operation of strategies aiming to beat some benchmark with alphas of 300 basis points or more. In other words, strategies derived from the index fund concept were less risky than conventional asset management.

The burgeoning index fund business provided Wells Fargo with another significant advantage in reducing transactions costs. By holding so many different stocks in the index funds and related strategies, many transactions could be crossed in-house at zero transactions cost. Crossing occurs when one in-house account is the seller of what a different in-house account wants to buy, so the computer can simply move the assets from one account to another at no cost to either party. That way, a large volume of transactions can be executed without hitting the formal cost structure of the Street, with no commissions, no bid-ask spreads, no market impacts.

I asked Grauer why there seemed to be such a generous source of securities to take the other side of these trades. He pointed out as an example that assets investors were transferring into one of the index funds came primarily from portfolios previously held by active managers, providing either more of some stock the index fund needed to hold or that could fulfill the need of one of the active management strategies. Clients were also constantly changing managers or manager assignments as well as adding or withdrawing money. Today, as a result, Wells Fargo in its modern incarnation as Barclays Global Investors operates the largest internal zero-cost marketplace in the world.

This whole panoply of policies, concepts, and careful execution would have been impossible in the days of human bookkeepers and mountains of paper. Technology and infrastructure were critical to the success of turning BGI into "an innovation powerhouse," as Grauer describes it.[4] The computer was central, not only in its frequent role as stock picker, but also in making possible the volume of daily transactions and portfolios owning hundreds of stocks, along with all the associated record-keeping they produced. Without the computer, the validity and commercial applicability of the theoretical work could never have been confirmed.

How did Wells Fargo Investment Advisors turn into Barclays Global Investors? The first step took place in 1989, when Wells Fargo formed a joint venture with Nikko Investment Advisors in Tokyo, in which each party owned 50 percent of the WFIA business. The association was serendipitous. Nikko was already oriented in a quantitative direction but had a lot to learn from the Wells Fargo side. Nikko also had extensive connections, not only in Japan but also throughout Asia, where foreigners had great difficulty penetrating the market for investment management of pension funds.

By the mid-1990s, the senior management of WFIA's parent company, Wells Fargo Bank, began to have second thoughts about whether they wanted their institution to continue in the global asset management market. The bank had no global footprint but did enjoy a strong competitive edge as a regional institution, and had every intention of remaining with that business plan. WFIA-Nikko, although profitable, was a distraction that absorbed resources Wells Fargo managers believed would earn more in the commercial banking business. Patricia Dunn, then co-CEO of WFIA with Grauer, attempted a management-led buyout, but her endeavor was unsuccessful.

Wells Fargo finally sold the whole business to Barclays Bank in London, a major British bank with interests all around the world. Barclays also had an experienced professional quantitative division that would be philosophically compatible with the WFIA group. Barclays Global Investors, or BGI, became WFIA's new name, but the fundamental character of WFIA's business and modes of operation was transplanted under the new rubric. The major change was an intensified focus on global markets with the cooperation of Barclays Bank to help BGI build scale, the secret of its profitability, and the unusually strong competitive position in markets where Barclays offered products.

From that point forward, as Grauer describes it, "We walked a different path. We made ourselves into an organization that could regenerate itself and sustain itself through the use of science and technology." What Grossman portrays as "a pivotal event" occurred in 1994, when BGI recruited Richard Grinold as director of research. Grinold had been director of research and then president of BARRA, the successful investment research consulting firm started by Barr Rosenberg in 1973, from which he had departed in 1985 to start his own portfolio management company (see *Capital Ideas,* p. 262). Four years later, Grinold was joined by his former BARRA colleague, Ron Kahn. In 1995, Grinold and Kahn had published a book called *Active Portfolio Management: Quantitative Theory and Applications.**

The title of this important book is an accurate description of its contents. The book has become a bible at BGI for people at all levels,

---

* Originally published by Probus, a Chicago publisher that no longer exists. The second edition was published in 2000 by McGraw-Hill.

and, in opening the path to maximizing BGI's capabilities, it has had an impact far beyond just shaping strategies. The book ultimately identified the management objectives that would differentiate BGI from its competitors. In addition, *Active Portfolio Management* defines three concepts that provided theoretical backing for strategic ideas long under development at Wells Fargo and BGI. These three features, to use Grinold and Kahn's nomenclature, are the Information Coefficient (the IC), Breadth, and the Information Ratio (the IR).

The Information Coefficient is the correlation between forecasts of returns and the actual events subsequently realized. The IC is therefore a measure of skill. But investment success depends on more than accurate forecasts of residual return. Breadth refers to the number of opportunities a successful portfolio management organization has to apply its skills. As Grinold and Kahn put it, "[Breadth] is the number of times we can use our skill. If our skill level is the same, then it is arguably better to be able to forecast the returns on 1,000 stocks than on 100 stocks."[5]

For example, one trouble with tactical asset allocation is the limited number of asset classes you deal with—primarily stocks, bonds, and cash—as well as the low frequency of new bets to make. Thus, "Betting on the market's direction once every quarter does not provide much breadth, even if we have skill."[6] In contrast, a strategy that works in many markets around the world instead of just in the U.S. market would be one with superior breadth.

The end result is the Information Ratio, which is the key to portfolio management nirvana: The IR is "the residual component of the return uncorrelated with the benchmark return," or alpha, divided by the volatility of that residual return.[7] The goal, in other words, is not just the conventional one of trying to outperform the benchmark but to do so with sufficient consistency so that there would be no dispute as to whether the alpha is really there or just a flash in the pan. Looking smart is one thing, but being smart without rigorous control of risk would get you nowhere.

It is "the Information Ratio [that] defines the opportunities available to the active manager. The [higher] the Information Ratio, the [greater] the possibility for active management."[8] All of this adds up to Grinold's and Kahn's Fundamental Law of Active Management, which tells us "that our Information Ratio grows in proportion to the skill (IC) and in proportion to the square root of the Breadth (BR). Hence, the equation $IR = IC \times \sqrt{BR}$."[9]

Daniel Kahneman, Professor of Psychology at Princeton, received a Nobel Prize in 2002 for his ground-breaking work in the development of Behavioral Economics. His writings analyze the quirks of decision making, such as how attitudes about risk differ depending on whether gains or losses are involved. But Kahneman would deny that most people are irrational. Rather, he believes "the failure in the rational model is . . . in the human brain it requires. Who could design a brain that could perform in the way this model mandates? Every single one of us would have to know and understand everything, completely, and at once."

Richard Thaler is a busy man. He is Professor of Behavioral Science and Economics, and Director of the Center for Decision Research, at the Graduate School of Business of the University of Chicago. He is also a principal in an investment management firm whose strategies are based on Behavioral Finance and has compiled an impressive track record. While he has assembled a long list of behaviors that go against the predictions of the standard models in finance, Thaler rejects any description of his work as proving investors are irrational. "People are not blithering idiots," he argues, "but they are a long way from hyperrational automatons."

In 1969, **Paul Samuelson** won the first Nobel Prize in Economics. In *Capital Ideas*, he describes the stock market as "no easy pickings." He goes even further today: "A respect for evidence compels me to incline toward the hypothesis that most portfolio decision makers should go out of business—take up plumbing, teach Greek, or help produce the annual GNP by serving as corporate executives (*sic*). . . . No book can make you rich; few can keep you rich; many will speed up your loss of fortune." As a result, Samuelson continues to have deep respect for the risk management strategy of wide portfolio diversification.

Robert Merton won a Nobel Prize in 1990 for his work on the option pricing model. A popular professor at Harvard Business School, Merton also runs a busy consulting firm, where he seeks to redesign the financial system from today's jumble into a dynamic mechanism for risk sharing and for helping individuals invest for retirement. Merton sees himself as "a plumber" who wants to use all the available tools to do the job. "The answers given by Capital Ideas are still valid," he says. "My point is understanding institutions and how they make implementation of these ideas possible." (Photo by Bachrach.)

Andrew Lo is Professor of Finance and Director of the Laboratory for Financial Engineering at the MIT Sloan School of Management. He is also active in the real world of finance as the co-founder and Chief Scientific Officer of a hedge fund. Lo sees institutions as central to the functioning of financial markets, but recognizes that institutions change over time, in part as a result of "purposeful decisions by human beings," but also in response to the forces of evolution. Lo's Adaptive Market Hypothesis blends these views into a powerful vision of how markets work and what forces are driving new developments in the marketplace.

Robert Shiller of the Cowles Foundation at Yale has published over two hundred papers and five books, including the worldwide best seller, *Irrational Exuberance*. "Finance is what changes the way things actually happen," he says, and institutions transmit those changes. Volatility—a fancy word for what happens when we are taken by surprise—has been the primary factor in all of Shiller's efforts to manage risks in many aspects of economics and finance. He has even invented new financial instruments for hedging against the risks inherent in home ownership, the salaries of employees, and fluctuations in output and employment throughout the economy.

Bill Sharpe, Professor Emeritus at Stanford, won a Nobel Prize in 1990 for his pioneering 1964 paper that developed the Capital Asset Pricing Model, a paradigm for how markets would line up risk and return under conditions of equilibrium. This model is the source for the "alpha" and "beta" strategies now dominating institutional investment management. Like the other theorists in this book, Sharpe is more involved today in implementation of theory than in development of new theories. He was cofounder of Financial Engines, a successful Silicon Valley business venture employing the computer to provide corporate employees with sophisticated advice on asset allocation and risk management.

Nobel Prize-winner **Harry Markowitz** launched Capital Ideas in 1952 with his theory of portfolio selection, based upon optimizing the trade-off between risk and return and composing the result into a diversified investment portfolio. But Markowitz has lost faith in "equilibrium models . . . that make unrealistic—absurd —assumptions about the actors." He has become a financial engineer working in a laboratory on an ambitious project that involves complex computer programming to explore in detail how stock prices would behave in a market where some investors have behavioral quirks while others are coolly rational. "By the time you are through," he says, "you have a little world."

Myron Scholes won a Nobel Prize in 1990 for his contribution to the Black-Scholes-Merton option pricing model, but his contacts with academia today are incidental. He is co-managing partner of a $2.6 billion hedge fund that makes no forecasts of beta or alpha. Instead, Scholes and his associates trade in the capital markets to make money by providing what Scholes describes as "liquidity and risk transfer services." These strategies involve taking on risks that a wide variety of investors and business firms do not wish to carry and are willing to pay others to assume for them. "This is a great business," Scholes says.

Blake Grossman is CEO of Barclays Global Investors, a latter-day version of Wells Fargo Investment Advisors, extolled in Chapter 12 of *Capital Ideas*. BGI is one of the largest portfolio managers of institutional assets in the world, including $1.3 trillion in indexed assets and exchange-traded funds. Almost every actively managed strategy—across equity, fixed income, asset allocation, and currencies—has delivered positive alpha since inception. "The heritage of our product line goes back directly to the original theories of Markowitz, Sharpe, Modigliani-Miller, and Black-Scholes," says Grossman. "Their theoretical models are still the core of our work. They color everything we do."

Since **David Swensen** became Chief Investment Officer of the Yale endowment fund in 1985, Yale has outperformed the S&P 500 by a wide margin, and has ranked at the top of the universe of educational endowment funds. Swensen has achieved this remarkable track record by depending on Markowitz's methods for optimizing the risk/return trade-off and out of deep respect for the Efficient Market Hypothesis. Yet he has done so by "establishing and maintaining an unconventional investment profile [requiring] acceptance of portfolios which frequently appear . . . imprudent in the eyes of conventional wisdom." Today, it is Swensen's approach that has become conventional wisdom.

Before **Eugene Fama** of the University of Chicago Business School set forth the principles of the Efficient Market Hypothesis in 1965, there was no theory to explain why the market is so hard to beat and not even a recognition such a possibility might exist. Since then, Fama has become a principal in a major mutual fund company and, in cooperation with his frequent co-author Kenneth French of Dartmouth's Tuck School, he has enhanced the empirical performance of the Capital Asset Pricing Model by adding two new variables—size of market capitalization and the ratio of price to book value.

Jack Treynor's bold model for asset pricing in 1964 closely resembled Sharpe's but was never published. In 1973, Treynor and Fischer Black established the groundwork for today's strategy of portable alpha, asserting that "two managers with radically different expectations regarding the general market but the same specific information regarding individual securities will select active portfolios with the same relative proportions." Like the other theorists in this book, Treynor is now more concerned with how models work in practice than in devising new models. He likes to tell people about stocks he finds attractive, but he invests only when his friends just don't get it. (Photo by Keith Skelton.)

Bill Gross, a founder and now Chief Investment Officer of Pacific Investment Management Company (Pimco), oversees the management of over $600 billion of fixed-income securities. His biography, *The Bond King*, sums up his legendary capabilities in the bond market. Oddly enough for a bond firm, Pimco offers a strategy called StocksPLUS, which aims to outperform the stock market by adding Gross's outperformance of a short-term bond benchmark to the total return on the S&P 500. Launched over twenty years ago, StocksPLUS was a precursor of today's "portable alpha strategies" by seeking alpha from a source outside the fund's primary asset position.

In the early 1980s, **Marvin Damsma** was the Chief Investment Officer overseeing the billions in the pension funds of New York City employees for a salary "just enough to let me live on Nathan's hot dogs and pizza." In 1987, Damsma became Chief Investment Officer for the pension assets of BP-Amoco, where the company gave him leeway to experiment with innovative and unconventional perspectives on pension management. This freedom allowed Damsma to look at the whole portfolio risk management process in many ways that differed from the traditional model. Ideas once perceived as radical when Damsma started his innovations have become today's conventional strategies.

Martin Leibowitz is a phenomenon. After 26 years at the old Salomon Brothers, he became Chief Investment Officer of TIAA-CREF; he is now a Managing Director at Morgan Stanley. His 1972 book with Sidney Homer, *Inside the Yield Book: New Tools for Bond Market Strategy*, was a trail-blazer for a field where most bonds were traditionally held on a buy-and-hold basis. He has repeatedly demonstrated how much power theory can contribute to practice. Recently, Leibowitz has turned his attention to the roots of the Capital Asset Pricing Model to create an entirely new design for the process of institutional asset allocation. (Photo by Bachrach.)

In 1986, when **Bob Litterman** was applying for a job at Goldman Sachs, Fischer Black asked him whether an econometrician could contribute anything to Wall Street. Litterman had plenty to contribute, such as coauthoring an article with Black on the role of equilibrium and rising to high responsibilities in Goldman's hugely successful asset management business. "Volatility is a central consideration in all our decisions and in all our strategies at Goldman," Litterman observes, "but equilibrium, and the notion of the world moving toward equilibrium, is at the heart of the way we think about the world. I know the Invisible Hand is still there."

At BGI, Information Ratios of over 0.75 are common, and an occasional score of over 1.00 also occurs. These achievements compare with more typical Information Ratios of zero in other major asset management organizations.

Here, too, state-of-the art technology was essential, not just in record-keeping but also in executing portfolio management in accordance with the Fundamental Law of Active Management. Preserving the Information Ratio requires constant recalculation of the risk structure and tracking how the alphas evolve as prices change in the market. The prominent role of technology in all these operations converted BGI into a capital-intensive business in an industry where most investment management firms had only modest investments in fixed capital. BGI saw this difference as an advantage, because the capital intensity required by its strategies tended to keep the competition at bay.

Beyond having to learn how to be comfortable with all the machinery and the masses of computer printouts, BGI staff had to cut loose from traditional ways of thinking about portfolio management and market behavior. Over time, they also had to learn to break free from their own recent achievements to keep the menu of strategies refreshed and ahead of any competition that might be hot on their heels.

All of this required strong and creative leadership from Grinold. The trick was tapping into his passion to innovate, to see theory and data translate into alpha as a way of keeping score on just how smart you are—every day. The discipline mandated by Grinold's approach significantly increased the pace of new product development. There were only six full-time people in research when he arrived. The firm has been "progressively marching upward ever since," as Grossman puts it. BGI now has well over a hundred people worldwide in the research function, developing a bewildering combination of high-breadth, derivatives-based, relative-value strategies across the capital markets from stocks to bonds to cash. The technology budget continues to increase in order for BGI managers to capture the increased complexity brought on by the heavy use of derivatives.*

---

* Quoted, in part, from "The New Think Tank," by Allan Kunigis in *Currents*, BGI's quarterly publication, April 2006.

Grinold's objective was to transfer to active management the discipline and technology of managing the benchmark itself—most frequently the S&P 500. "There was no point in having a good idea if the market got away from you," Grauer pointed out, "especially when our active bet products were guaranteeing correlations as close as 0.98 with the benchmark."

The direction was set by the components of Grinold's and Kahn's Fundamental Law of Active Management. The emphasis continued to be on strategies developed from the index fund concept: high breadth, tight control of risk, and minimal transactions costs, permitting a search for small alphas with low variability and strategies that would work across large numbers of stocks in as many different markets as possible. The most important range of strategies includes enhanced indexing or "tilts," where small active bets are taken against the index fund in a large number of stocks, but the resulting portfolio will have just about the same level of risk, or variability of returns, as the index fund even as enhanced indexing makes specific bets against the index returns.

These types of strategies are the grandchildren of a strategy developed much earlier, the "Yield–Tilt" Fund—and that strategy itself was a kind of grandfather of strategies based on Behavioral Finance. The overweighting of high dividend yields over low yields was based on the theory that taxable investors are more interested in growth than in slower-growing companies with high-dividend payouts and lower levels of retained earnings. As a result of this bias, high-dividend payers tend to be underpriced compared to lower-yielding stocks. Institutional investors, most of which were tax-free, could take advantage of the yield tilt provided by the anti-yield bias of taxable investors. Indeed, I have never forgotten my first meeting with a new investment client who retained my investment counsel firm back in the 1960s. Reminding me how well he was doing in his business, he asserted, "I want you to be sure to remember one thing about me: I can't stand more income."

Enhanced indexing began at BGI with about $3 billion under management, promising a tracking error of no more than 2 percent a year against the relevant passive index. Today BGI has over $100 billion in enhanced indexing in the United States alone. The patterns and alphas of the whole class of enhanced indexing strategies have varied continuously with the passage of time, even though the basic technology and structure has been relatively constant. In markets as dynamic as today's capital markets, Grauer explains, "The half-life of alphas is short—sometimes even in minutes!" As a result, BGI brought in waves of Ph.D.s for the research process with the goal of finding "green alphas," which had long half-lives and lurked in behavioral biases and in new databases other managers were not using.

One familiar behavioral phenomenon is stock momentum, when stocks keep moving because investors believe a stock that is moving will continue to move. These investors then buy the stock and move it further, in a process that can repeat itself for an extended period. BGI has studied this phenomenon with care to discover signals from market data that the momentum is about to break, such as variations in the total volume of trading, the retail share of the total trading volume, and the development of the stock's outperformance of the general market. The firm—more precisely, the firm's computers—constantly watches 7,000 to 8,000 stocks for these indicators in markets around the world, a capacity few other firms could match.

Managing people was as important to BGI profitability as managing portfolios. Grauer describes the basic personnel policy of the firm as searching for people who are "bright, nice, and [with] a fire in their bellies. We would not consider or retain anyone who did not have all three of those characteristics." Training is intense and prolonged to instill loyalty to the organization and to show people how to maximize their capabilities. The firm promotes people early and frequently, which is expensive but keeps morale and enthusiasm high.

Patricia Dunn was one of the most impressive examples of the BGI approach to promoting people "early and frequently." Dunn graduated from the University of California at Berkeley with a major in journalism; she had joined the old Wells Fargo in the early 1970s as a part-time secretary. She rose to the position of co–CEO with Fred Grauer from March 1997 to June 1998, and then sole CEO for the next four years until she retired from full-time duties for health reasons.[*] She no longer has any connection with official BGI.

---

[*]Dunn became Nonexecutive Director of Hewlett-Packard and served in that position until her resignation in the autumn of 2006.

Under her régime, and against considerable opposition at first, BGI entered early on into the business of issuing exchange-traded funds or ETFs. Today BGI's *i*Shares issues number 116, of which 42 are international; the total universe of ETFs in the United States is on the order of 280 funds.* The total market value of the *i*Shares funds involves over $210 billion, compared to about $360 billion in the U.S. ETF market as a whole. In addition, BGI added a wrinkle on the ETF concept in 2006 in the form of what it calls *iPath* ETNs, unsecured thirty-year notes rather than shares, which track various commodity indexes. At maturity, holders of these notes receive their principal plus a payment equivalent to the return of the underlying index during the note's term. A similar arrangement would apply on a weekly basis to noteholders who wish to redeem before maturity.

Grauer has emphasized that even the selling of BGI's services was carried out in an unusual fashion. Instead of a professional sales staff, the chief investment officers of the five main sections of the operation constituted the primary sales force. The CIOs turned out to be great salespeople—they had no difficulty getting in to see the top executives at the firms they were soliciting. Once in the door, they could engage these executives in scientifically based dialogue in which they could play the role of consultant rather than plain-vanilla salesperson.

In tracing through all this history, Grossman depicts the evolution of active management of BGI as "renovating" the early enhanced index strategies under a critically important assumption: "The markets are very efficient, very dynamic, constantly reaching greater levels of efficiency that make them more and more difficult to beat. The half-lives of our strategies were shrinking. Under these circumstances," he continues, "we recognized we had to build a continuous process of innovation." And innovation has developed into a complex process at BGI, involving theoretical as well as empirical consideration, the transactions costs that will be involved, the format of the product, the sales effort to be called upon, the daily portfolio management requirements, and even legal issues.

---

*The ETFs issued by BGI have their origin in an instrument called SuperTrust, innovated in 1990 by Leland, O'Brien, and Rubinstein, who originally developed portfolio insurance. See *Capital Ideas,* Chapter 14, "The Ultimate Invention."

The biggest step forward was the introduction of long/short strate-gies in 1996, promoted by a few people on the staff who were big be-lievers. This approach—an aggressive idea without much acceptance at the time—appeared to BGI to be a more efficient way to manage money than under long-only conditions. Short-selling offered a major increase in Breadth, and therefore in the critically important Informa-tion Ratio, because selling stocks short instead of just buying them dou-bled the opportunities to put return forecasts to good use.

Short-selling turned out to be even more effective in fixed-income management. With stocks, the upside may be infinite and the downside may be zero, but as a practical matter the upside and downside are roughly equal. Not so with bonds. The ultimate bond payoff at par is a powerful anchor holding prices close to 100. Unless interest rates take an unusually steep fall, and unless the bonds in question are also non-callable, bonds have a much smaller upside than downside. The result is that short sales in the bond market have less risk and greater potential profitability than buying long.

At the beginning, just four or five key clients understood what long/short could accomplish for them and stepped forward to provide the seed money. Assets under management in this area, however, were stagnant for four or five years. But around 2000, the business took off. Today, BGI claims to be among the biggest managers of hedge fund money in the world, including in funds of funds. Long/short strategies are also available outside the hedge fund area, especially in a rapidly de-veloping pace of short-selling strategies for fixed-income securities.

Grossman enjoys discussing the role of basic finance theory in the development of BGI products and in their implementation. "I think the heritage of our product line goes back directly to the original theories of Markowitz, Sharpe, Modigliani-Miller, and Black-Scholes," he told me. "They provided the intellectual platform and foundation for every-thing we do. When we developed the whole idea of separating alpha strategies from beta strategies like indexing related only to market forces, we were drawing directly on CAPM for understanding what was involved and how to put it to good use. Much of what we do also draws on Barr Rosenberg's innovation of multifactor models, in which

Barr went beyond beta in the search for the drivers of return and for shaping risk control structures" (see *Capital Ideas*, Chapter 13). Thus, despite the complexity BGI has added to the whole process, the basic framework of financial theory supports the entire edifice.

At this point, I mentioned a discussion I had had with Jack Treynor about CAPM and its role in portfolio management in today's world. Treynor had mentioned that "CAPM is about expectations. All the other asset pricing models are about surprise." Grossman agreed. "CAPM is about what *should* hold in equilibrium," he observed, "whereas multifactor models like Fama and French's models incorporate the size effect and the value/growth effect" (see *Capital Ideas*, pp. 201, 277).[*10]

In fact, Grossman added, much of the work, especially by practitioners, is not as much about theory as it is about ways to capture what is priced or not priced in the marketplace. That is precisely what applications of Behavioral Finance are all about: Grossman believes Behavioral Finance does provide insights into profitable opportunities even though it has insufficient theory behind it. That is also how Bill Sharpe feels on this matter:

> The optimal situation involves theory that proceeds from sensible assumptions, is carefully and logically constructed, and is broadly consistent with the data. You want to avoid empirical results that have no basis in theory and blindly say, "It seems to have worked in the past, so it will work in the future" (Burton, 1998, pp. 20–28).

Then Grossman posed a related question: "What about constraints? Theory is silent about constraints and assumes they do not exist. But in the real world investors seldom follow religiously the asset allocation that comes out of Markowitz's procedure of mean/variance." They invest less than proportionately in markets other than the market of their own country—or even their own state and city. Although mean/variance tends to favor less liquid assets like real estate or timber that have low

---

[*] In correspondence, Treynor has emphasized that beta is a measure of volatility, which means that it, too, is a function of surprise: "Beta estimates are based on data dominated by surprise," he told me, because the best estimates of beta are based on short time intervals, where surprise is more dominant than in long-run estimates.

correlations with more conventional assets, many investors, and individual investors in particular, prefer assets that are liquid and easy to trade. In most instances, security selection and manager performance are based on some benchmark instead of on the absolute expected return relative to risk exposure. Investors have different time horizons.

"These kinds of constraints," Grossman explains, "have a significant impact on investment results, often for the worse, but we would not understand that if we did not have capital market theories to explain the fundamental drivers of investment returns and risk exposures. Those theories were truly a great development. And now, finally, we see broad acceptance of the hedge fund structure, where the whole design is aimed at breaking out of the constraints."

Grossman then made a provocative observation: "There doesn't seem to be much of a middle ground right now between the advocates of hedge funds and the advocates of index funds. That doesn't make sense." Here Grossman is reflecting the basic philosophy at BGI. Any active strategy that offers the prospect of a high Information Ratio is worth considering as long as it is consistent with BGI's competitive edge—it must require scale, or substantial sums under management to be profitable, it must be developed from proprietary technology, and it must be quantitatively driven instead of based on visiting companies or anything resembling that kind of research process. If the strategy meets those conditions, it can be anything from enhanced indexing to the most aggressive kind of hedge fund.

At this point, our discussion turned to the high-tech bubble of the 1990s and what it has taught investors about financial theory in action and about successful investment management. I commented that Modigliani and Miller, way back in 1958, had conceived the big idea that drove the bubble to such fantastic heights. It was M&M who declared that any investment project and its associated financing plan must pass only one test—whether the project as financed will increase the market value of the company's shares. The market knows all. Only when the price of the stock goes up is the company earning its cost of capital. This was the philosophical justification for the bubble and the total emphasis on anything, including cooking the books, that would make a company's stock price go up (see *Capital Ideas,* pp. 174–178).

Grossman responded, "I wish we had a better understanding of the drivers. There is a great lesson in how there can be such hysterical periods despite the increase in sophistication among the major investors in the stock market. After all, these people were well aware that stocks were overvalued. Yet they could not take the big business risk of being on the wrong side when the market was roaring ahead like that. Maybe they could have gone short on some of those things, but in many cases they could not borrow the stock so the whole arbitrage mechanism failed in its mission of keeping the market efficient. I wonder how much conviction investment managers did have in what they were doing."

BGI's investment management structure led it to keep making bets on stocks with rational values at lower price-earnings ratios than the big winners of the moment. As a result, BGI's enhanced indexing business was "beaten up—almost wiped out." Clients were also restless, repeatedly asking "When are you guys going to change what you are doing?"

BGI held out. Managers were confident of the long-term validity of what their models were telling them. On the other hand, this argument did not sound like a very satisfactory answer at that moment, even though BGI's approach had been tested and proven valid over an extended time period reaching back to the early efforts of Bill Fouse and Jim Vertin in the 1970s. Yet, despite all the turmoil, BGI lost only a few clients during the hectic days of the bubble.

I then commented on my own conviction about this problem. In my experience as a money manager in the late 1960s and as a consultant and observer since then, bubbles are more often made by clients than by managers, because it is scary for a manager to remain steadfast when long-time clients start walking out the door. Only the most tough-minded can resist that kind of pressure.

And what of the future? Grossman believes much has been learned from the experience with the bubble. The terrible losses incurred in the crash made short-selling appear much more respectable. On the other hand, short-selling and the rapid growth of the hedge fund universe are making the market more efficiently priced as mispricings disappear more rapidly. So the market is even more difficult to beat than it was in the first place. Alpha does not grow on trees, ripe for the picking, even for management organizations as sophisticated as BGI.

As a result, BGI is turning to entirely new approaches. As an application of what it has learned from the teachings of Behavioral Finance, the firm now has a large number of CPAs and accounting Ph.D.s just studying corporate accounting reports. Grossman chuckles, "If you had told me twelve years ago that we would be harnessing our strategies to behavioral in general and accounting in particular, I would have been mighty skeptical. But we are studying the accounting data with fresh viewpoints to assess the quality and sustainability of earnings and to understand where the real drivers of earnings come from."

Although this work has its origins in Graham and Dodd, it is much more rigorous. BGI has found vast quantities of data and is uncovering many different sources of growth other investors are ignoring. The trick now is to discover how—or whether—the market prices these facts.

❖

"It was an evangelical undertaking," Grossman declared as he looked back over the whole story from the struggles of the 1970s onward. "Indexing and computer-driven strategies based on theoretical models are still the core of our work. They color everything we do."

And so the BGI story goes forward, a robust and faithful child of the academic work of the past while creating a new future as it continues to bring the gown to town. It finally succeeded in Vertin's task of "pushin' the rock uphill."

11

The Yale
Endowment Fund
Uninstitutional Behavior

W hen David Swensen earned his Ph.D. in economics at Yale in 1975, the possibility of ending up as Chief Investment Officer of the Yale University endowment was the last thing that might have crossed his mind. Exactly ten years later, he took the job.

The day he said "yes" was one of the luckiest days in the long history of Yale University. Its endowment at that time had a market value of only a little over $1 billion compared with $18 billion on June 30, 2006, the end of the last fiscal year. For the ten years ending 1983, $1.00 in Yale's endowment grew to $2.55, an annual rate of 9.8 percent. Since Swensen took over management of the endowment in 1985, Yale's annual total return has been just about double his predecessor's and has ranked at the very top of the universe of large institutional investors.

Over the past ten years, the endowment has increased 3.7 times— and that is after substantial contributions to the university spending stream—while the S&P 500 Index increased only 2.2 times, but the S&P data include reinvestment of all dividends and no deductions for any kind of expenditure. The entire universe of endowment funds has not even kept pace with the S&P 500. Yale's annual returns since 1985 have beaten inflation in every year except for 1988 and 1991. During the big bear market of 2001–2002, the S&P 500 shrank by 30 percent while the Yale portfolio *increased* by 10 percent. Meanwhile, the endowment's annual contribution to Yale's spending needs has grown over twelvefold, to more than $618 million, or from 10 percent to 34 percent of the university's budget. All these positive developments were accompanied by a decline in portfolio volatility from 15 percent a year to under 11 percent.

These results would be impressive for any investor, but managing a university endowment is a daunting task. In the first place, the job is a scary one. Unlike most professional investors, Swensen has only one client—Yale's Investment Committee. If he fails to keep it happy, he will find himself back on the job market. Sustained success has given him a lot of wiggle room, but Swensen had to start off with no track record, and even now he must have anxious moments in the watches of the night. After all, the committee itself has to answer to its critics, which tend to multiply rapidly in number when performance falls short.

The investment problem for a university endowment is particularly complex, because the endowment has to satisfy competing goals. High returns are crucial, because the endowment is not just a pool of money but a stream of revenue to help pay for faculty and administration salaries, student aid, and maintenance of the physical plant. The alumni, the students, the faculty, and the administration all agree they want the university to exist into eternity, which means that preserving the capital of the endowment fund has a high priority. Skilled risk management is essential. On the other hand, playing it safe in investing will seldom earn high returns.

Consequently, those extraordinary rates of return produced by Swensen's team and Yale's lead position in the world of endowment funds really matter. Education is a competitive enterprise today—the size and fecundity of the endowment fund are key variables. The level of professors' salaries, the amount of financial aid available for deserving students, and the attractiveness and operational efficiency of the physical plant can determine whether a university is a leader, able to attract the best of faculty and students, or just an also-ran without distinction.

Yale's financial position is sensitive to an even broader set of considerations. Thanks to Swensen's achievements, Yale is a much larger university than it would have been if the endowment had earned no more than the average rate of return. Its whole position in the community of universities has been transformed by the endowment's performance. Accordingly, Swensen's responsibilities are a lot tougher than when he started. When the portfolio contributed 10 percent to Yale's annual spending, a loss or underperformance here or there did not matter so much. But when the portfolio is contributing over a third of the budget, and has a responsibility to keep Yale so close to the top of the pile, defining goals and making decisions is much more complex than it was in the past.

Managing the endowment fund, then, demands the highest kind of financial sophistication. We shall see that Swensen has performed his task with a wide variety of tools and financial engineering. But his strategies begin with the basic theoretical structure of Capital Ideas, which shapes the asset allocation, risk management, and manager selection that has produced his stunning track record.

◈

Who is this man who could pull off such miracles in portfolio management? And how did he achieve so much in a world where consistency and high returns seldom go hand-in-hand?

Swensen graduated in economics from the University of Wisconsin in 1975 and went to Yale for his Ph.D., where he studied under James Tobin (see *Capital Ideas,* pp. 64–74) and Tobin's colleague, William Brainard. He devoted his doctoral dissertation to an analysis of "Tobin's Q," or the relation between the total market value of a firm and the replacement value of its fixed assets. As the total value of a firm includes its outstanding liabilities as well as the value of its equity, Swensen was interested in developing a model for the valuation of corporate bonds.

In 1979, in the course of seeking actual bond market data, he went to see the people at Salomon Brothers & Hutzler, then Wall Street's most active bond trading house, where he encountered Salomon's bond mathematician and local guru, Martin Leibowitz. Swensen was fascinated, even though he confesses that "I was not sure what an investment bank was."* He asked Leibowitz whether there might be a job for him

---

*Unless otherwise specified, all quotations are from personal interviews or correspondence.

at Salomon Brothers. Leibowitz told him, "You have a wonderful academic career ahead of you. This is no place for you." But Swensen was determined. He came back to Leibowitz, and said, flat out, "I want to work for you."

Swensen found the experience "fabulous—Salomon was a hungry and scrappy place." He stayed at Salomon for three years, in the course of which he structured the first financial swap transaction in history, between IBM and the World Bank, a transaction that was the genesis of what is now a mega-billion dollar market in an endless variety of transactions and instruments.*

Lehman Brothers lured Swensen away from Salomon Brothers, but the stint at Lehman would turn out to be brief. One day Tobin and Brainard called from New Haven to talk Swensen into taking over the management of the Yale endowment fund, a position that had been open for some time. Swensen balked, complaining, "I don't know anything about portfolio management." His former professors refused to take no for an answer. "That doesn't matter," they told him. "We always thought you were a smart guy, and Yale needs you." As a loyal Yale alumnus, they insisted, Swensen was obliged to take on the job. There are lots of jokes about economists and their hilarious failures at forecasting, but Swensen's track record goes a long way to demonstrate that Tobin and Brainard knew what they were doing when they flattered him into taking a position he never thought he would hold, much less aspire to.

Swallowing an 80 perccent cut in pay, Swensen said yes to Tobin and Brainard, and moved himself back to New Haven. His salary is now a respectable one by most standards, but far below what the major players at thousands of hedge funds and other investment organizations take home for their efforts. For Swensen, this job has been a labor of love.

None of this has deterred Swensen from carrying out his nonconformist vision of how Yale should manage its endowment. He has been a maverick every step of the way in an area where risk aversion

---

* And that Robert Merton, as we saw in Chapter 4, proposes as a simple way of helping entire nations diversify their GDP risks.

runs high and where, as John Maynard Keynes put it many years ago—and Swensen likes to recall—"Worldly wisdom teaches that it is better for reputation to fail conventionally than to succeed unconventionally." Swensen's basic approach does look more conventional today, but only because so many other endowments have attempted to follow in his footsteps. They continue to follow—but nobody has surpassed him as a pioneer.

As he phrases it himself in his excellent book, *Pioneering Investment Management,* "Active management strategies demand uninstitutional behavior from institutions, creating a paradox that few can unravel. Establishing and maintaining an unconventional investment profile requires acceptance of uncomfortably idiosyncratic portfolios, which frequently appear downright imprudent in the eyes of conventional wisdom" (p. 7).

But Swensen's results have been shaped by more than his exceptional design for the portfolio. As he sees it, a complex of human relationships is what determines the numbers on the bottom line and the subtleties, complexities, and risks of the investment process.

On the one hand, he has enjoyed a remarkable bond with the Yale Investment Committee. The members of the committee—many of them distinguished professional investors in their own right—have respected and accepted Swensen's unorthodox proposals to break with the crowd, giving him wide discretion in carving a new path through the thickets of portfolio structure, risk management, and manager selection. Then they have stood by him instead of losing confidence when outcomes have been less than expected, as inevitably happens to all investors. In addition, Swensen has chosen a staff of colleagues who could put his ideas into action—and do it right. Superb execution of the "uninstitutional" portfolio has been every bit as important to the results as the development of the concept itself.

Swensen is well aware of how much he owes the committee for his success. "They gradually shifted responsibility to me and my staff over a number of years," he told me. "I did not even recognize it was happening until after the fact."

There is an irony here. Way back in 1966, Jack Treynor was working on a project at the consulting firm of Arthur D. Little to figure out why Yale's hotshot investment managers were producing such mediocre results for the endowment. Treynor's recommendation was short and to the point: "It seems to us that the key to active portfolio management lies in giving the fund manager the freedom to determine his own style of investment management and to act independently and quickly."[1]

It took only a little less than twenty years, but Yale finally got the message.

◼

Swensen's response to the committee's transfer of authority was measured, in much the same way that its transfer of authority to him was measured. Even though he had a good idea of where he wanted to end up with that "uncomfortably idiosyncratic portfolio," he did not go to the committee with a fully developed plan to rip the old portfolio apart and install the new. "You must make sure you move the process in the right direction," he pointed out. "You have to go gradually to unorthodox positions. So I would suggest to the Committee, 'Why don't we establish a target of x percent for this asset class now and revisit this next year?' Then the target moves up over time." In fact, except for a small commitment to private equity in 1986, which was increased in 1987, the asset allocation of the endowment did not reflect substantive changes until 1991. At that time, Yale made a commitment to a group of hedge funds to provide "absolute returns," or returns earned from a roughly equal balance of long positions and short positions so that the portfolio's level of volatility is close to zero. Swensen financed this commitment with a substantial reduction in U.S. equities.

Through it all, Swensen has found that plain English is a critical ingredient of maintaining his relationship with his committee. As he describes it, "You can go to any trustee and ask their view of the trade-off between preserving purchasing power and providing a stable floor of resources to the budget. This is an intuitive concept even a nonfinancial person can grasp. But ask about utility functions and the efficient frontier and say 'here is its point of tangency,' and you have no hope of engaging them in the big decisions that have to be made."

◼

When Swensen began his task, the Yale endowment portfolio was indistinguishable from most university endowments. Within five years, it was well on its way to looking like an outlier. Yet Swensen was *more* orthodox than chief investment officers at other institutions, because the structure he built was founded on basic elements right out of the standard textbooks in finance. When I asked him whether he came in with the ultimate structure in mind, he laughed and retorted, "Efficient markets were a big thing in your book *Capital Ideas!*" His vision has never wavered from three central principles.

First, the capital markets are efficient in the sense that the prices of most publicly traded securities rapidly reflect current information. If the markets are efficient, then equities and equity-like investments should be priced to provide higher expected returns than fixed-income investments over the long run because equities are riskier than bonds. The long time horizon of Yale's portfolio should therefore justify a dominant allocation to equities and equity-like assets.

Second, if the markets are efficient, efforts to outperform the broad indexes would have little chance of success. The choice, therefore, would be between indexing equities and accepting a market return or finding equity-like investments that would tend to provide higher returns than the publicly traded markets. Again in light of the long time horizon, the Yale portfolio should seek to favor assets other than publicly traded securities in areas where competent investment managers could be identified.

Third, the future is always uncertain. Consequently, risk management is fundamental to the whole process. Indeed, risk management is the only part of the process under the control of the investor. Diversification is the most effective form of risk management, and every decision must be consistent with maintaining a high degree of diversification—or minimal covariance—throughout the portfolio.

After establishing these principles based on Capital Ideas, Swensen also turned to Modern Portfolio Theory and quantitative analysis to shape his strategies and to rationalize his asset allocation. "Quantitative analysis," he believes, "provides essential underpinning to the portfolio structuring process, forcing investors to take a disciplined approach."[2] Mean/variance is the optimization process developed by Markowitz in 1952 to guide investors in arriving at an appropriate asset mix (see *Capital Ideas,* pp. 54–55). The input to the optimization is supplied by the investor, who enters estimates of expected returns for each asset or asset class to be included in the portfolio, the estimated variance or volatility of returns for each asset, and the estimated covariance of each asset's return with the returns of all the others. A programmed computer does all the rest.

The output provided by the optimizer provides an array of recommended portfolios, one for every level of expected return (the "mean") or one each for every level of variance, or risk. All the portfolios along this array are classified as "efficient," in the sense that they offer the highest expected return per unit of risk or the lowest level of risk per unit of expected return. The array as a whole is known as the "efficient frontier."

In their calculations, optimizers typically put more weight on the covariance of the returns of the assets—the way their returns vary in relation to one another—than on the volatility of the individual assets or on their expected returns. Diversification, in other words, tends to dominate expected returns along the efficient frontier. But diversification is more than just spreading yourself around. Diversification means exposure to areas where the sense of discomfort and uncertainty can be unsettling—but those are often the sectors that produce the most exciting results.

Swensen describes the process this way: "Mean/variance was a powerful influence in causing us to move away from the standard institutional portfolio. You never get a recommendation of 65 percent equities from mean/variance—it's always telling you to move toward diversifying asset classes that promise equity-like returns. These kinds of results led us to emphasize private equity and venture capital, real estate, hedge funds offering long/short strategies or absolute returns, and investments in raw materials like timber. By the time we had cut back on the assets trading in public markets to make room for these new areas, our portfolio looked entirely different from other university endowment portfolios."

Unlike Swensen, most investors at that time, and particularly institutional investors, were reluctant to build "uninstitutional" portfolios with low weights assigned to stocks and bonds and large shares assigned to less liquid and less familiar asset classes.* Before the optimizer does its calculations, therefore, many institutions add constraints to the inputs that limit the maximum weight of the unconventional assets the optimizer

---

*In Chapter 14, we explore this point in greater detail, where these kinds of risks are described as "dragon risks."

can recommend. The motivation for interfering with the optimizer's un-constrained recommendations was in part a manager's fear of the career consequences if the unconventional assets fail to deliver their expected returns. To put it another way, their hesitation reflected uncertainty about their ability to select professional investment groups capable of managing these kinds of asset classes.

The end product of all these inputs and outputs, and the assumptions and the risks, is what Swensen describes as the Policy Portfolio. The Policy Portfolio is the university's ultimate statement of how the endowment is to be allocated among major asset classes over the long run. Yale has made only a few changes in its Policy Portfolio—and the adjustments were both infrequent and minor. In addition to providing a benchmark for how the university chooses to trade off risk versus expected return, the Policy Portfolio also serves as the overall yardstick against which the Investment Committee can judge the actual performance of Swensen and his staff. Jack Meyer, Swensen's counterpart at Harvard from 1990 to 2005, sees the Policy Portfolio in the same light: "If you use a policy portfolio that doesn't align precisely with your return goals, risk toler-ance, and basic asset mix, no amount of clever trading will save you."[3]

Nevertheless, the Yale committee's attachment to the Policy Port-folio has an aggressive as well as a defensive flavor. As the 1995 report describes it, "Because of the importance of maintaining policy tar-gets, the Investment Office closely monitors deviations of actual from target allocations in the Endowment. When markets rise and fall, the portfolio is rebalanced; that is, securities are bought and sold to maintain actual allocations at the policy targets. By adhering to policy targets, rebalancing imposes a disciplined 'buy low, sell high' strategy. . . . *While rebalancing is conducted primarily to control risk, the process adds value to the extent the market exhibits excess volatility*" (emphasis added).

Swensen is an outspoken and eloquent enemy of market timing—the effort to buy low and sell high—which he insists is like chasing rainbows and doomed to failure. He and I have an ongoing friendly dis-pute over this matter, in which I insist that Yale's strict rebalancing policy is a form of market timing, although mechanical rather than a matter of judgment. Indeed, daily rebalancing in the equity portfolio is not unusual. If the stock market rises on a given day, pushing the percentage allocation to equities above the prescribed Policy Portfolio allocation, Yale will sell off enough equities to restore the Policy Portfolio distribution, and vice versa if the stock market falls—or variations occur in any of the other liquid asset classes. There are big payoffs from this strategy when the market has big swings, such as in 1987 or 2002–2003, especially as faithful adherence to the policy, no matter what, prevents panicky or greedy reactions from getting in the way of buying low and selling high. Swensen defines the rebalancing policy as simply a means to assure "that Yale's policy targets are faithfully represented in the portfolio."

Because of his strong convictions about the right way to go, Swensen had no inhibitions about a Policy Portfolio with little resemblance to the portfolios at other institutions. Step-by-step, he liquidated what he perceived as an undiversified portfolio dominated by marketable securities and invested the proceeds into an entirely different portfolio that satisfied his view of true diversification. Indeed, as a result of his "huge respect for efficient markets," he began by dismissing most of the active managers in stocks and bonds and putting about half the equities and all the bonds into index funds. That was only a beginning. Swensen slashed Yale's exposure to marketable equities from over 60 percent of the portfolio at the outset to the low 20 percent area by the mid-1990s (when everybody else was rushing into the bull market), and even lower most of the time since then—an allocation sharply below the approximately 40 percent average allocation of other educational endowment funds.

A clear beginning of the shift had occurred by 1990, after Swensen's first five years on the job. Domestic equity investments were down from 62 percent to only 48 percent of the endowment fund, at a time when most institutional portfolios had as much as 65 percent in equities. The reduced share of the domestic equities was transferred to foreign equities and a foray into the bond market that Swensen reversed after 1993.

By 1995, the portfolio generally conformed to its current allocations. Domestic equities had been cut to 22 percent of the portfolio, or less than half the share only five years earlier. The allocation to bonds was reduced by five percentage points to 16.5 percent and was on the way down to the 5 percent area—compared with an average of about 20 percent among other educational institutions. Today, the single justification for Yale's bond portfolio is to hedge the endowment fund against the risk of an extended period of deflation in the economy. Stability of income and principal are subordinate objectives. Yet the Capital Market group's astute in-house active management of the bond portfolio, including security selection as well as a willingness to accept illiquidity, has consistently outperformed its benchmark, the Lehman Brothers Government Bond Index.

On the other hand, nontraditional assets—hedge funds, private equity, venture capital, real estate, and timber—which had been only 10 percent of the portfolio in 1985 and 15 percent in 1990, had soared to 52 percent of the total in 1995. At latest count, about 69 percent of Yale's endowment is in this group, compared to an average of only 26 percent in the endowment funds of other educational institutions.

Swensen makes a strong argument for these moves, based on his view of where markets are efficient, in line with capital market theory, and where they are not. Capital Ideas are ultimately about liquid markets and have much less meaning for the uninstitutional investment area. This perspective shapes Swensen's vision of how chief investment officers of endowment assets should carry out their mission. In his 1995 report, he makes the case this way:

> In efficient markets, active portfolio management, like market timing, tends to detract from aggregate investment performance. In the context of relative performance, security selection is a negative sum game. . . . Both overweighted and underweighted investors incur transaction costs and create market impact in establishing their positions. . . . Hence, as a group, active managers will underperform passive, index-matching strategies.

The 2004 report extols the strategy of moving away from markets where efficiency prevails to areas where investment skill can have higher odds of a positive payoff:

In July 1990, Yale became the first institutional investor to pursue absolute return strategies as a distinct asset class. . . . Unlike traditional marketable securities, absolute return investments provide returns largely independent of overall market moves. . . . An important attribute of Yale's investment strategy concerns the alignment of interests between investors and investment managers [especially relating to] many of the pitfalls of the principal-agent relationship. . . .

Private equity offers extremely attractive long-term risk-adjusted return characteristics, stemming from the University's strong stable of value-added managers that exploit market inefficiencies. . . .

Real estate, oil and gas, and timberland provide attractive return prospects, excellent portfolio diversification, [are] a hedge against unanticipated inflation, [and] an opportunity to exploit inefficiencies. . . . The real assets portfolio plays a meaningful role in the Endowment as a powerful diversifying tool and a generator of strong returns.

Along the way, Swensen has been faithful to one of Harry Markowitz's favorite observations about asset allocation: "It's not the variance you have to worry about, it's the covariance." Diversification is an obsession with Swensen, but he pursues it in his own way. In the 1995 endowment report, he summed it up in a few words: "Yale seeks diversification without the opportunity costs of investing in fixed-income by identifying high-return asset classes that are not highly correlated with domestic marketable securities. . . . [Under these conditions], a portfolio can be constructed that offers both high returns and diversification."

In other words, you can hold plenty of risky assets with high expected returns as long as they fluctuate independently rather than in step with one another. This is nothing more than Markowitz's theory of diversification. From the very beginning of Swensen's régime, Yale has consistently aimed for the maximum possible level of diversification while selecting assets with expected rates of return higher than returns available from conventional asset classes. Yale does more than apply this concept religiously; Yale has been the pioneer leading the rest of the institutional investing world in this direction.

Superb execution of these strategies has been the secret of the success in the drive to establish an "uninstitutional portfolio." Few chief investment officers anywhere have been able to match the uncanny talent Swensen and his staff have exhibited in choosing skilled managers for each strategy.

The experience with U.S. equities is a clear example of how Swensen operates. Yale hired no big-name managers in this market, and all the managers of U.S. equity run specialized portfolios with relatively few holdings. One manager, for example, invests only in energy-related stocks, another only in real estate stocks, another only in biotech, and so forth. Moreover, these portfolios are highly concentrated in only a few stocks; the largest manager tends to hold only five to ten stocks, and at one point was down to three.

The result is a huge tracking error against any of the major indexes like the S&P 500 or the Wilshire 5000. "There is no way you can succeed with active management if you try to control benchmark risk," Swensen declares: "You must be willing to deviate from the benchmark if you want to earn returns commensurate with the risks of owning equities. And you must be patient. These managers often lag, but they have done their homework and have no hesitation in just hanging in."

This is not a recipe for smooth returns, and the Yale U.S. equity portfolio has had a sequence of bumpy short-term rides to reach its spectacular longer-run performance. For example, consider the situation at the beginning of December 1994, when the value of the U.S. equity portfolio was approximately $800 million. At that point, the portfolio began to lag its benchmark and was a cumulative $273 million under water by December 1998. In January 1999, the shortfall peaked at $295 million. Four years later, as of December 2002, Yale's U.S. equities, totaling $1,154 million in value, were $689 million ahead of their benchmark. And the bulk of the assets was managed by the same managers in the dark days of 1998 as in the glorious recovery at the end of 2002—and beyond.

If the choice of managers in the equity area is not a recipe for smooth returns, it does appear to be a recipe for high returns. Over the five fiscal years ending June 2006, Yale outperformed the stock market by a cumulative 27 percentage points. Over the ten years ending 2006, the domestic portfolio produced an annual total return of 14.2 percent per year, outperforming the broad Wilshire 5000 index by 5.7 percent a year, an excess that enabled the portfolio to generate $763 million relative to the portfolio's benchmark. The foreign equity portfolio performed even better than that.

Like it or not, however, making judgments about manager performance has to involve benchmarks. Benchmarks are no problem in the case of the marketable securities, but a lot more complicated for the alternative asset classes where passive yardsticks are either unavailable or doubtful in their relevance to a portfolio like Yale's. In the case of real assets like real estate and timber, Swensen chose to construct benchmarks relating to the manager's contribution to the expected long-run return of the asset class.

But Swensen is convinced a different kind of benchmark, a softer yardstick, is essential. Here two factors come into play: understanding the manager's investment process and monitoring the manager's attitude toward Yale as a client.

At the beginning, Swensen or members of his staff would base their judgments on a manager's track record and a careful analysis of the models employed in selecting choices for the portfolio. That approach has diminished in importance over the years. The track record and models are still important, but now the staff also spends a lot of time with each manager, discussing in detail every real-time transaction and the motivation for selecting each holding. "You cannot be a partner with somebody who has a black box," Swensen points out.

This last comment sums up Swensen's current philosophy. As he describes the approach:

> The whole investment management area is cluttered with conflicts of interest and agency problems. When we choose a manager or invest in a fund, we want people side-by-side with us rather than as agents, which means people who put the interest of the investors front and center. We look for people who are going to be good partners: people who will operate with intelligence and integrity, people who will refrain from taking a step if it in any way violated fiduciary principles or would be against the interest of their clients or limited partners. Ability is important—we have to recognize that—but overcoming agent/principal conflicts is overwhelming.

What about terminating managers? "You have to be heartless on behalf of Yale and fire people when circumstances demand it," Swensen replied. "Thank goodness, that has been a rare event. The average relationship here is fourteen or fifteen years, even longer. Growth in assets under management or the departure of key personnel have been the main reasons we have terminated people. It's all about the people."

Although Swensen relies heavily on mean/variance in setting the policy asset allocation of the portfolio, he views this tool as only a starting point: "Mean/variance does not tell you where you should be. It provides only a range of choices. Most important, it cannot take into consideration the most important purpose of the whole exercise—how much Yale is spending, should spend, and could afford to spend." Risk management, in other words, is at the heart of the whole process.

For this purpose, Swensen begins with Monte Carlo simulations, the same procedure underlying Harry Markowitz's complex replication of a stock market described in Chapter 8 and the investment advice on retirement provided by Bill Sharpe's Financial Engines described in Chapter 7. This exercise enables Swensen to make meaningful estimates of the risks of future outcomes for the portfolio based on varying assumptions of spending policies and investment policies under a wide variety of scenarios. All of these results can then be analyzed in terms of the two goals of the investment management process—to preserve the long-term purchasing power of the endowment and, in the short run, to provide a stable flow of resources for the operating budget.

Using thousands of simulations based on the same assumptions employed in the mean/variance analysis, Swensen and his staff have been able to estimate the probability of losing 50 percent of the endowment over a fifty-year horizon, an unhappy possibility they call Impairment Risk. They were also able to calculate the probability that they might have to cut their contribution to the university's budget by 10 precent after inflation over a five-year period, or Spending Disruption Risk. The staff carries out this exercise every year, often with the advice of outside experts to help refine the concepts and assumptions of the process.

In 1990, when allocations to alternative asset classes accounted for only 15 percent of the total portfolio at Yale, Swensen's estimates indicated close to a 35 percent probability of Spending Disruption Risk and a probability of 31 percent for Impairment Risk. These results were cause for concern, but calculations for university endowments in general indicated Yale was in much better shape than the others. Swensen's strategies over the years have succeeded in reducing the probability of Disruptive Spending Drop Risk to about 20 percent and Impairment Risk to close to 10 percent.

Endowment spending—the fund's contribution to Yale's operating budget—is also under strict control. The procedure aims to make certain the spending stream reflects the growth in the portfolio but also includes a smoothing device so that fluctuations in market values will not disrupt university operations in the short run. The formula in use comes in two parts. The portfolio's expected long-term contribution was originally estimated at 4.5 percent of its market value after adjustment for inflation, but that number has been raised three times in Swensen's régime. Twenty percent of the endowment's annual contribution to Yale's budget is based on the long-run estimate of 5.25 percent of the value of the portfolio (increased from 5.00 percent in 2004), after adjustment for inflation. The balance is 80 percent of the previous year's spending from the endowment fund; the formula had been 70/30 but was changed to 80/20 in 2004. Under this formula, the endowment's contribution to Yale's overall annual budget has risen from 14 percent in 1993 to about 35 percent at the present time.

Swensen has strong opinions about how markets work and about the validity of the theories included in Capital Ideas. He simultaneously supports and rejects these ideas.

On the one hand, he sees inefficiencies in pricing in both individual securities and the markets as a whole, but "they are incredibly difficult to exploit, especially for the mass of investors—including institutions—who operate on time horizons that are far too short. So what good are those inefficiencies in the first place?"

The tendency of managers in efficient markets to hug their benchmarks is a phenomenon that fascinates him. Why do they do it? In *Pioneering Investment Management,* he answers this question as follows: "Consider the business consequences to investment managers holding portfolios that differ markedly from the market portfolio. Substantial deviations in security holdings cause portfolios to vary dramatically from the benchmark. Underperforming managers lose clients. . . . Because markets price securities efficiently, success will be transitory . . . and stem from luck, not skill" (2000, pp. 74–75).

In large part, this viewpoint explains why Swensen has so much of Yale's money invested in less efficient markets like real estate and private equity. Managers in these areas display a greater variability in returns because there are no generally accepted benchmarks for them to hug. Inefficient pricing in these kinds of markets permits managers with real skill and an aptitude for hard work to produce high excess returns from processing superior information. Here it is relatively easy to separate the men from the boys, and results tend to reflect skill rather than luck.

On the other hand, when asked about Behavioral Finance, Swensen replies, "I love it!" He considers the main benefit of Behavioral Finance as helping him and his staff to understand the limitations of the different filters Yale brings to the investment process. Swensen is a great admirer of Robert Shiller—but speculates on how to preserve the notion of the Capital Asset Pricing Model and efficient markets if Shiller's views on the market's excess volatility are valid.

Swensen resolves the dilemmas of efficient markets by differentiating between the great mass of individual investors and major institutional investors. He believes most investors should recognize that markets are almost impossible to beat with any consistency, after adjustment for risk. These investors simply lack the resources and training of institutional staffs—and anyway most of the institutions still come out with results that do no better than index fund returns. His recent book expounds at length on the risks individual investors face when they try to emulate institutional strategies.[4] "After all," Swensen asserts, "at Yale we have twenty professionals devoting their lives to the investment process, and they are really good at their jobs." With all those smart people handling big money, small investors have poor chances of success in active management. Swensen also has little faith in most of the mutual fund industry, which he believes is more interested in taking care of its own fortunes than the finances of the customers.

Nevertheless, he considers Capital Ideas to be the indispensable structure for investors confronting the uncertainties and promises in the world of finance. "The basic framework is far superior to anything else that's out there. In short, it is incredibly valuable."

12

CAPM II: The Great Alpha Dream Machine

We Don't See Expected Returns

H ere is a paradox. In today's world of investing, the Capital Asset Pricing Model has turned into the most fascinating and perhaps the most influential of all the theoretical developments described in *Capital Ideas*. Yet repeated empirical tests of the original Sharpe-Treynor-Lintner-Mossin CAPM, dating all the way back to the 1960s, have failed to demonstrate that the theoretical model works in practice. In addition, we have already seen Harry Markowitz's misgivings about the underlying assumptions of the model, as set forth above in Chapter 8.

At the conclusion of an extended paper on the status of CAPM published in 2004, Eugene Fama of Chicago and Kenneth French of Dartmouth described the status of CAPM in these words:

> The attraction of the CAPM is its powerfully simple logic and intuitively pleasing predictions about how to measure risk and about the relation between expected return and risk. Unfortunately, perhaps because of its simplicity, the empirical record of the model is poor— poor enough to invalidate the way it is used in applications. . . . The CAPM, like Markowitz's portfolio model on which it is built, is . . . a theoretical tour de force. We continue to teach the CAPM

as an introduction to the fundamentals of portfolio theory and asset pricing . . . but we also warn students that, despite its seductive simplicity, the CAPM's empirical problems probably invalidate its use in applications.[1]

I would rephrase Fama's and French's gloomy conclusion about CAPM's empirical problems. Those problems invalidate the model's use in *some* applications. But the model's power has turned out to be astonishing where its use is appropriate. In recent years, CAPM has inspired widespread and radical changes in the way institutional investors allocate assets, and the order in which they sequence their allocation decisions. CAPM also influences the way investors arrive at judgments between active and passive investing, select active managers, and confront the risks imbedded in their portfolio decisions. CAPM is indeed alive and well as an effective tool of portfolio management, although in ways that none of its developers would ever have predicted.

What is the Capital Asset Pricing Model all about? The answer to that question depends in part on which of the living originators of this model you ask, Jack Treynor or Bill Sharpe. Although Treynor and Sharpe started developing their models independently at almost the same moment, and although they ended up in pretty much the same place, they approached the model from different perspectives.

Treynor had been involved in helping clients of the consulting firm, Arthur D. Little, determine whether prospective investments in new productive facilities would be sufficiently profitable to justify taking the risk of building them. He was impatient with the traditional approach of using the internal rate of return for this purpose because the IRR was "clearly an idea that isolated the company from the capital market."[2] Sharpe had been working with Harry Markowitz on methods to simplify the application of Markowitz's approach to optimizing the trade-off between risk and return.

Both men were attempting to solve the problem of how to quantify investment risk and then to explore the implications of the relationships in the marketplace between risk and return. While Treynor was launching his approach from the real economy, Sharpe tackled it from the viewpoint of an investor in the capital markets.

As each pursued his own goal, they both recognized the similarity of the larger issues involved, and their ultimate solutions bore a remarkable resemblance despite the wide difference in starting points.* The ultimate determinant of asset valuation in both cases turned out to be the covariance with a "common factor." As Treynor put it, "The risk premium per share is proportional to the covariance of the investment with the total value of all investments in the market."[3] (For a more detailed account, see *Capital Ideas,* pp. 183–189.)

Both models, furthermore, specify how everything would work out *under conditions of equilibrium,* in which everyone shares the same information and interprets it in similar fashion, and in which expected returns as reflected in asset prices inevitably line up in relation to a commonly shared definition of risk. In addition, investors can borrow or lend unlimited amounts at the riskless rate of interest. Under those conditions, every asset is correctly priced, and nobody has any further incentive to trade.

Harry Markowitz is not the only authority to have expressed misgivings about the unreality of these assumptions. My objective here, however, is to demonstrate how, *despite its shortcomings,* CAPM has been transformed into a powerful, real-world tool for managing money and estimating performance.

◈

The equation Sharpe developed to specify the model defines how individual assets are priced in the marketplace in which they trade. The significant elements in the pricing process are expected returns and volatility relative to the market.

Here is Sharpe's algebraic specification of CAPM in his original 1964 paper on this subject (see *Capital Ideas,* pp. 191–193):

$$E_i = \alpha_i + R_f + (E_m - R_f)\,\beta_i$$

---

*See Treynor (1961) and Sharpe (1963) and (1964).

where:

E_i = Expected return on asset i

α_i = Alpha, or the residual return on asset i, with expectation of zero

R_f = Risk-free rate, such as the rate on a Treasury bill;

E_m = Expected return on the market

β_i = Beta of asset i

The equation is simple and straightforward. In words, it says that an individual asset (i) such as General Electric or a U.S. Treasury bond due in 2015 would be priced so that its expected return (E_i) is equal to the expected return of the market as a whole (E_m) less the return on a riskless asset like a Treasury bill ($E_m - R_f$), multiplied by the asset's "beta" (β_i).[*]

The Capital Asset Pricing Model of how assets are priced in the market makes no mention of any of the unique characteristics of any individual asset, be it General Electric or a Treasury bond. The entire risk in owning these assets is in their beta, which is a measure of their covariance with the market, reflecting how the fluctuations in the return earned on that asset compare with the volatility of the market as a whole. Stocks with greater volatility than the market have betas of more than 1.0, while less volatile stocks have betas of less than 1.0. Stocks fluctuating precisely with the market would have betas of 1.0. Note that beta reflects only volatility *relative to the volatility of the market;* the returns on some stocks can be very volatile and still have a low correlation with the market and therefore a low beta.

André Perold of the Harvard Business School describes beta this way: "Beta offers a method of measuring the risk of an asset that cannot be diversified away."[4] This simple statement tells the whole story about CAPM. *The market as a whole is the only influence on the return of individual assets, and risk is conceived and measured only in terms of the relation between the volatility of the individual security and the volatility of the market as a whole.* In Perold's words, "The CAPM is based on the idea that not all risks should affect asset prices. In particular, *a risk that can be diversified away when held along with other in-*

---

[*] The excess return, or ($E_m - R_f$), is known as the risk premium of the market. In theory, investors would shun risky markets where the expected return is less than they could earn on, say, U.S. Treasury bills.

vestments in a portfolio is, in a very real way, not a risk at all" (emphasis added). Stock picking is a waste of time!

Perold is describing a miracle, a kind of free lunch. As a result of diversification, the risk of the portfolio as a whole will be lower than the average of the individual risks that compose it. Perold does not mean that there is no risk in investing—indeed, CAPM's essential feature is its concentration on risk, where the risk of a portfolio depends upon its exposure to the market as a whole, rather than residing in its diversifiable individual components.

But in theory rational investors are risk-averse, so that valuation and perceptions of risk are closely linked. Investors will refuse to buy the riskier assets unless those assets provide compensation for above-average risks in the form of an expected return higher than the market's. Thus, according to CAPM theory, investors tend to place a lower valuation on riskier assets with high betas than they would place on less risky assets with low betas. CAPM does not hold literally in real life, because investors fail to recognize the magnitude of risks. They overprice risky assets because of glamour or a sense of adventure, or they simply ignore risks.

What about that other element of the model—that α_i right up at the very front of Sharpe's equation? α_i is an admission that nothing is perfect, as I just suggested. The actual realized return on any individual asset often differs from what its beta predicts, because future events are likely to vary from the consensus expectations reflected in today's valuation. α_i represents that residual return. It measures the difference between an asset's actual return and the model's predicted return. Alpha is known only after the fact, but a positive alpha would mean the asset "beat the market." Nobody expects the market to value every asset exactly in conformance with CAPM, but efficient market theory asserts that investors' errors will cancel one another out, so that, *on the average,* assets will be valued as CAPM predicts and alpha for the market as a whole averages out to zero.*

But there is gold in them thar hills when an investment manager can employ superior information and analysis to discover where mispricings—or expected positive alphas—exist. Alpha is the nirvana all active managers claim they can consistently produce for their clients. BGI offers many products that aim to beat the market in addition to offering index funds. Alpha plays an active role in the way David Swensen has

---

*Joanne Hill, a Managing Director at Goldman Sachs, has made the case that alpha is not a zero-sum game. See Hill (2006).

organized the Yale portfolio. Alpha is the focus of attention in most of what follows in this book. As we shall see, the widespread struggle to earn a return above what the market earns, after adjustment for risk, has become increasingly sophisticated and elaborate.

Nevertheless, the search for alpha is a zero-sum game. Total alpha in excess of or lower than the return of the market as a whole is an impossibility, because the return on the market is the return on the market, no more and no less. There is no way every stock could beat the market, just as there is no way every stock could underperform the market. *Most* stocks could beat the market by a little if the underperformers were all disasters.

As a matter of luck, any portfolio manager can end up beating the market in short periods of time. Luck puts other managers below the market for short periods of time. Only a tiny contingent of managers have delivered positive alphas with high consistency over extended periods of time. (Warren Buffett of Berkshire Hathaway or Bill Miller of Legg Mason are outstanding examples.)

Even when super-managers exist, identifying them in advance is a task of extraordinary difficulty. Few people are as skilled as David Swensen at that task. Furthermore, unless those super-managers limit the size of the assets under their management, they will incur rising transactions costs as they grow bigger.* Then their alphas will vanish. All these obstacles have led many investors, small as well as large, to turn to index funds and other passive strategies that promise nothing more than the return of the market as a whole—a Wells Fargo innovation in 1971, and, as we have seen, indexing is still a major source of business at BGI.

Much of the time, this skepticism about active management turns out to be valid as the market's return tends to be superior to what eager active managers or individual investors can produce, especially after transactions costs and adjustment for the network of unsystematic risks embedded in active management. As one investor's positive alpha is earned at the expense of another investor's underpaying or overpaying for some asset, there is a loser for every winner, and who knows on which side any particular manager will land?

---

*Both Buffett and Miller operate at turnover rates way below the average.

In the late 1960s and early 1970s, when the professors began promoting CAPM's insights among practitioners, the model failed to receive much acceptance. Widespread skepticism was summed up in the typically dismissive assertion in 1971 that, "These people with math and computer backgrounds . . . who think they can assign precise degrees of risk to five or six decimal places are nothing but charlatans. . . . Beta is nothing but a fad, a gimmick. . . . These knaves must be driven from the temple!" The speaker was none other than a senior economist at the widely respected management consulting firm of Booz Allen Hamilton (*Capital Ideas,* pp. 189–190).

Wall Street's critics need not have worried so much about CAPM as first presented. A long series of empirical tests raised serious doubts about its validity, including tests by such renowned scholars as Fischer Black. Other academics have tried to "fix" CAPM in one way or another. The most notable effort in this direction has been by Eugene Fama of the University of Chicago and Kenneth French of the Tuck School at Dartmouth, in 1992, when they identified two new independent variables in addition to the market: the ratio of book value to market value, and a stock's total valuation in the marketplace. Empirical tests of Fama's and French's work indicated that returns for "value" stocks and small stocks tended to be higher than CAPM's original beta alone would predict, and returns for growth stocks and large-capitalization stocks tended to be lower.[5] Even earlier, in 1966, Barr Rosenberg studied covariance models and introduced the notion of adding "factors" to the market return to explain the valuation of individual securities (see *Capital Ideas,* Chapter 13, "The Accountant for Risk").

Treynor has made an important observation about models like Fama-French or Rosenberg. In a recent interview, he put it this way, "One of the challenges to the CAPM is the idea that the market factor is not the only systematic factor in the market. However, the CAPM is utterly silent on whether there's one systematic factor in the market or two or three or ten. The CAPM still holds if there are other systematic factors, but it does say that if there are systematic factors they will have risk premiums that are proportional to the covariance with the market portfolio."[6] In other words, models involving additional factors in effect sit on top of rather than demolishing the basic premises of Treynor's and Sharpe's models.

Nevertheless, more recent critical work suggests other kinds of critiques of CAPM, as illustrated by only two examples. One would think that the best-managed and most successful companies in the country would be too highly valued by investors to produce returns higher than the return from just an index fund on the market as a whole. Yet Jeff Anderson of Mellon Financial Corporation and Gary Smith of Pomona College prove just the opposite in a paper titled "A Great Company Can Be a Great Investment."[7]

Anderson and Smith studied the performance of *Fortune*'s ten "most admired companies in the United States" from 1983 through 2004 and found that "A portfolio of these stocks outperformed the market by a substantial and significantly significant margin." At the opposite end of the spectrum, John Campbell of Harvard and two colleagues explored the pricing of financially distressed companies from 1963 to 2003. The stocks of these companies had much higher volatility than stocks with a low probability of failure, but these stocks also produced lower rates of return. Clearly, investors failed to price the risk of failure adequately.[8]

As a result of many discrepancies of this nature, CAPM in its pure form has never played much of a role in stock selection, even though some institutions give it lip service and a few have found ways to put it to use. The issue in any case does not turn primarily on empirical testing. Empirical testing of CAPM may be an impossibility, and even favorable results from such tests are likely to be suspect.

Bill Sharpe himself is emphatic about this view of the matter. When asked whether individual stocks will have higher expected returns if they have higher betas relative to the market, he responds, "It would be irresponsible to assume that is not true. [But] *that doesn't mean we can confirm the data.* We don't see expected returns; we see realized returns. We don't see *ex ante* measures of beta; we see realized beta" (emphasis added).[9]

That is just the beginning of the story of the Capital Asset Pricing Model. The knaves have *not* been driven from the temple. Times have changed, and changed in a big way. Practitioners now look at CAPM in a new light. The model is no longer just an abstract theoretical formula.

On the contrary, CAPM today frames the marching orders and responsibilities involved in the whole investment process.

Investors have learned from CAPM that they must recognize the fundamental distinction between investing in an asset class and selecting individual securities on which they hope to earn an extra return. The choice of asset classes—for example, stocks, bonds, emerging market equities, real estate, or subdivisions of those markets—is in essence the choice of beta risks, or the volatility of entire markets rather than their individual components. The search for alpha, or residual and uncorrelated risks, means taking an extra risk beyond the beta risk in the hope of earning a return over and above the expected returns from the asset classes in the portfolio.

It is important to note the frequency with which the word "risk" appears in this discussion. As mentioned at the outset, the key elements in the pricing process are risk and the central role of diversification, or risk management. In his introduction to *Asymmetric Returns: The Future of Active Asset Management,* Alexander Ineichen of UBS argues that: "The key tools required to extract alpha are risk management tools. In our view, investors cannot manage returns but they can manage risk. Achieving sustainable positive absolute returns [is] the result, we believe, of taking and managing risk wisely."[10]

In today's terminology, strategic asset allocation begins with formulation of the overall asset allocation in light of the beta risks. The results of this selection process compose a portfolio of asset classes known as the policy portfolio. The policy portfolio reflects the views of the board of trustees—or an individual investor—about the primary risks they want the portfolio to be exposed to over the long run.

On the other hand, the search for alpha, or for returns over and above the expected returns from the beta exposures, is a tactical proposition, quite separate from the strategic decisions. The management of alpha risks is usually the responsibility of the chief investment officer and the staff.

The growing distinction between strategic and tactical risks, or between beta risks and the search for alpha, reveals how CAPM is motivating a fundamental transformation of investing. CAPM makes it clear that alpha and beta are uncorrelated sources of return, but investors had never explored the full implications of that distinction. The distinction is a powerful one. If returns from taking beta risks and returns from taking alpha risk are independent, finding a new method for combining the two might even reduce total portfolio risk instead of increasing it. Furthermore, investors are now asking why they should retain the same managers to produce both the beta return and the hoped-for alpha return.[*]

For most of market history, the only alternative to managing your own money was your friendly broker, or a bank trust department, or an insurance company, or, less frequently, mutual funds. Beginning in the 1950s and at a more rapid rate since the 1960s, investors have turned to independent investment advisers who charge a fee based on the amount of the client's assets. All those outside management facilities contend they can outperform the market. Otherwise, they would never have attracted any business.

Under this conventional arrangement, the manager buys a portfolio of stocks or bonds that simultaneously delivers the market's return (now known as the beta return) plus a tracking error from the market's return the manager claims will be on the positive side rather than the negative side (the alpha return). *But why pay full fees for receiving the return on the market, when today passively managed index funds make the market return available at fees of ten basis points or less?*

The expectation of earning alpha—beating the market—is the only justification for paying more than index fund fees. But now investors are asking, "Why not separate the management of beta returns and alpha returns instead of leaving them conjoined as they always had been?" This step would not just reduce the costs of portfolio management; it would focus attention where attention should be focused: on returns in excess of market returns, after adjustment for risk exposures.

The wonder is that so much time had passed before anybody even thought of raising this question. As far back as 1973, Jack Treynor and Fischer Black had made clear that the search for alpha was independent of the decisions relating to exposure to the market as a whole:

> Optimal selection in the active portfolio depends only on appraisal risk and appraisal premiums and not at all on market risk or market premium; nor on investor objectives as regards the relative impor-

---

[*]For an extended description of this whole process, see Anson (2005).

tance to him of expected return versus risk; nor on the investment manager's expectations regarding the general market. Two managers with radically different expectations regarding the general market but the same specific information regarding individual securities will select active portfolios with the same relative proportions.[11]

Treynor's and Black's paper including this paragraph, "How to Use Security Analysis to Improve Portfolio Selection," has an interesting history. Treynor and Black first presented their case in 1967 at a University of Chicago seminar and then sent it off to the Chicago-based *Journal of Business* for publication. According to Treynor: "They hated it. Basically, they believed markets were efficient and that therefore security analysis was a waste of time. We were trying to prove a rational, systematic way to use security analysis if you really thought it was worthwhile. It took years for the *Journal of Business* to come around, but they finally published it in 1973."[12]

And then another thirteen years had to pass before the practitioner community began to stir. In 1986, three colleagues at Goldman Sachs, Eduardo Schwarz, Joanne Hill, and Thomas Schneeweis, published an extended essay on the nature and usefulness of financial futures. In the course of their discussion, they point out that, "Futures allow long-term investors to separate the broad asset allocation decision (stocks versus bonds versus cash) from the choice among assets in each of these categories. This separation [of investment tasks] facilitates specialization in investment management and thereby encourages the development of new money management products. . . . The opportunity to capitalize on specialized investment management skills has yet to be utilized in the long-term money management business."[13]

But nobody was paying much attention. Even though this reasoning makes eminent good sense, the actions it involved in the 1980s were so novel, so far from established procedures, that broad acceptance and practical applications were slow to develop. As late as 1996, the lonely voices of Marvin Damsma, Chief Investment Officer for the pension assets of Amoco Oil (subsequently BP-Amoco), and his colleague, Gregory Williamson, wrote,

Consider for a moment how we tend to think about investment return: most of us see performance figures as one whole number representing the *total annualized return* of a strategy (stocks, bonds, etc.) for a given period. . . . Thus, we tend to *see and compare* data on a one-dimensional plane. Instead, what might happen if we take the total return number and divide it into two key parts: a market return component representing the index return of the asset class invested in, and a second component, the alpha or value-added return? . . . Would it be possible to separate the two? . . . After a little experimenting we determined that the answer is "yes" and we recognized a greatly expanded world of investment opportunity [emphasis in the original].[14]

As the full implication of these strategies began to sink in, investors recognized that they need not pay one manager for both services, alpha and beta. Portable alpha is now the rage. Consider how Mark Anson, former Chief Investment Officer for the huge California Public Employees' Retirement System, or CalPERS, has recently capsulated the new view:

Divide a portfolio into two asset classes, one called Beta and one called Alpha. The Beta Drivers [are] a fund's overall exposure to the financial markets [and] are the domain of the Board of Trustees [who] establish the Policy Risk of the fund. The Board establishes the asset class targets and benchmarks used to drive the beta performance. Alpha Drivers are used to generate added value . . . when markets are misaligned. They are used as a tactical bet to outperform a benchmark. . . . Alpha risk measures a fund's deviation from beta risk.[15]

How could anyone accomplish the feat of disconnecting beta returns from alpha returns? Before the recognition of the wide variety of functions performed by derivatives like options and swaps, and before hedge funds had made short-selling a respectable activity, investors were unaware of any effective way to employ separate sources for the beta drivers and the alpha drivers of their returns. Today, in response to the rapid pace of financial innovation—often called financial engineering—the process of separating beta management and alpha management is commonplace.

These innovations have muted all the obeisance paid over the years to the notion that consistently outperforming the market is an almost impossible task. Instead, investors now talk about alpha as though it grows on trees. One has only to find an effective and reliable manager to pick the luscious fruit.

These new techniques of separating alpha from beta are without question a valuable set of innovations in investment management. Yet, as we shall see in more detail below, their long-run impact will tend to make markets more efficient and alpha more difficult to find, because these strategies will intensify and broaden the search for alpha by sophisticated managers whose quest is for higher fee revenues. Therefore, we should keep in mind investors' exaggerated hopes for what these complex systems may be capable of producing over time.

Today's markets offer many different ways to accomplish the separation of alpha bets from beta bets in the portfolio. As a result, the beta bets—the basic asset allocation that optimally achieves the investor's long-term goals—need not restrict or constrain the allocation of the alpha portfolio among different asset classes. Short-selling, borrowing, and the use of derivatives can finance the alpha portfolio in such a way that the basic asset allocation strategy of the beta portfolio remains untouched. And careful diversification of alpha bets can limit the amount of variance generated by the search for alpha.*

CAPM is no longer a toy or a theoretical curiosity with dubious empirical credentials. It has become the centerpiece of sophisticated institutional portfolio management. Some practitioners even dare to claim CAPM has blasted the Efficient Market Hypothesis into smithereens.

The motivation for this revolutionary development was more than a new perspective on what CAPM could do for investors. After the stock market bubble of the 1990s burst between the end of 2000 and the middle of 2003, many investors were convinced the expected real return on equities in the years ahead would be below the long-term average of around 7 percent. This view was fortified by long-term interest rates on Treasury securities lingering well below the average of 7.1 percent from 1959 to 1999 or 6.5 percent during the bubble years of 1995–1999.

These developments left investors scraping for any opportunity to improve returns without taking on an excessive amount of risk. The wholesale move into so-called alternative investments such as hedge

---

*For a lucid and authoritative analysis of how to optimally combine the beta portfolio with the alpha portfolio, see Kritzman and Thomas (2004).

funds, real estate, private equity, venture capital, and oil and timber would probably have never come about, or allocations would never have reached the substantial degree they did reach, if expected returns on conventional equities and bonds had not sunk to such disturbingly low levels. As a result, this state of expectations made the separation of beta and alpha a more attractive strategy than it might have been if investors had higher hopes for what they could earn in the usual places.

The next two chapters present real-life examples of where these changed perceptions have led. The first example involves a simple solution to the separation of alpha and beta management, developed by the famous bond manager Bill Gross in 1986 almost as an afterthought but clearly in line with these basic concepts. The second example demonstrates how Marvin Damsma moved the Amoco portfolio in the direction he was so early in recognizing as optimal. The third example, from Barclays Global Investors, provides insights into how elaborate the process of separating of alpha from beta can be. Then we turn to another methodology that also focuses on separating alpha from beta, but from a different and novel perspective.

13

Making Alpha Portable

"*That's Become the New Mantra*"

It may seem odd to turn to the world's largest and best-known firm in the fixed-income management business to enhance returns on a stock market portfolio. Nevertheless, an enhanced stock market return is precisely what Pimco Investment Management of Newport Beach, California, has delivered since the late 1980s under the direction of Pimco's CEO, Bill Gross. Gross is the subject of a biography called *The Bond King,* which aptly sums up both his fame and his legendary capabilities in the bond market.[1]

Called StocksPLUS, Pimco's strategy has provided a consistent alpha, or excess return over the S&P 500 Index fund since the late 1980s at no increase in risk. That includes beating the S&P 500 in the worst of the bear market of 2000–2002 by 150 basis points before fees and 120 points after fees.

So far as I know, this product was the first to seek alpha from a source outside the primary asset holding in a fund. The alpha in the StocksPLUS strategy comes from the return on an actively managed bond portfolio. In modern parlance—but an expression never used by Pimco—StocksPLUS "ports" the alpha from the bond portfolio to the S&P 500 Index fund, and that is why these kinds of arrangements are called "portable alpha."

StocksPLUS has delivered a positive alpha over the S&P 500 return in 194 of the 195 rolling three-year periods from July 1989 through

September 2005. Over the ten years ending September 2005, Stocks-PLUS outperformed the S&P 500 50 basis points a year after fees, with a total return showing a 99.9 percent correlation with the S&P 500. The volatility of the two portfolios was almost identical: The monthly standard deviation of StocksPLUS returns was 4.49 percent compared with 4.44 percent for the S&P 500.

StocksPLUS started out small. By 1995, only five clients held a total of $1 billion in the fund. By 2000, the number of participants had quadrupled, but the assets under management had grown tenfold. At latest count, the fund held twenty-seven portfolios and $18 billion in assets, including about $1 billion in an open-end mutual fund—minimum purchase for institutions $5 million.

◈

Who dreamed up such an odd combination in the first place? The inspiration for the StocksPLUS strategy came from a passing remark by Myron Scholes, who was a Pimco director in the mid- to late 1980s. Scholes was so impressed with Pimco's many talents in bond management he suggested to Gross that the Pimco team should be able to transfer those talents to new areas beyond plain-vanilla fixed-income strategies.

Although Scholes was no more specific, he provoked Gross to dream up a novel direction in which to deploy Pimco's skills. Gross's first idea never got anywhere because his partners thought it was too far out and it involved managing equities. But the second idea—"Myron's lightbulb," as Gross describes it—drew directly on a relatively new product called BondsPLUS. Gross recognized at once that the design of BondsPLUS could work just as well for equities as for bonds.[*]

Both strategies are simple in concept and in execution. The tough part in both instances depends on skilled active bond management to provide the bonus return, or alpha. The basic methodology involves buying futures contracts instead of the actual security that clients want to own—in BondsPLUS the actual security is a Treasury issue or a high-grade corporate bond, while in StocksPLUS the actual security is an S&P 500 Index fund.

---

[*]Unless otherwise specified, all quotations are from personal interviews or correspondence.

In BondsPLUS, assume that Pimco wants to maintain exposure to a particular Treasury note in its actively managed fixed-income portfolios. Thanks to the development of an active and sophisticated market for futures contracts in Treasury issues, Pimco can achieve the desired exposure to the Treasury note by buying a futures contract on that issue rather than purchasing the note directly. A futures contract gives the holder the right to ask for delivery of the actual issue at a specified date and will fluctuate in price exactly as the underlying issue fluctuates. Why futures? Buyers of Treasury futures do not have to put up cash equal to more than about 5 percent of the actual purchase price and can cover the difference with collateral typically consisting of high-grade debt securities.

But there are no free lunches. The price of a futures contract includes an allowance for a financing rate to cover the 95 percent of the purchase price that has not been provided in cash.* In BondsPLUS, Pimco aims to invest the collateral to take advantage of inefficiencies in the market for short-term Treasury securities as a means to outperform the embedded financing rate in the futures contract.

For example, Gross had noted that yields on the shortest-term paper in the money markets were significantly lower than the returns available in the six- to twelve-month portion of the market. He smelled a chance for alpha. As he explains the excessively large spread in yields, overnight liquidity was so essential for money market funds, and even some institutional equity managers, these investors had no choice but to accept yields deemed "too low" under more normal circumstances. Liquidity was more important than return in such cases.

This insight was just one of several opportunities Gross perceived for outperforming the embedded interest rate in Treasury futures. By exploiting these kinds of inefficiencies, Pimco could deliver to its clients the return on Treasury issue they wanted to hold plus more than enough to cover the financing costs involved in the futures contract.

---

* The financing rate is typically three-month LIBOR, which is the customary financing rate in many financial transactions similar to this one. LIBOR is the London Interbank Offered Rate, essentially the same kind of high-quality credit as the rate on federal funds in the United States, which is the rate commercial banks charge one another for overnight borrowing of reserve balances at the Federal Reserve Banks. The price of the S&P 500 futures contract also includes an adjustment for the expected dividends on the S&P 500 over the life of the contract, which will not accrue to the holder of the futures.

In StocksPLUS, the basic exposure is an S&P 500 Index fund, while the alpha is derived in the fixed-income market in much the same way as in BondsPLUS. The StocksPLUS strategy does not buy the S&P 500 Index fund. Rather, it invests in futures contracts on the S&P 500, just as the bond strategy invests in futures contracts on issues it wanted to hold in the basic fixed-income portfolio. The operational methodology in the two cases is identical. In StocksPLUS, investors buy futures contracts on the S&P 500 by putting up about 5 percent margin and borrowing the remainder, secured by collateral. If Pimco can invest the collateral so that it returns more than the financing cost embedded in the futures contract, the client will have earned the return on the S&P 500 Index plus the extra return on the collateral. That extra return will have been ported to the S&P 500 Index fund from the returns of the collateral investments.

The alpha in this arrangement is in that excess—or shortfall, as the case may be. Thus, the beta exposure, the S&P 500, is separate from the alpha exposure from fixed-income investing, and the whole procedure is essentially self-financing.

◈

Pimco opened the pathway to portable alpha, but by now that pathway is jam-packed. Bob Jones, Managing Director at Goldman Sachs Asset Management, described portable alpha in the spring of 2006 as, "That's become the new mantra."[2]

Three money management firms were involved in portable alpha strategies back in the late 1980s: Jacobs Levy, Martingale Asset Management, and Numeric Investors. But, so far as I have been able to discover, one of the first programs along these lines for a pension fund was developed by Marvin Damsma and his team at the Amoco Oil Company (later BP–Amoco and now plain BP).

I first met Damsma in the 1980s, when his job was Third Deputy Controller of New York City. Despite his unassuming title, Damsma was responsible for many billions of dollars of pension money for the New York City Employees Retirement System (NYCERS), as well as the retirement systems of the city's police force, firefighters, teachers, and the Board of Education. For his efforts, the City paid him $72,000 a year, which he describes as just enough "to let me live on Nathan's hot dogs and pizza." Nevertheless, Damsma is grateful for this experience. He told me he had an excellent relationship with the trustees, who were particularly helpful in their support of a new, innovative bond investment program. This program not only produced better returns for the city's pension funds, but also helped establish several new bond indexes that are in wide use in today's bond market.

Damsma is an iconoclast with an iconoclastic sense of humor, wide-ranging curiosity, and a determination to get things done. For example, his cynical description of typical pension fund sponsor issues includes the following:

Set time frames:
    —Pension Fund: 10–20 years
    —Trustees and Management: 1 quarter
Typical investment goals:
    —Risk: "Don't Lose!!! Ever!!!"
    —Compliance: "Stay in bounds."
    —Liabilities: "Match 'em! Beat 'em!"

Damsma is most critical of conventional pension fund planning for the basic portfolio structure, where asset class allocation—the beta choices—drives all the efforts to earn alpha. Under conventional planning, the process begins when the sponsor, often with the assistance of an outside consultant, hires active managers for major asset classes like large-capitalization U.S. equities or foreign equities. Nothing odd about that, but then the sponsor also expects the managers to outperform their benchmarks. Damsma is convinced that performance and efficiency can be significantly improved when the two forms of risk—beta and alpha—are viewed under two separate lenses.* The rest of this story explains why Damsma feels so strongly about that viewpoint and how he implements his own fund's separation of the risks of market exposure from the risks of seeking excess return.

---

*That does not mean the two have to be under two separate managers, but they usually are these days.

After about two years of political pressures and carping from a few overseers with no serious knowledge of investments and finance in New York, Damsma was happy to accept an invitation in March 1987 from the Amoco Corporation in Chicago to assume the more impressive title of Director—Trust Investments and a salary rather higher than what New York City was willing to pay him. His primary responsibilities covered a defined-benefit pension fund whose assets today exceed $7 billion plus a company savings plan now worth some $9 billion. Together, these two employee benefit packages account for nearly 40 percent of the company's total trust assets. Their performance matters.

The new association at Amoco provided Damsma with more than just a salary commensurate with his responsibilities. Damsma persuaded the company to give him the leeway to experiment with an innovative but clearly unconventional perspective on pension management he and his team had developed. He was convinced this approach would make a significant difference to the company's bottom line. Today, increasing numbers of pension funds and many other kinds of fiduciary funds are following in Damsma's wake. What was once perceived as radical has become today's conventional.

Damsma's goal was to separate the search for alpha from the basic asset allocation decisions of the pension fund's policy (or beta) portfolio. The effort to take a different tack began in 1990–1991, long before investing in hedge funds was a popular development in pension fund management. Damsma hired six market neutral managers. As these managers held both short and long positions, Damsma believed they could double the expected alphas that a skilled long-only manager would have earned in conventional strategies.* But Amoco still wanted to end up with a beta (policy) portfolio of 55 percent in U.S. equities, 20 percent in foreign equities, 16 percent in fixed income, 9 percent in alternatives, and nothing in cash.

Damsma provided the resources for these market neutral managers by selling off part of the pension fund's active exposure to the U.S. stock market. While this action resulted in a reduction in the portfolio's allocation to U.S. stocks, that return stream could easily be re-

---

*Market neutral managers hold both short and long positions that roughly offset each other. When properly managed, the portfolio is relatively immune to fluctuations upward or downward in the market as a whole.

stored by simultaneously purchasing futures contracts on the S&P 500. The long/short (market neutral) strategies effectively canceled out their equity exposure and provided a cash return resulting from the broker's rebate on the short position, plus—Damsma hoped—an alpha return.

As in the Pimco case, purchasing the futures contracts generally required only a small cash deposit (e.g., margin of about 5 percent to 6 percent) on the notional value. By structuring the investment process into two components—the S&P 500 and the return of the market neutral strategies—Damsma's team was able to "port" the alpha (excess return) from one strategy to the asset class (or beta) needed to maintain the desired policy portfolio asset class weightings.

The key to this process is the separation of the alpha decision from the beta decision. There are many different ways to accomplish that step, and the hedge fund structure is only one. For example, the separation can take place from a long-only strategy, from a strategy of earning some short-term interest rate target (LIBOR plus), currencies, convertible arbitrage, and even from a strategy of investing in real estate via real estate investment trusts.

Philosophically, this approach is precisely what Jack Treynor and Fischer Black had in mind in 1973 when they said, "Optimal selection in the portfolio depends only on appraisal risk . . . and not at all on market risk." It also is the same approach as Bill Gross's in StocksPLUS, where the market return comes from the investment in S&P 500 futures, but the alpha comes from bond management, with the cash collateral for the futures funding Gross's activities in the bond market. In this case, the alpha on the bond market return is "ported" back to the position in the S&P 500.

There is a practical difference between StocksPLUS and the former Amoco strategy, however. Pimco (usually Gross himself) manages what is called the "alpha engine," the pool of funds he invests in the bond market in the hope of generating an alpha return. At BP–Amoco, Damsma hires outside managers for both the basic asset class beta return and the search for alpha.

At this point, Damsma provided me with an interesting comment on what he had been able to accomplish: "We were quickly learning that one of the biggest benefits was not only in alpha land but in risk control. As we all know in the investment business, risk is guaranteed; return is not. We were learning that uncorrelated alphas allowed us to manage and potentially reduce the residual risk—the tracking error against a stated benchmark (e.g., the S&P 500)—for a better overall trade-off between volatility and total returns. The BP team also recognized that separating alpha and beta into their individual components was allowing them to look at the whole portfolio risk management process in new and different ways from the traditional model of long positions in asset class exposures only."

Today Damsma and his team are still pursuing this general framework but in a more sophisticated fashion and with more satisfactory return patterns (at least to date). As Damsma describes it, "We are embarking on a 'new strategic partnership structure.' Our goal is to build a more efficient alpha engine by allowing managers greater freedom to use their 'alpha frontier' to construct an alpha portfolio geared to our risk/return targets. In other words, managers are free to select from a preapproved universe of their strategies to build a portfolio targeted to our desired alpha and residual risk ranges. We refer to this entire combination as *the alpha engine*. After that, we assign the desired beta or benchmark portfolio for the manager that best meets our policy needs."

Under Damsma's supervision, the manager making the beta adjustments uses futures or swaps as required (the porting process). In short, BP is asking managers to develop an "internal" fund of funds for alpha purposes only and then adjusting the betas (or asset classes) back to their desired benchmarks or policy portfolio (which could be a traditional market or a liability-targeted return stream). One minor disadvantage: "It does create some additional costs that will modestly reduce the overall net alpha to be earned."

On the other hand, there are several subtle benefits to this multi-strategy concept. Damsma is giving managers more freedom to act within their capabilities. Most important, the managers in this new structure now assume a greater role in the search for and production of alpha, which means they go beyond providing just a product universe or menu to choose from. Assuming the managers have genuine skill, they can choose among many strategies in their tool kits (i.e., asset classes or betas) to produce a more consistent target alpha via better management of residual risk.

There is a valuable by-product of this process. Freedom means the manager is clearly accountable for the results. The manager cannot pass the blame for poor performance back to Damsma or the BP investment committee. At the same time, the expectation of success is greater, and the specifications of what is required are well defined. The arrangements also get away from talking about the usual criteria, such as beating the median manager or being in the second quartile with its broad range of outcomes. Furthermore, this system makes the manager responsible for risk parameters as well as returns. But it also involves a need for greater governance at the sponsor level to monitor whether the manager's procedures and behaviors are consistent with guidelines or agreement terms and are generally prudent.

Under this system, Damsma's fund can more effectively tailor the incentive structure to align the interests of managers with the fund. The system is, in fact, similar to the types of performance fee models often used in the hedge fund world. Unconventional as this structure may be for plain-vanilla management of stocks and bonds, it may in fact be more beneficial than the usual setup when a multitude of strategies are involved. Finally, the sponsor workload shifts from asset class performance and quartile comparisons to a greater focus on the optimal policy risk/return structure (which can be market or liability related), a more complex governance program, and new opportunities to create alpha and manage risk in terms of a more inclusive manager framework.

What is Damsma actually up to? He explains his approach to the separation of beta management from alpha management in terms of several key points:

- The whole methodology involves a different way of thinking about the investment process for all kinds of institutions—not just pension funds but endowments, foundations, insurance companies, other trusts.
- It is a process for financially reengineering the return streams from various asset classes.
- It is a process offering new ways to manage risk.

- It does not create alpha. It merely separates the search for alpha from the search for basic asset class returns. Alpha and beta are generated in separate strategies.
- The methodology does not eliminate risk. It rearranges the sources of risk.

The process begins with judgments about the total return a portfolio is expected to achieve in both "alpha" and market (beta) return space. I use quotation marks around the alpha here, because the alpha return is the amount by which the portfolio's actual return differs from the market return or a target benchmark return. There is no guarantee the alpha return stream will be positive. In many, if not most, cases, alpha will tend to be negative, particularly after fees.

What about risk? Elroy Dimson of the London Business School once described risk as meaning more things can happen than will happen.[3] This is really a fancy way of saying we do not know what is going to happen. Nevertheless, it provides a useful framework for thinking about risk. As Damsma emphasizes, the beta return has a distribution of possible outcomes that differs from the distribution of outcomes for the residual, or alpha. This distinction is the key to Damsma's whole process, because it means the investor can separate the management of the two components of total return. That capability is what has made the whole conceptual analysis so appealing to Damsma's team and has led them to pursue what they learned from the experience with the six long/short managers back in 1991. As Damsma describes it, the procedure is "a form of investment Legos."

An example illustrates how Damsma might port an equity-produced alpha to a bond return (such as the Lehman Aggregate Index) to create a "synthetic bond strategy" with an equity-like alpha. As in the case of StocksPLUS, the goal would be to improve the overall return of the bond segment of the portfolio. In order to accomplish this goal, Damsma would generally begin by taking funds from various bond strategies and reallocating them to an equity strategy.

For simplicity, we will assume here that the equity strategy is a strategy to outperform the S&P 500. If the assets were invested in a strategy to extract an expected alpha of 200 basis points from the index, the manager would simultaneously seek to eliminate or neutralize the equity market return in order to produce only the residual return, or alpha and its residual risk structure. Remember, the objective here is only to earn the alpha from an equity strategy, not to take fund resources away from the bond portfolio to invest in equities as an asset class.

This goal can be achieved via several methods. For example, the manager could initiate a swap with an appropriate counterparty, where Damsma's fund would swap the S&P 500 return directly for the return of the asset class (or beta) needed—in this case, bonds. Or, the sponsor could sell S&P 500 futures short and then purchase futures on a bond index. It could also short individual stocks, where the sponsor is not allowed to hold the cash proceeds—the broker involved holds the cash—but the broker pays the sponsor a small amount, called the cash rebate, from the interest the proceeds of the short sale will generate. Then the sponsor could buy futures to reintroduce the desired new beta exposure to the bond market.

Either way, the equity return (or equity beta) producing the alpha would be eliminated and replaced with the bond return. Assuming the equity manager can produce the 200 basis points of alpha, that alpha in the equity area would now sit atop the bond return.* The overall policy allocation would remain intact, and the only difference would be a higher overall alpha (in this case 200 bp as against a traditional bond alpha of, say, 50–100 bp). Note, once again, that some additional cost may be incurred so the overall alpha could be less than 200 basis points. Regardless of the level of alpha ported, negative as well as positive, this modest amount of financial reengineering could help build better overall alpha return streams Amoco can then blend with traditionally produced alpha streams.

Damsma's approach does not limit the variety of different strategies the investor can employ to produce alpha. That is one of its great attractions. The investor's choices cover a wide range, including traditional long-only strategies designed to outperform the market or some segment of it, strategies designed simply to outperform the cash

---

* Note that we are assuming a positive alpha of 200 basis points. It could just as easily go the other way, with a negative alpha.

return (LIBOR plus), arbitrage strategies, long/short equity or hedge fund strategies, various fixed-income strategies, and currencies—among others.

As the returns among this group of possibilities are uncorrelated, they do not add any systematic risk to the total portfolio. Each strategy is risky, but the distribution of possible outcomes in each strategy has no relation to the distribution of possible outcomes of the other strategies—or of the basic exposure to the market represented in the policy portfolio. The beta portfolios that produce the alpha are likely to be eliminated or neutralized, so there will be no reason to be concerned about their risk impact. Consequently, this process provides freedom to seek alphas wherever the manager believes they might be found.

The bottom line of Damsma's team's current thinking is what he calls "asset allocation goes 2×." That is, asset allocation for alpha, and asset allocation for beta. Traditionally, sponsors begin with the asset allocation decision—for example, stocks, bonds, cash, or real estate. Under this process, the investor must accept the alpha that goes with the primary beta allocation. While this has been accepted practice, such a process may be limiting the opportunity to earn additional alpha or reduce a sponsor's risk levels. Under the new model, investors start with the decision on how to allocate the assets into alpha-seeking strategies, and then focus on the beta decisions.

Damsma sums it up this way: "We think of our portfolio as simply a set of alphas and betas. They do not have to be directly linked or connected to each other as in the traditional long-only model. In addition to better risk control, there are many other benefits." One of the primary benefits from separating the management of beta bets and exposure to alpha opportunities is in how it helps simplify replacing an underperforming manager or maintaining a successful manager. In the traditional setup, where a long-only manager is responsible for both an asset class (beta) and producing an alpha in that asset class, Damsma could not replace Manager A with Manager B unless Manager B had the same beta exposure. In short, Damsma could pick only from managers within the same asset class so as to prevent the fund's policy portfolio from getting out of balance.

The reverse is also true. If a manager under the traditional arrangements produces an alpha, but due to policy targets the fund now exceeds its target allocations to that particular asset class, the sponsor is often forced to reallocate money from the manager to fix the over-weight. Goodbye alpha! By separating the management of beta bets and the efforts to earn alpha, the search for alpha need not interfere with maintaining the desired exposure to the basic asset classes.

Treynor and Black had it right: "Optimal selection in the active portfolio depends only on appraisal risk and appraisal premiums and not at all on market risk or market premium."

Jeff Hord is a Managing Director at Barclays Global Investors responsible for developing innovative strategies to provide clients with the basic asset allocations their policy portfolios require—the beta bets—while still seeking to generate alpha independently of the beta bets. Hord's teams have a worldwide focus and work with pension plans, foundations, endowments, and individual investors.

In the autumn of 2002 Hord developed a strategy called the Asset Trust platform that enables investors to make independent alpha and beta decisions, that outperforms traditional methods, and that accomplishes these objectives in a cost-effective fashion. His innovation was to use a trust format to bring together two clients with radically different investment objectives in a single account to improve the return each client is expecting to receive.

One of these investors, called the Active Investor, typically has retained an active manager who expects to contribute an alpha return over its benchmark. The other investor, called the Index Investor, prefers the passive approach of index fund investing but participates because the Trust promises to pay an extra margin over the index fund return without any increase in risk.

How does Hord accommodate under one roof two investors with such different approaches to the investment problem? The Index Investor facilitates the objectives of the Active Investor by contributing the shares of an index fund to the Trust. As an incentive to make this move, the Index Investor receives the precise return on the index plus a specified spread over the index as compensation for providing its capital to the Trust.

These arrangements have four additional attractions to the Index Investor. The Index Investor pays no management fee; is guaranteed against any tracking error against the return of the chosen index; pays no transactions costs; and has a priority claim on the assets of the trust. The Index Investor is therefore better off as a participant in the Trust than just holding the index fund position in a conventional manner.

The Active Investor has made the high-octane choice of utilizing the Index Investor's capital. The Active Investor assumes all the risks and pays all the costs, but will also receive whatever is left over from the performance of the investments in the Trust after the Index Investor has been paid. Collateral provided by the Active Investor will insure the Index Investor against loss if those residual earnings in the trust—the alpha—are negative instead of positive.

In an example, suppose the Active Investor is a charitable foundation with total assets of around $2 billion and the policy asset allocation structure: 55 percent in U.S. marketable equities, 10 percent in fixed-income, and 35 percent in a package of alternative investments like private equity and hedge funds. Some of these assets are invested passively in index funds; others are under active management.

At a recent meeting of the foundation's investment committee, one member draws the attention of his colleagues to the absence of any international equities. He recognizes that this omission is motivated by a strong conviction that the U.S. markets would outperform the international markets. On the other hand, a short time ago he had heard a presentation by an active international equity manager with an outstanding record of outperforming the international markets. Highly impressed with this manager's many original insights into the finer points of international investing, the committee member says he wishes they could find a way to turn over $200 million of the foundation's assets to this manager while still preserving the basic asset allocation.

But then where would that $200 million come from? After much discussion, the committee agrees it should stay with the basic policy asset allocation but, at the same time, admits it would like to take advantage of this international manager's talents. The committee's consultant suggests asking BGI to help it find a solution to this dilemma (almost all the foundation's assets were already under either active or passive management at BGI).

The committee meets with a number of BGI strategists. The most interesting proposal comes from Hord, who explains how he could satisfy the foundation's interest in turning over $200 million to the international manager without liquidating any current holdings to finance the shift. His assertion sounds like an impossibility to the committee members, but Hord does have a structure to meet their needs—$200 million to the international manager with no alteration in current asset allocations.

Hord proposes the Asset Trust platform to accomplish that objective. The foundation would be the Active Investor, and Hord assures the committee he would have no trouble finding a suitable Index Investor with a current $200 million investment in BGI's international index fund. BGI would liquidate that international index fund investment and transfer the proceeds to the active international manager. Hord explains that the Index Investor would still be guaranteed the return on the international index fund, and that guarantee would be collateralized by $200 million transferred to the Asset Trust from the foundation's fixed-income assets. For safety's sake, the fixed-income allocation would be converted from BGI's active management to the BGI fixed-income index fund, but the fixed-income return would continue to accrue to the foundation. All earnings on all assets involved would be reinvested.

Let us review what has happened. The Index Investor's holding in the BGI international equity fund has been liquidated, with the proceeds transferred to the foundation's outside active international equity manager. Meanwhile, the Index Investor continues to earn the return on the international index fund, at no cost and zero tracking error, plus the promised spread over that return to compensate it for contributing assets to the Trust. The foundation's actively managed fixed-income portfolio has been converted into an index fund and is now held in the Trust as collateral against the Index Investor's advance of its international equity assets.

How do matters appear at the end of the first year? Let us assume that the active international manager will have provided an annual total return of 12 percent as against the 9 percent annual return on the international index fund. The original $200 million will have grown to $224 million under the active manager's skilled care, while the international index fund would have grown only to $218 million. The active manager will have produced an alpha of 3 percent, or $6 million, for the foundation *without using a penny of the foundation's money.* Nevertheless, the Active Investor—the foundation—has also continued to earn the return on its fixed-income fund, while the Index Investor has accumulated a claim equal to the 9 percent return on the international index fund, just as would have happened if nobody had ever done anything in the first place.

What happens when the foundation decides the time has come to unwind this contraption? Let us assume that this decision arrives after five years and that the return on the active international portfolio has continued to compound at 12 percent a year, while the international index fund's annual total return was 9 percent a year. This means the foundation's assets will have grown to $352 million over the five years, and the index fund liability to the Index Investor would have grown to $308 million. There is an alpha here equal to $44 million.

The active international equity manager will liquidate the portfolio and deliver $352 million to the foundation. BGI would then liquidate the Trust's holdings and turn over $308 million of that money to the Index Investor for reinvestment in the international equity index fund. This leaves a net profit of $44 million on the foundation's account plus the performance on the fixed-income fund within the Trust. Thus, the alpha of $44 million was "ported" from the active international manager to the foundation's fixed-income fund that collateralized the deal.

The story is not necessarily destined to have such a happy ending. Suppose the returns were reversed, with the index fund earning 12 percent a year and the active manager stumbling behind at 9 percent. Now the foundation would have accumulated only $308 million, while the Index Investor would have accumulated a claim of $352 million. The foundation would have to liquidate $44 million from its fixed-income portfolio in order to make good on its guarantee to the Index Investor. There is still a portable alpha in the deal, but the alpha would be negative instead of positive. The Active Investor's choice is far from riskless.

※

Each of these strategies derived from the alpha and beta concepts of CAPM appears to take a different path in order to separate the risks of searching for alpha returns from the risks of investing in asset classes such as stocks and bonds. Yet the underlying structure is the same in every case. The investor adds an active manager to the current set of management teams but does not disturb the underlying asset allocation. The financing of the active manager comes from somewhere else.

The source of that financing can come from many different kinds of sources. In the Pimco BondsPLUS and StocksPLUS strategies, the financing came from the use of futures contracts requiring an up-front payment of cash equal to only 5 percent of the amount involved. At BP–Amoco, Damsma used a variety of techniques to find the cash that financed the search for alpha while strictly maintaining the basic asset allocation mandated by his policy portfolio.

In the BGI Asset Trust case, the Index Investor contributed the assets to be liquidated to finance the active international equity manager in return for a collateralized guarantee from the Active Investor. More frequently, and in more elaborate situations, complex and specifically designed instruments in the derivatives markets provide the necessary financing.

◈

Assuming investors can actually create, recognize, and execute the necessary transactions, portable alpha is more than just a major development in the uses and understanding of the Capital Asset Pricing Model. Its relevance to Capital Ideas goes further than that. Without the use of a variety of forms of options, and the Black-Scholes-Merton option pricing model to price them, the whole process might have languished on the pages of learned treatises like Joanne Hill's, as a brilliant idea without a means of implementation. In many ways, the active and incessantly creative markets for derivatives make the whole process possible.

Nevertheless, the tricks and treats of portable alpha are not the only new perspective on asset allocation and the search for excess returns. Indeed, the next chapter discusses a different and novel approach that provides us with an even deeper understanding of what CAPM is all about. This approach offers a strikingly effective way to solve the policy portfolio problem by providing higher probabilities of achieving alphas with possibly less risk and surely no more risk than with portable alpha strategies.

14

Martin Leibowitz

CAPM in a New Suit of Clothes

I n the world of investment management, Martin Leibowitz is a phenomenon. His collected papers as of 1992 filled a volume of over
1,100 pages—printed in the kind of small type that does not lend itself to skimming or fast reading.[1]

His output since 1992 has shown no signs of diminishing in quan-
tity or quality. Both the *Financial Analysts Journal* and *The Journal of
Portfolio Management* cite Leibowitz as having contributed more articles than anyone else. At the *Financial Analysts Journal,* he has won
eight coveted Graham & Dodd awards for one of the best articles in any
one year (again more than anyone else).

He is the author or coauthor of four additional books. Although he
began his career in finance as a fixed-income guru, Leibowitz turned
early on to the analysis of equity markets as well and has made important
contributions to that area. His career has spanned twenty-six years at the
old Salomon Brothers; nine years as Chief Investment Officer of TIAA-
CREF, the massive pension fund for members of university faculties; and,
since March 2004, at Morgan Stanley, where he is free to write and talk
on any subject that suits his fancy. Just incidentally, he won the Junior
Chess Championship of Tennessee at the age of fourteen, and then, a year
later, a Ford Foundation scholarship from the University of Chicago.

In recent years, Leibowitz has turned his attention to the Capital
Asset Pricing Model as a tool for practitioners in decisions relating to

asset allocation, risk management, and performance measurement. His work bears some relationship to the use of CAPM in structuring portable alpha strategies, but his innovative insights on this model have wider applicability. Indeed, over Leibowitz's long career, he has demonstrated repeatedly how much power theory can contribute to practice.

❖

After studying physics at the University of Chicago from 1951 to 1956, Leibowitz headed west.[*] He told me that when he first saw San Francisco, he "could not believe this place existed on this earth—I gotta move here."[†] He worked for a while at the Stanford Research Institute on projects involving operations research, but in 1959, despite San Francisco's charms, he decided he had to go to New York City: Moving to New York for a year was a decision every young man should make at least once in his life.

His first job in New York was at a computer simulation laboratory, Systems Research Group, where, in a small world, he encountered Harry Markowitz, then developing a computer language he dubbed Simscript. Most of Leibowitz's colleagues at this firm held Ph.D.s in math, which Leibowitz had never bothered to pursue. Math seemed so easy to him there was no point spending time taking courses in it (Leibowitz now characterizes himself at that time as "an arrogant stupid kid"). But later he thought better of that snap decision. He began by taking evening courses at NYU and pretty soon found himself going through the grind of earning a Ph.D. at night.

One day it was time to start earning a proper living. With hindsight, we can say the first steps in that direction were in quite the opposite direction of where Leibowitz has ended up, but in fact the linkages would turn out to be closer than he had any idea at the time. In 1964, he took a job at a carpet manufacturing company owned by a friend's father, a brilliant businessman who had developed a new process for nylon carpeting. Although Leibowitz was convinced that going into business happened to other people, he was instantly intrigued and

---

[*]Leibowitz earned a B.A. degree in 1955 and his Master of Science in physics the following year. At that point, he was still only twenty years old.

[†]Unless otherwise noted, all quotations are from personal conversations or correspondence.

soon decided he loved it. His boss gave him increasing responsibilities in every area of the firm from finding locations and organizing processes for factories to negotiating options for the purchase of land. In the process, he earned two patents in materials handling, while his math turned out to have a practical application when he had to figure out how to cut a roll of carpet for a whole series of jobs with minimum waste.

◼

Now two threads that would change his life started to come together. First, the carpet business was growing so large, Leibowitz tried to persuade his boss it should go public. Second, his new wife's uncle, Sidney Homer, liked to sing carols at home with his family at Christmas time. Homer just happened to be a senior partner at the major Wall Street bond trading firm of Salomon Brothers and Hutzler, where he had moved after a career managing fixed-income securities at the prestigious investment management firm of Scudder, Stevens, & Clark. Leibowitz knew Homer was somehow involved with Wall Street, but he had never heard of Salomon Brothers and had never given a thought to having anything to do with the world of finance. On the contrary.

During a break between Christmas carols, Leibowitz casually asked Homer about what would be involved in the carpet company going public. Salomon Brothers in 1967 was only beginning to move into corporate finance, but Homer said he would look around and see what he could recommend. Meanwhile, however, Homer wondered how much Leibowitz might know about bonds. "Bonds?" asked Leibowitz, "why ask me about bonds?" "Because you are a mathematician," responded Homer, "and I have spent some time trying to write a book about the mathematics of bonds. My calculations failed to work out, so I put the whole thing away and let it gather dust. Maybe you could look at it and tell me where I went astray."

Leibowitz soon found the problem in Homer's work, but he was incredulous that Salomon Brothers had no trained mathematician on its staff. Although Leibowitz had inherited a distaste for Wall Street and finance, he was now fascinated. He switched gears and began trying to persuade Homer to make him Salomon's in-house mathematician.

Homer took a dim view: "Salomon is too crass an outfit for the likes of you," he explained to Leibowitz. Leibowitz was not to be turned off. He asked Homer to let him talk to some of the people and make up his own mind.

What he saw only made the prospects even more irresistible. The main participants in the bond market in the 1960s had been there from the earliest days—commercial banks, savings banks, and insurance companies. There was little trading activity, as most bonds were traditionally buy-and-hold investments. But in 1969, when fears of inflation were running strong, most bonds were selling below par, or their original issue price of 100. The people at Salomon Brothers were trying to figure out how they could arrange swaps of bonds between institutions, establishing losses for tax purposes but without any shrinkage in the expected yield to maturity of the bond positions. They were not having much success in working out a procedure for the necessary calculations, so almost every trade was figured on an ad hoc basis.

Leibowitz found the whole scene irresistible. In June 1969 he bade farewell to the carpet company, took a cut in salary, and installed himself at Salomon Brothers right on the trading floor at a tiny desk but with access to a huge time-share mainframe IBM computer. Soon he was solving the problem the others had been wrestling with for so long. Now even senior partners were joining the line at his desk to find out how they could work out these swap-loss deals for their customers.

Then something even more wonderful happened to make Leibowitz just about the most important man at Salomon Brothers. In those days, nobody at Salomon Brothers knew how to calculate the price of a bond even when they knew the yield to maturity as well as the coupons that were clipped semiannually to collect the income on the bond. And vice versa: Given a price and the coupon, they did not know how to calculate the yield. But all was not lost. Everybody had a copy of what was called "the yield book," and could look up the answers there. The yield book was a great fat volume, easily confused with a bible from a distance. But the yields in the yield book only went as high as 8 percent, and, as fears of inflation heated up in 1970, long-term bond yields rose above 8 percent. What to do? Nobody had the slightest idea of how to price a bond with a yield above 8 percent.

Leibowitz had no trouble doing the calculations on his time-sharing computer in a matter of seconds, and pretty soon he was more in demand than anyone else at the firm. The line to his desk was even longer than in the past. As he described it to me, "I had the only yield mechanism in town—maybe in the whole world. Now they really needed me. With the senior partners fighting with each other to be at the head of the line, *I became discovered!* I had gained a little footing at Salomon Brothers." He even received a title, Director of Investment Systems. At that point, Leibowitz was also Adjunct Assistant Professor in Quantitative Analysis at the NYU Graduate School of Business Administration.

The turmoil in the financial markets persuaded Sidney Homer to pick up the threads of his book, and soon he and Leibowitz were writing it together. The manuscript turned into *Inside the Yield Book: New Tools for Bond Market Strategy,* published in 1972 by Prentice-Hall and the New York Institute of Finance.[2] The very notion of a bond market *strategy* was revolutionary in a field where, as I mentioned earlier, bonds had been traditionally bought on a buy-and-hold basis.

Active management of bond portfolios followed quickly in the wake of the book's publication, while buy-and-hold almost vanished. The bond market has never been the same, and fixed-income investing has become more elaborate, more complex, more challenging—and often more risky—than the stock market. Thanks to the work of Homer and Leibowitz, theory now played an important role in helping to transform the practice of bond management in ways no one had in any way anticipated. In his testimonial to Leibowitz's update of 2004, Andrew Carter, one of the pioneers in active fixed-income management, had this to say about the book: "Sidney was the historian, and Marty is the poet, of the most important financial market on earth: bonds."

In 1995, after having been at Salomon Brothers for twenty-six years, Leibowitz received a call from John Biggs, chairman of the university retirement fund TIAA-CREF, then the largest pension fund in the world with assets of $300 billion. Biggs invited Leibowitz to take over as Chief Investment Officer of CREF—the equities portfolio of TIAA-CREF. Leibowitz's first instinct was to turn the invitation down, as life at Salomon Brothers was exciting, rewarding, fun, and educational.

Biggs called on some of the TIAA-CREF trustees to bring pressure on Leibowitz, and his resistance gave way when he began hearing from Steve Ross and Bob Merton about how much they needed him. "It was wonderful," Leibowitz recalled. "I was into everything, with terrific people." In fact, Leibowitz soon became Chief Investment Officer for all TIAA-CREF investments, which included equities and bonds and substantial positions in real estate. He was so valuable to the organization that in 2001 TIAA-CREF managed to keep him on three years beyond the normal employee retirement age.

By 2004 Leibowitz had no choice but to look around for a job, for the first time in many years. Morgan Stanley came along, and, as Leibowitz describes it, "clasped me to their bosom. I was made a Managing Director of the firm and given a position where I could pursue anything I wished, study any area of finance, write as much or as little as caught my fancy." Who could resist that opportunity? Leibowitz's irrepressible curiosity was soon let loose.

New and interesting questions came into view as Leibowitz became involved as a trustee or adviser to the investment offices of major institutions such as the Carnegie Foundation, Harvard, the University of Chicago, and the Institute for Advanced Study at Princeton. All these institutions were wrestling with the same set of problems. Expected returns on the conventional policy portfolio were insufficient to meet their needs. At the same time, the search for higher expected returns seemed inevitably to lead to higher risks than investment committees deemed to be appropriate.

Every time investment committees and investment staffs looked into the matter, they bumped into the same barrier: They could not achieve their investment objectives unless they could liberate themselves from the constraints of the traditional asset classes. In many ways, this was the easy part. More complex puzzles were awaiting solution, such as understanding the nature of the risks institutions might be taking on in the search for higher returns, or clarifying the impact of new asset classes on the portfolio's overall level of risk.

Institutions needed an entirely new design for the process of asset allocation. At the same time, they were going to have to confront greater or different kinds of risks if they hoped to generate higher returns.

Putting this kind of problem before Leibowitz was like handing him a lifetime supply of vintage wines from Bordeaux. He thought the matter through and came up with what he is convinced can develop into a powerful solution to the dilemma. The plan he developed, as he describes it, is "only part of Markowitz, part of Sharpe, part of Grinold-Kahn." All the rest of it is Leibowitz. His scheme has roots in CAPM but turns important parts of CAPM on their heads.

❖

The path to the solution struck Leibowitz quite by accident in 2003, when he happened to be preparing for a presentation to a large group of endowment fund managers. This particular group had been in the forefront of diversifying portfolios away from the traditional stock–bond mix into a much wider range of asset classes such as real estate investment trusts (REITs), direct investments in real estate, hedge funds, private equity, venture capital, and, to a lesser extent, direct investments in raw materials such as oil and timber. These alternative asset classes had expected returns higher than the returns on equities, or they were assets like market neutral hedge funds with lower expected returns than equities but with lower-than-proportionate volatility of returns.

Determining the fundamental risk characteristics of an overall portfolio with this widely varied mix of assets was far from obvious. Leibowitz recognized that any portfolio would always have a primary risk factor—a source that would dominate the overall risk of a portfolio. Leibowitz began his search by attempting to understand how the various pieces of the portfolio would interact and how the relative volatilities of the different asset classes would affect the overall volatility of the portfolio.*

In the old days, everybody was 60 percent U.S. equities and 40 percent bonds, more or less. Then the percentage allocation to U.S. equities was the primary source of risk in institutional portfolios, and therefore one could easily gauge the risk level of the overall fund by that explicit percentage number. But the results of that calculation could be irrelevant in portfolios where the traditional exposure to stocks and bonds had been cut back significantly and a proliferation of different— and often less liquid—kinds of asset classes had been introduced. In this

---

*In much of the work described in the following pages, Anthony Bova, Leibowitz's colleague at Morgan Stanley, was coauthor of the published material.

new world, the answer to the portfolio's risk structure was a lot less obvious. U.S. equities were still there, but a smaller proportion of the total portfolio than in the past.

Nevertheless, there would be no way for investment officers to understand the fundamental impact on risk of the new asset classes unless they had a means for calculating the comovement between the new asset classes and U.S. equities—a relation Leibowitz refers to as "implicit beta effects." To give himself an example to work through, Leibowitz put together a covariance matrix, which is a table showing the cross-correlations of each asset class with each of the others. For clarity of explanation, Leibowitz added to the table the expected return and volatility (standard deviation of annual returns) of each asset class.

Here is is an oversimplified view of what Leibowitz's covariance table looked like in his example, together with how he employed this covariance matrix to calculate the implicit betas of the new asset classes. For the purposes of this particular example, Leibowitz combined REITs with the traditional assets classes of U.S. stocks and bonds. Note, for later reference, that Leibowitz assumes here that the expected risk premium on U.S. equities works out to be 5.75 percent, or the expected return on equities at 7.25 percent less the expected return on cash of 1.50 percent. U.S. equities also all assumed to have a beta of 1.00.

Leibowitz's Return/Covariance Matrix

			Correlations			
Asset Class	Expected Return	Volatility[*]	REITs	U.S. Equities	U.S. Bonds	Cash
REITs	6.50	14.50	1.00	0.55	0.30	0.00
U.S. equity	7.25	16.50	0.55	1.00	0.30	0.00
U.S. bonds	3.75	7.50	0.30	0.30	1.00	0.00
Cash	1.50	0.00	0.00	0.00	0.00	1.00

$$\text{REIT beta} = \text{Correlation with U.S. equities} \times \frac{\text{Volatility of REITs}}{\text{Volatility of U.S. equity}}$$

$$= 0.55 \times \frac{14.5}{16.5}$$

$$= 0.55 \times 0.8788$$

$$= 0.4833$$

[*]Standard deviation of annual returns.

By weighting each of these individually calculated implicit betas by the weight of the asset class in the total portfolio, Leibowitz was able to calculate the overall beta of the portfolio. He then proceeded to perform this set of calculations for each portfolio in the endowment group. Once the job was done, and Leibowitz looked over the results of his effort, he encountered three surprises—outcomes he had not expected to find.

First, despite the wide variations in asset allocation, the total beta values of all the different funds fell into a narrow range of between 0.55 and 0.65. The funds looked different from one another, but at their cores, the similarity was profound.

Second, the total volatility of almost every fund also fell in a narrow range, in this case between about 10 percent and 11.5 percent. As with the betas, this tight range prevailed despite wide variations in asset class distributions in this group of funds. The surprise here was even bigger than that. Back when most portfolios were 60/40 stocks versus bonds, the total volatility of the portfolio also fell in the range of about 10.0 percent to 11.5 percent, and equities were the primary source of risk. *With all the fiddling around, these investors had not changed the portfolio's primary source of risk—U.S. equities!*

Finally, the total betas of the portfolios—the weighted comovements of each asset class with equities—explain more than 90 percent of the total volatility of each portfolio. U.S. equities remain as the prime source of risk, or volatility. The volatility of the portfolios is essentially unchanged, even though chunks of the original allocations to stocks and bonds had been moved into multiple asset classes whose market behavior did not appear to have any resemblance to the performance of stocks and bonds. Equally interesting, the volatility of each of the funds is about the same as it had been even though every fund is more diversified than it had been in the past. On the basis of what Leibowitz had already learned from this exercise, and in view of what additional analysis would produce, he summed up his approach for me: "It asks new questions, but it also cuts through a lot of the mustard."

And why had nobody ever noticed this strange state of affairs before? What could explain these bewildering results? All the institutions had reduced their U.S. equity positions, and some had slashed their bond allocations to single-digit percentages of the total in order to fund the new asset classes they were adding. On a dollar-weighted basis, university endowments had cut their U.S. equity positions from 45 percent of the total portfolio in 1995 to 32 percent in 2005, while fixed-income and cash fell from 30 percent to 20 percent. This contraction in holdings of conventional assets, involving just about a quarter of the total portfolio, had been redistributed in varying proportions to foreign equity, absolute return (hedge funds), private equity, and real assets.*

On an equal-weighted basis, the changes were less dramatic but in the same direction, with U.S. equity down to 46 percent from 49 percent and fixed-income plus cash down to 26 percent from 37 percent. The difference between the dollar-weighted and equal-weighted data indicates that the larger institutions dominated this process. Nevertheless, the smaller institutions were heading in the same direction, especially in reducing their allocations to cash and bonds.

Charitable foundations followed a similar path. According to the leading consultant firm in this area, Cambridge Associates, foundation allocations to U.S. equities shrank from 43 percent in 1995 to only 27 percent in 2005; holdings of bonds and cash over the same ten years dropped from 33 percent to 15 percent. The dollars liberated from U.S. equities and bonds were transferred to global equities other than U.S., to both marketable and nonmarketable alternatives, and to equity real estate.†

With such radically changed patterns of risk and interactions within investment portfolios, one would have expected entirely different patterns of volatility and other metrics of risk. But Leibowitz could find almost no alteration in the risk of these portfolios after the major transformations had taken place on the asset side.

The answer to this puzzle, he discovered, lay in the cutbacks in *both* stock and bond positions, the conventional asset classes. If the drawdown had been only from U.S. equities or only from U.S. bonds, the results would have been different from what actually took place, especially among the larger institutions. If only the relatively volatile asset class of

---

*All data in this paragraph and the following are from the National Association of College and University Business Officers (NACUBO), kindness of the Yale Endowment Office.

†Data from Foundation Conference Group Asset Allocations, Cambridge Associates LLC, courtesy Dwight Keating of the Benedum Foundation.

equities had been the funding source for the less volatile alternative asset classes, both the beta and overall volatility of the total portfolio would tend to fall. Using only the relatively stable asset class of bonds as the funding source, both the beta and overall volatility of the total portfolio would tend to rise. But using the *combination* of high-beta equities and low-beta bonds to finance the move to mid-beta alternatives was kind of a wash, leaving the basic risk structure of the portfolio more or less as it was before the alternatives were even under consideration.

As Leibowitz and Bova express it, "The exchange of a mid-beta funding package for a new mid-beta asset results in a relatively unchanged portfolio beta. Moreover, the allocations to alternatives tend to be fragmented, so the *total* beta (calculated by weighting the individual betas by the asset class weight in the portfolio) dominates the fund's volatility."[3]

And this finding led Leibowitz to arrive at another counter-intuitive conclusion: "Contrary to conventional wisdom, diversification, as typically pursued, has a relatively minor impact on fund volatility." It is the betas—the exposure to U.S. equities—that define the riskiness of the total fund.

So much for the betas. How can all these elaborate calculations of risk exposure help us in discovering and measuring alpha, the excess return of an asset or portfolio after adjustment for risk? In Leibowitz's framework, the answer to this question appears at first to go back directly to the Capital Asset Pricing Model. With a closer look, important differences from CAPM make their appearance.

Each asset class has an expected return, or investors would shun that asset class. And some component of the return expected from each asset is derived from its comovement with U.S. equities. But that comovement has to be less than 100 percent, or the fund would be investing in U.S. equities! As a result, Leibowitz points out, "These residual returns—the difference between the total expected return and the expected return due to the comovements of these asset classes with equities (the beta, in other words)—can be viewed as 'alpha-like' and variously referred to as structural alphas, diversification alphas, allocation alphas, embedded alphas, or, most important, implicit alphas."

Note that Leibowitz does not use the word alpha without a qualifier. This is the point at which his vision of the structure of portfolio risks and returns begins to part way with the pure formulation of the Capital Asset Pricing Model. In a paper published in the September/ October 2005 issue of the *Financial Analysts Journal* and carrying the imaginative title, "Alpha Hunters and Beta Grazers," Leibowitz makes this distinction clear:

> Unlike truly active alphas, *allocation* alphas are broadly accessible through a semipassive process of moving [a fund] toward an effective strategic allocation. . . . [Thus], allocation alphas are quite distinct . . . from the truly active alphas derived from tracking down— and bagging—the fleeting and elusive opportunities that arise from market inefficiencies. . . . They are quite different concepts . . . and are pursued in different ways.[4]

Whatever you call them, Leibowitz's alphas are passive "in the sense that there is no presumption of positive outcomes from the selection of superior managers or from direct active investment by an asset managers." The source of these passive alphas is varied: They may derive from market inefficiencies, the volatility structure of the typical institutional portfolio, and how much the fund ends up holding U.S. equities as the fundamental risk factor instead of a global market index or a policy portfolio baseline.

Leibowitz calculates these passive alphas quite in the spirit of the CAPM. Taking REITs once again as an example, Leibowitz provides the steps necessary to calculate the passive alpha for REITs under certain plausible assumptions. In the table below, the assumptions are in plain text while the results of the calculations are in bold type:

Calculation of Passive Alphas: The Example of REITs[*]

Total expected return on REITs	6.50%
Less risk-free rate	−1.50%
REIT risk premium over cash	**5.00%**
Less REIT beta × Equity risk premium at 5.75% = 0.4833 × 0.0575 =	−2.78%
Passive REIT alpha	**2.22%**

[*] The equity risk premium of 5.75 percent in this example is derived in Exhibit 1 on page 2 of Leibowitz and Bova (2005b), where it is assumed to be a total equity expected return of 7.25 percent minus the return of 1.50 percent on cash.

All alphas calculated in this manner add directly to the portfolio return. In this instance, REITs will add 2.22 percentage points to the total expected return of the portfolio, adjusted for the weight of their position in the portfolio. The REIT alpha is passive, or implicit, in the sense that it is not the outcome of active management, but it is nonetheless real, because it is an excess return adjusted for its beta factor. That is precisely what CAPM specifies.

On the other hand, this perception of alphas introduces three features that are not part of the traditional CAPM line of analysis, which is why Leibowitz at the outset described his approach as "only part of Markowitz, part of Sharpe, part of Grinold-Kahn."

First, "all alphas add directly to the portfolio return, [because] these passive alphas will always have a zero correlation with U.S. equity." But second, these alphas will tend to add little or nothing to the volatility of the portfolio as a whole, because the allocation to each is relatively small and the set of assets involved are only weakly correlated with one another—except through their correlation with equities. The combination of small allocations and weak correlations among the alternative asset classes adds the third and equally surprising feature of the analysis: "The benefit from multiasset diversification is to be found not in reduced volatilities, but rather in enhanced fund returns."

Essentially, these enhanced returns are the result of choosing asset classes that produce more return than would be expected merely on the basis of their betas. Assuming, for the sake of example, that returns on REITs have no correlation with equities, moving cash—a zero-beta asset—into REITs has no impact on portfolio volatility, but REITs do have a higher return than cash. This example is extreme, but it illustrates Leibowitz's point that the attraction of multiasset diversification is in higher returns rather than lower volatility.

As usual, there are no free lunches. More realistically, if we move from cash to REITs, the volatility of the portfolio is going to increase. Every time you add any asset class from cash, the beta of the portfolio will rise. Investors who wish to add a new asset class but at the same time feel obliged to hold the portfolio volatility constant will have to take some kind of counter-step to get back to the prescribed volatility level. In many instances, that step will involve making a modest cutback in the equity position, even though less in equities will mean some reduction in expected return.

The arithmetic in a simple example would work out like this. Assume, as above, that REITs have an expected return premium over cash of 5.0 percentage points and a beta of 0.48 and that equities have an expected return premium over cash of 5.25 percentage points and a beta of 1.00. Now assume we take 10 percent of the portfolio that is sitting in cash and buy an equivalent amount of REITs. We would be adding 50 basis points (10 percent of 5.0 percent) of additional return to the portfolio. But we cannot count on that full 50 basis point addition, because we have also added 0.048 of beta. Liquidating 5 percent of our equity position, with a beta of 1.00, would restore the desired portfolio volatility but at a cost of 29 basis points of expected return (5.00 percent of 5.75 percent). As a result, the net gain in expected return from buying the REITs works out to 21 basis points (50 − 29).

This example involves moving from cash with zero volatility to a new asset class with positive beta volatility. When a new asset class is funded by liquidations from asset classes other than cash, the results will differ from this example. When the beta-based volatility of the liquidated asset classes varies only slightly from the beta-based volatility of the added asset classes, adjustments are either unnecessary or minor in impact.

Leibowitz seems to have found the pot of gold at the end of the rainbow. These alternative assets with returns higher than equities add to the portfolio's return without adding to the portfolio's total risk. Why not have it all? Why bother to hold any conventional stocks and bonds except as a token? Instead, why not stuff the portfolio with alternative assets like hedge funds and private equity? Why not go even further, and just stuff the portfolio with the single highest alpha source instead of spreading the weight across multiple alpha assets?

Good questions, but in fact the chief investment officers of major institutional investment funds have chosen *not* to have it all. They must have a clear and widely held answer to these questions or they would not hold such responsible positions.

The answer is the familiar word "constraints," which really means "you can't have it all even though you may want to have it all." Leibowitz has another expression, "dragon risks," taken from ancient mythology when people believed the earth was flat and feared "there be dragons in the spaces beyond." As he puts it, dragon risks "capture the cornucopia of concerns that lead to these constraints." Or, to put it differently, there are "beyond-model" risks—risks whose precise nature and structure are unknown.

These are the kinds of risks fiduciaries shun, not for lack of temptation, but because of the *consequences* of taking such risks based on assumptions that—like all assumptions—could turn out to be wrong. Many unrewarded risks will be forgiven by investment committees and trustees, but dragon risks are the ones where being wrong has major consequences for the institution and surely for the investment officer, and where nobody is going to be much interested in the nature of the original expectations on which the risk may have been based.

Just as examples of dragon risks—and with full recognition that his list is partial—Leibowitz lists: "underdeveloped financial markets, liquidity concerns, limited access to acceptable investment vehicles or first-class managers, problematic fee structures, regulatory or organizational strictures, peer-based standards, 'headline risk,' and insufficient or unreliable historical data."[5] To this extended list, we could add the probabilities that these assets will perform entirely differently from expectations or that the distribution of outcomes will include higher probabilities for extreme outcomes than allowed for in the original planning. Under these circumstances, the whole process could turn into a disastrous mess that would be far from easy to unwind. No wonder chief investment officers have chosen not to have it all.

And now we come to a curious but inevitable conclusion, a concern that owes more than just a part to Harry Markowitz and his single-minded emphasis on the importance of diversification. In financial markets, the notion of too much of a good thing has a lot of truth to it. If institutional investors begin to swallow their inhibitions about dragon risks and load up on alternative assets at the expense of traditional investments like U.S. stocks and bonds, a point will come when outcomes will be entirely different from what was anticipated. For one thing, as Leibowitz phrases it, "In those cases where the alpha core can be expanded beyond the usual boundaries, the alpha volatility and excessive dragon risks may begin to challenge the fund's beta dominance."[6] In other words, the whole scheme could fall apart if the field becomes overcrowded. And in addition to that unhappy eventuality, return expectations could turn out to have been exaggerated because the arrival of too many investors drives up asset prices and reduces prospective returns.

In an ironic sense, the Capital Asset Pricing Model and the Efficient Market Hypothesis would become descriptions of reality rather than abstract models. Everybody would want to own the same portfolio, and that portfolio in effect would become The Market. Then all prices would clear without variation, everyone would have the same risk tolerance, everyone would earn same rate of return, and everyone would be taking on the same level of risk.

To some extent, this process is already well under way. REITs are a conversion of real estate from an asset you can kick to a piece of paper trading in the financial markets. Private equity used to be priced in a negotiation between seller and buyer; now private equity is priced in auction markets. And this transformation is spreading to other formerly nonliquid asset classes like timber and commodity markets in general. When even the measurement of alpha is a matter of debate, the market behavior of any asset class—even stocks and bonds—is likely to be unstable and unpredictable.

These developments are more than idle curiosity. It is the fashion today for institutional investors like pension funds, university endowment funds, and charitable foundations to decide upon an overall asset allocation structure to be in place for the indefinite future. The resulting portfolio, known as the Policy Portfolio, is the benchmark against which actual returns are measured and the guiding policy statement of the fund's desired exposures in the marketplace. When new and different players are entering asset markets they never even considered before, and when the whirlwind of new derivatives products affects every corner of the financial markets, the pricing, volatility, and expected returns of asset classes are not stable. They are subject to change without notice. In that world, Policy Portfolios should not be a constant star but a variable, subject to constant review and testing.

Despite these varied concerns, Leibowitz finds the opportunities compelling when he views the risk/return trade-off of nontraditional assets from the perspective of the overall portfolio. He pays due respect to dragon risks, but he believes investment committees should arrive at their asset allocation decision in a direction opposite from what most such investors employ.

Instead of just thrusting these assets into the portfolio through "tortured reoptimizing," as opportunities come along, or as consultants, salespeople, and peer pressures may suggest, Leibowitz would *begin* the asset allocation process by settling right up front on the maximum acceptable limits for these nontraditional asset classes, or the "alpha core." He would then optimize these alternative assets to produce the highest return for any acceptable level of standard volatility risk as well as the dragon risks. Then, and only then, would he turn to the equities and fixed-income positions—the "swing assets" as Leibowitz calls them—and adjust the allocation of those assets to achieve the desired risk level for the portfolio as a whole.

Under Leibowitz's recommended strategy, the traditional view of the risk/return trade-off is still in place, but the focus has undergone a dramatic shift. The source of return now derives from the alpha core. The source of total portfolio risk management derives from the allocations between equities and fixed-income. Now portfolio volatility management is the sole purpose of the swing assets while the alpha core is the source of portfolio expected return. In this framework, then, the appointed tasks of the portfolio's components are clear and the opportunities for maximizing expected returns while controlling the risks—optimization, in other words—are no longer cluttered with extraneous considerations.

The analysis in this chapter covers just a small sample of Leibowitz's innovative contributions to portfolio management and investors' understanding of the driving forces in capital markets. From *Inside the Yield Book* in 1972 to the more recent series of essays on beta-based asset allocation, Leibowitz's work covers an enormous range as well as remarkable depth of analysis.

On pages 85–86 of *Capital Ideas,* I recount Leibowitz's celebration of Bill Sharpe in October 1990 when the news arrived at a professional meeting that Sharpe had won the Nobel Prize. In reciting Sharpe's many extraordinary contributions, Leibowitz used the word that Jews always recite at Passover, "Dayenu," which means what God has done for us already would be more than enough even if He had never helped us again. As Leibowitz proceeded to list Sharpe's achievements, he added "Dayenu!" at the end of each item.

In May 2005, Leibowitz received the Award for Professional Excellence, the highest award given by the CFA Institute, and I had the honor of participating in the ceremonies. Taking up Leibowitz's own theme, this is what I had to say on the occasion:

> If he had only given us *Inside the Yield Book*—Dayenu!
>
> If he had only given us immunization of pension fund portfolios—Dayenu!
>
> If he had only stuck to fixed-income and never even fussed around with equities—Dayenu!
>
> If he had only given us the franchise factor—Dayenu!
>
> If he had only given us beta-plus, structural alphas, portfolio triage, and core alpha—Dayenu!
>
> If he had only given us thirty-three articles in the *Financial Analysts Journal* and nineteen in *The Journal of Portfolio Management*—Dayenu!
>
> If he had only given us all the wonders I have omitted—Dayenu!
>
> If he had only been the nicest, the most generous, the most entertaining friend all of us are honored to have—Dayenu!

15

Goldman Sachs Asset Management

"I Know the Invisible Hand Is Still There"

Fischer Black moved from MIT to Goldman Sachs in 1984. Shortly after his arrival in New York, Black expressed one of his most enduring observations: "The market appears a lot more efficient on the banks of the Charles River than it does on the banks of the Hudson."

Black's quip was welcome news to his associates at Goldman. Goldman has always been among the most aggressive trading firms on Wall Street, and aggressive trading did not look like a matchup with Black's unshakeable devotion to a world shaped in every dimension by the Capital Asset Pricing Model and equilibrium. There was a sigh of relief at Black's recognition that Wall Street and Cambridge, Massachusetts, are different places. Indeed, Black soon became an enthusiastic guide to the development of quantitative modeling for a wide range of profitable strategies, in fixed-income as well as in equities, while the Goldman staff gradually learned how to take advantage of Black's quirky methods and personality.

One day in 1986, Black interviewed a man named Bob Litterman for a position in fixed-income research. Litterman was a Ph.D. from the University of Minnesota who also had had a stint of teaching at MIT, but his primary interest was in econometrics—the application of statistical methods to economic and financial forecasting. Black took a dim view of econometrics, because it failed to take equilibrium into consideration as a determining force. In fact, two years later, in a paper carrying the blunt title of "The Trouble with Econometric Models," Black asserted that "Certain economic quantities are so hard to estimate that I call them 'unobservables.' Two of these are the expected return on the stock market and the risk premium on bonds."[1] Yet the econometricians kept trying.

Black began the interview with Litterman by asking, "What makes you think that an econometrician has something to contribute to Wall Street?"[2] Litterman defended himself to a point where Black decided not to oppose Litterman's application, despite his doubts about the value of econometrics. Even though Litterman never converted Black to an enthusiastic econometrician, Black and Litterman ended up in a remarkably creative partnership that involved an ironic turnabout: Black succeeded in converting Litterman into an enthusiast for equilibrium. As Litterman put it to me, "Fischer's insights became my career."[*]

Soon they were working together to build models for derivatives, for hedging strategies, for risk management, and for asset allocation strategies. All of this work culminated in 1992 in a model immortalized as Black-Litterman.[3] The Black-Litterman model performs the remarkable feat of combining the notion of equilibrium expected returns with a wide variety of active management strategies. This achievement is the equivalent of putting a Yankee fan and a Red Sox fan in the same room without any arguments starting up between them.

Litterman has explained equilibrium expected returns in these words: "Equilibrium is a state of the world in which expected returns of assets are proportional to their exposure to priced risks. The Capital Asset Pricing Model is a useful approximation, although one can entertain more complicated, and perhaps more realistic, equilibrium models with multiple periods and multiple priced risks."[†]

---

[*] Unless otherwise specified, all quotations are from personal interviews or correspondence.
[†] See Markowitz's criticism of CAPM, above, pp. 104–108. As Markowitz has pointed out in a more recent article, if investors are constrained in how much they can borrow and sell short, "the Black-Litterman expected returns will typically not imply the specified market holdings." See Markowitz (2006).

Litterman started his career at Goldman in fixed-income research, but he was later transferred to head of risk management for the firm as a whole. This was an interesting assignment, carrying a lot of authority, but Litterman hoped he could reach a point where Goldman would transfer him from a staff responsibility to responsibility for managing a business. He was eager to find an opportunity to put into practice the theoretical tool kits he and Black had been developing. In 1993, he tried to persuade Jon Corzine, then managing partner of the firm (subsequently Senator from New Jersey and then Governor), to shift him to portfolio management, but Corzine's response was, "Nah, Bob, we have much more important things in line for you."

Litterman watched developments in the asset management business with close attention. Cliff Asness, a Chicago Ph.D. in finance and Eugene Fama's former teaching assistant, had organized the quantitative research group in 1994. In 1995, Asness launched the Global Alpha Fund, with returns "off the charts"—92.8 percent in 1996, followed by 34.8 percent in 1997. Litterman was fascinated: "That looked like a pretty easy way to make money," he told me. Asness would leave Goldman with part of his group at the end of 1997 to start AQR Capital Management, now a flourishing, $30 billion investment management organization.

Following Asness's departure, Litterman finally landed on the asset management side, with responsibilities for both quantitative strategies and creation of a risk management function (he was relieved of the risk management responsibility later, when Jacob Rosengarten, the head of risk management, was elevated to report directly to the division heads). Litterman is now responsible for Quantitative Equities, a group headed since its inception eighteen years ago by Bob Jones, and which manages approximately $100 billion in a variety of equity portfolios. Most of these portfolios are in long-only format, but a small portion is positioned in long/short strategies, including hedge funds. Litterman is also responsible for Quantitative Strategies, which manages everything else, primarily hedge funds, fixed-income, and global tactical asset allocation (GTAA). This group is coheaded by Mark Carhart and Ray Iwanowski. In addition, Litterman oversees Global Investment Strategies, a consulting operation for clients headed by Kurt Winkelmann that covers risk budgeting, asset allocation, and asset/liability management. Litterman describes his job as "the baseball coach, not one of the players on the field." Returns have been high and growth rapid throughout Litterman's domain, with assets running into the hundreds of billions.

When I asked Litterman the precise size of assets under management, he responded, "One thing is certain—we used to be a low-risk quantitative shop, but now we are far and away the biggest hedge fund manager in the world in terms of hedge funds managed directly in-house. Beyond that statement, I should have a simple answer, but the reality is a little more complex." He was right: The answer he provided was complex, but it reveals a lot about how the Goldman asset management business functions.

"We have two different metrics for assets under management, not including the volatility adjustment we employ," Litterman explained. "Part of the money under management is in conventional strategies in which the assets are owned directly by the clients. The remainder consists of managing portable alpha strategies, or what we usually refer to as overlays."

Litterman then offered an example. "Suppose a client asks us to manage some money on a notional portfolio of a billion dollars in a portable alpha strategy that would track a designated benchmark with an average error over time of no more than 100 basis points (one percentage point). At the end of the day, that request is really asking us to produce $10 million of active risk, or tracking error, for the client, as opposed to passive strategies like index funds. But as this is a portable alpha strategy, we are not actually investing $1 billion of the client's money. We are working it out with a derivatives strategy that requires perhaps $40 million of margin to cover the financing of the strategy." And then he added another view of the same concept: "The client could just as well contract for 50 basis points of active risk on $2 billion, in a straightforward management proposition instead of a portable alpha strategy. Then we would be managing the same $40 million of capital in the same way but now calling it $2 billion of notional assets."

The result is a multipart set of calculations of assets under management. Litterman takes the position that simply adding up notional assets tells you little about Goldman's level of activity. Goldman distinguishes between low-volatility portfolios and high-volatility portfolios, and considers this distinction especially important in hedge fund and portable alpha strategies. A portfolio of $10.0 billion at 4 percent volatility is roughly the equivalent of $2.5 billion at 16 percent volatility.

"The key point is that volatility is a central consideration in all our decisions and in all our strategies," Litterman observes. "We do not shun risk, because, along with Fischer, we are convinced that expected returns vary directly with risk—that is what Fischer meant and what I mean when I refer to 'equilibrium.' This belief is at the core of all our strategies. Equilibrium, and the notion of the world moving toward equilibrium, is at the heart of the way we think about the world. I know the Invisible Hand is still there."

◈

Day-to-day portfolio management has to go forward, and Litterman recognizes you cannot just sit back and let the forces of equilibrium run the show: "We are determined to keep volatility under tight control so that it does not exceed the clients' specifications as to how much benchmark risk and tracking error they can tolerate. Volatility is never easy to live with."

Because volatility is difficult to live with, investors must also control how much active risk their managers are taking. How far are managers' bets driving the portfolio away from its benchmark guidelines? How closely does the actual portfolio at any given moment differ from the policy portfolio reflecting the client's risk aversion and long-term view of expected returns in the markets?

As Litterman sees it, "Composing portfolios is all about allocating your risk appropriately. Most people miss on that and don't spend enough resources on it."

The risk of any portfolio is inherently a finite commodity. More important, the client's overall capacity for risk taking is also inherently a finite commodity. The client has presumably allocated that scarce resource to various managers, and risk management is therefore a process of resource allocation in a scarce environment for both the client and for the portfolio manager. This point has broader relevance. It is not just the risk of the portfolio that is a finite commodity—the client's overall capacity for taking risk also has a limit. The more clearly that limit is defined, the more successful the portfolio management process will be.

As with allocation of any scarce resource, a budget is appropriate. In the words of Litterman's colleague, Jason Gottlieb, the risk budget is "the diagnostic tool of risk decomposition [whose] aim is to identify the sources and magnitudes of risk taken in the aggregate portfolio . . . to help us understand whether a program is being adequately rewarded for its active risks."[4]

The risk budget sets forth in detail the misalignment between the client's policy portfolio and the actual portfolio in three areas: asset allocation; beta or "the sensitivity of the manager's portfolio to the swings of its underlying benchmark"; and stock selection risk, which is revealed in the tracking error incurred after adjusting for the beta effects. "A high ratio of stock selection risk," Gottlieb explains, "is typically a sign of high-quality risk taking."

Stock selection is "high-quality risk," because adding value from the selection of individual securities—difficult as it may be—is less of a challenge than timing markets or making bets on sectors (for example, capital goods versus consumer staples) or making bets on style (for example, growth versus value). Bets in security selection are easy to diversify because there are thousands of choices available, while the risks of over- or underweighting entire asset classes and styles or sectors involve choices among only a few opportunities. This means the consequences of being wrong in any one bet in market timing or style management are more serious than the consequences of being wrong in choosing between Stock A over Stock B in a portfolio composed of a large number of individual positions.

※

The optimal route to successful investing requires the investor to take a position on market efficiency as an essential first step, by asking, "How likely is it that we will be able to outperform our benchmarks, after adjustment for risks taken?" The answer to that question then leads to the next choice: "How do we divide up the assets between active and passive management?" The stronger the belief in market efficiency, the higher the allocation to passive management should be.

This dialogue should come at the very beginning of the investment process. "You have to decide on the allocation between beta and alpha," Litterman explains. "Yale and Harvard have expressed the view that markets are not perfectly efficient and that returns can be generated from risks uncorrelated with the market, so they go right for alpha." Litterman takes a different viewpoint: "I take a view similar to

Fischer Black's, which is that markets are very efficient, but not perfectly efficient."

That statement about market efficiency is the foundation on which Black and Litterman built their model; a view on market efficiency continues to be a critical element in all asset management under Litterman's responsibility. Litterman extends Black's observation with an argument directly out of *Capital Ideas*. "It is guys like us," he pointed out to me, "highly disciplined and creative portfolio managers, who cause the markets to move toward efficiency. With the returns we have been generating, I am not worried that markets are fully efficient—yet. But they are becoming more efficient all the time, and fast. The world is going quant, and there are no secrets! Alpha is in limited supply and hard to find. The devil is in the details, and there are a lot of details, thank goodness. That is how quants like us can generate the kinds of returns we have produced."

Litterman enjoys translating his concepts into visual terms. "It's like fishing," he suggests. "In the past, when you wanted to catch fish, you threw your line out and waited. Now there are many fewer fish out there, which means you have to use better technology than just throwing your line out. Only a few places understand that, and they are catching a lot of fish. Nevertheless, we're pushing the world toward equilibrium, where risks and expected returns line up and making money from active management becomes more and more difficult."

This vision is the same vision Black had thirty years ago. "We see it every day in the markets," Litterman continues. "We operate in the most liquid markets in the world, but we have an impact on prices even in those markets. We are having increasing difficulty determining whether something is attractive or unattractive. Is the expected return above or below its equilibrium value? If you don't have equilibrium, you're floating in space. We are never going to reach equilibrium, but *equilibrium is the center of gravity*. The market is doing its job."

This peroration is not just philosophical musing. It translates into specific views of how to operate in a market that is close to efficiency. For example, Litterman explains, "Short-term trading opportunities like Sell-Ford-Buy-GM are now arbitraged away rapidly. Only those with the most efficient processes for executing transactions continue to make money. We focus on longer-term prospects. We search in all areas—currency, stocks, bonds—for attractive opportunities. Those investments take too long for the traders. That's fine for us—we can hold it that long."

Jeremy Grantham, Chief Strategist and Chairman of the investment management firm, Grantham, Mayo, Van Otterloo, is well-acquainted with major institutional investors addicted to short-term opportunities and fearful and impatient when offered investments that take longer to pay off. Echoing what Paul Samuelson has to say on this subject, Grantham explained this bias in a letter to his clients, "Very long time horizons are fine in theory, but committees in real life have to deal with an investment tolerance of about three years, far too short to receive the main risk reduction benefits of mean reversion. Committees still generally respond to pain by moving away from it."

Grantham draws a notable conclusion from the tendency of investors of all stripes to respond to pain by moving away from it. The process has caused stocks to become more volatile than they would be if longer-term views prevailed, and "that being the case . . . outlier events like the 1929 crash pack their full enormous punch. . . . The irony for now is that most institutions have been given the glorious, natural advantages of a long horizon and choose in most cases not to use it."[5]

Goldman, on the other hand, welcomes volatility as opportunity as long as they can control it. Diversification is the primary form of volatility control, and all the Goldman strategies diversify by investing in markets around the world. But alpha is the name of the game in active management, and the freedom to make longer-term bets increases the opportunity to create alpha. The result is the gold at the end of the investor's rainbow: a high Sharpe Ratio. The Sharpe Ratio is a measure of return relative to risk. Specifically, the Sharpe Ratio is the ratio of a portfolio's realized return, minus the return on a riskless asset, divided by the volatility of that return. Higher is always better than lower—a bigger bang for the buck.

Litterman pays close attention to the Sharpe Ratios of the portfolios under his supervision. "We still lose money all the time, between the good months. Nothing is easy. Nevertheless, we have been creating a Sharpe Ratio of 1.0 for ten years running, and that's huge. In the market as a whole, the volatility is between three and five times as high as the expected return." I asked Litterman whether he thought Goldman could sustain a Sharpe Ratio that high into the indefinite future. "Absolutely not," he responded. "Neither can we create unlimited wealth. Something has to give. . . . New competitors show up every day, and they know a lot. The academics have been describing this environment for fifty years."

As Litterman says over and over, "It's all about managing risks." The focus on risk management, however, does not mean that Litterman believes in any way that low risk is preferable to high risk. Control is what matters. Higher risk at a given Sharpe Ratio means more return, because the ratio is return divided by risk; holding the ratio constant, taking increased risk should lead to higher returns.

Litterman is fascinated that so many investors are averse to taking active risk. Given a basic exposure to the equity markets—that is, beta—he believes there is an optimal amount of active risk associated with whatever Sharpe Ratio you assume. Most investors take too little active risk, with 90 percent or more of their total risk coming from beta—from the volatility of the market itself. In that case, they are behaving as though the ratio of alpha they expect to earn relative to the volatility of that active risk will work out to be only 0.01 percent to 0.05 percent. That is a razor-thin number. Litterman goes on to explain further: "If, for example, you expect a Sharpe Ratio of only 0.25, which is the approximate Sharpe Ratio of the equity market, then you should allocate your risk equally between beta and active risk. If you expect a Sharpe Ratio above 0.5—a return as high as one-half the volatility you experience—then clearly you want active risk to be the dominant risk in your portfolio."

Conservative investors holding a diversified portfolio half in equities and half in fixed-income can expect positive returns *in the long run,* but need to be realistic. Litterman's group estimates the long-run equity premium at about 3 to 4 percentage points above bonds, although many economists currently expect less than that. This 50–50 portfolio, then, would create a real (inflation-adjusted) return of roughly 1.5 percent to 2.0 percent over the long run—before fees and taxes. "There is no way to obtain a higher return without taking more risk," Litterman argues. "But you do not necessarily have to put the entire portfolio into a mode of higher risk. If you can find skilled active managers who can get concentrated exposures to their capabilities to generate alpha, you can hope to generate a lot higher return with relatively little increase in overall portfolio risk."

In addition, many investors fail to recognize what diversification can accomplish for them in reaching for higher returns. "Consider hedge fund returns," Litterman suggests. And then he adds, "You would have to put 100 percent of your capital in hedge funds to get 3 percent active risk, because the returns are so diversified. And institutional investors put less than 10 percent in hedge funds—which doesn't even move the needle."

Goldman's quantitatively managed business is attracted to high volatility the way bees love nectar. If, as Litterman believes, risk and return are closely related in markets that are constantly driving toward equilibrium, volatility is a good way of extending your capital. Assuming you can live with returns that vary a lot in the short run, the odds are good you will earn a higher return over time. Thus, you will make more money on a billion dollars invested for your clients at high volatility than you would earn on the same billion at low volatility.

"In the best case," Litterman adds, "when a skilled manager offers a high volatility fund containing only alpha—with no systematic exposure to variations in the market itself—an investor can always manage exposure to this risk simply by determining how much capital to put into it. This is a sharp contrast to what the investor has to do with a low-volatility fund: Use leverage and pay higher fees in order to arrive at the same capacity for return generation."

This observation has important implications for investors in hedge funds. Many hedge funds do not offer pure alpha. Instead, they provide a rather opaque mix of alpha and beta, making the investor's ability to manage overall portfolio risk much more complicated. In order to generate higher levels of exposure to a skilled hedge fund manager's alpha, the investor would have to invest additional capital in the fund. This move would involve paying higher fees, and then the client would still be exposed to the relatively obscure higher beta risk. Attempts to hedge against such a risk would be no simple matter.

Risk management and an appetite for risk may be crucial, but they are only one side of the coin of high returns. In this environment, transactions costs make all the difference, because low transactions costs permit the execution of active strategies that would underperform at higher transactions costs.

Thanks to technology and competition, the quant team now pays a fraction of a cent per share in trading equities—and sometimes even zero. That result requires high skill in all of the most sophisticated trading techniques. For example, there are electronic networks in which investors transact anonymously with each other across computers, or program trading in which dealers bid on large stock portfolios on the basis of their characteristics rather than knowing the individual names held. In algorithmic trading, a relatively new procedure, positions are either liquidated or accumulated in a series of transactions instead of in just one big transaction. The computer then makes the decision to trade, depending on whether price movements indicate the market will be receptive at any given moment, or to refuse to trade if it appears the transaction would drive the price away from the price at which the investor hopes to settle.

"The process permits new strategies," Litterman continues, "but then we are constantly getting bigger, which means our impact on prices when we trade may also grow bigger. And so, we are intensely focused on minimizing transactions costs. Paper portfolios make money all the time, but the question is reality. For an investor as large as Goldman, measuring and minimizing market impact is essential. Market impact even matters in the process of asset allocation. Through our trading, we are, in effect, experimenting with markets every day all around the world. Whenever we trade, we watch for the ripples of our actions, which, big as we are, are still hard to spot. We want to make sure it stays that way."

Much of Goldman's work in asset management derives from the Black-Litterman model devised in 1992. Black and Litterman derived the model from the counter-intuitive notion that investors can combine active management with passive management in the same portfolio. Accordingly, Black-Litterman describes a strategy for a single portfolio built around two separate subportfolios, one reflecting equilibrium—expected returns lining up in relation to the covariance of portfolio with the market—while the other is a portfolio expressing a manager's active views of expected returns from asset classes or from individual securities within asset classes. The trick is in how Black and Litterman manage to combine a portfolio based on market efficiency and a portfolio based on bets on inefficiency into one portfolio incorporating both viewpoints.

This strange blend of equilibrium and active management was developed as a solution to a stubborn problem in the mean/variance optimization process, the fundamental approach to asset allocation dating back to Harry Markowitz's famous 1952 article, "Portfolio Selection" (see *Capital Ideas,* pp. 41–60). In this article, Markowitz sets forth the concept of an "efficient portfolio" as a portfolio that maximizes expected return per unit of risk (variance or volatility) or that minimizes risk per unit of return. The optimizer selects efficient portfolios from the assets under consideration by combining the estimates of expected return and risk for each asset with the covariance (or sympathetic movement up and down) of each asset with each of the other assets under consideration. The goal is to maximize the portfolio's expected return while minimizing all the covariances so that the portfolio is as diversified as possible.

Optimizers present a difficult problem, however. As professional investors describe it, optimizers are not "well behaved." Optimizers are typically partial to assets showing low covariances with the other assets or combinations of assets with high correlations. These features tend to dominate estimates of expected return or risk for each of the individual assets under consideration. Any inconsistency between two sets of inputs like expected returns and risk—which happens frequently when these two inputs are estimated separately—is treated by the optimizer as an opportunity. Many of the assets the optimizer tends to favor—such as real estate, timber, private equity, and emerging market equities—have relatively low liquidity or high-volatility returns or fall under the rubric of Leibowitz's dragon risks. Owners of conventional portfolios are uncomfortable with badly behaved optimizers that recommend too high an allocation to those kinds of assets, because trading them can be ruinously expensive or because they are too risky or too unconventional for conservative tastes. When that happens, the optimizer has been "badly behaved."

The optimizer's behavior can be improved by instructing the optimizer to allocate no more than a designated percentage of the total portfolio to assets that are uncomfortable to own. But while these constraints may make the optimizer better behaved, they also create a new dilemma: Too many constraints dilute the advantages of using the optimizer in the first place.

The problem of how optimizers misbehave first came to the attention of the quantitative analysts at Goldman Sachs in 1989, not long after Litterman had become head of fixed-income research. The head of fixed-income management in Goldman's Tokyo office had asked Litterman to develop a model for building global fixed-income portfolios that would be appropriate for Japanese investors. The task soon expanded to building a global model for composing fixed-income portfolios for Goldman's clients all over the world.

Litterman was uncertain as to how should he begin this assignment, and decided to consult Black. Black was interested in the challenge, but it was not his habit to think of models in terms of the real world. Equilibrium, as always, was the launching pad for his approach, but now Litterman feared Black was going to leave him more confused than enlightened. As he recalls this episode: "To me, asking questions of what would happen in equilibrium, well, was an interesting exercise in algebra, but not a serious question. Nevertheless, Fischer told me the whole problem could be solved in a simple mean/variance optimization. So I went off to the computers to fire up the optimizer and discovered what everyone knew: the optimizer was badly behaved—at least everyone knew it but me. I had never carried out an optimization."

This problem was especially serious in working on global bond portfolios in developed markets, because bond yields and foreign currency rates tend to be highly correlated with one another across international boundaries. This combination will inevitably provoke bad behavior by the optimizer. In this instance, the inputs were forecasts of bond yields six months out. A change of just one-twentieth of a percentage point, or 5 basis points (and the uncertainties in the Litterman's data were much greater than 5 basis points) in the forecast for one country would dramatically change the recommended weights in the portfolio. Major constraints on both maximum and minimum holdings were essential if the final output were to look in any way like an acceptable portfolio. Under these conditions, the optimizer was, without question, badly behaved and virtually useless.

In desperation, Litterman went back to Black and complained about the optimizer's behavior. "The bad behavior is well known," Black replied, "which is why most people using optimizers put constraints on the outputs." Litterman resisted the suggestion. "No value from that," he argued. "You put in what you want to get out of it."

Black suggested an alternative approach. He happened to have just published a paper that developed an equilibrium solution to the problem of how much foreign currency risk to hedge in global portfolios.[6] The paper makes no reference to the behavior of optimizers; its focus was on currency hedging. Litterman thought Black's idea sounded awfully academic and remained skeptical of the practical value of this approach.

But Litterman learned that trying out Black's recommendations was more productive than staring at a brick wall. He recognized that the currency issue is critical in global portfolios, but he had been unable to determine how far to go in hedging against currency fluctuations. Black's article on universal hedging suggests you can derive the answer to that question by optimizing the trade-off between the risk of currency fluctuations and the expected return of the portfolio. With no constraints and no views, you put into the optimizer the equilibrium expected returns for the fixed-income assets and the currencies along with the volatilities and covariances for each asset under consideration. Then, the optimizer will tell you to hold the global fixed-income market portfolio with the currencies hedged according to Fischer's universal hedging ratio. "That's great—it gives a perfect starting point," was Litterman's first reaction. "If you have no views, then hold the market cap portfolio."

This was an important first step. The economists' inputs Litterman had been using had led to what he called "crazy portfolios" reflecting the optimizer's sensitivity to those inputs. "As the portfolio reflecting our economists' views didn't make sense," he figured, "I should follow Fischer's suggestion and shrink the assumptions toward the equilibrium situation in which all the expected returns are proportionate to the assets' covariance with the market. Then, I can then take an average of the equilibrium assumptions and the economists' views." It sounds easy, but Litterman's first attempt, in which he took a linear combination of the two inputs, still failed to make sense unless the investor put almost all the weight on Fischer's side—on the equilibrium inputs. Even after that adjustment, the deviations from the market portfolio failed to make sense.

Litterman was not ready to give up. He drew on another key insight to combine the two sources of information—equilibrium and the economists' views—by using a Bayesian approach to combining new information with information already in place.[*] This Bayesian analysis

---

[*] For an explanation of Bayesian analysis, see *Against the Gods: The Remarkable Story of Risk,* pp. 129–133.

takes correlations into account. The approach he took makes use of the insight that two assets with similar behavior should have similar expected returns. Furthermore, the Bayesian approach provides a great deal of freedom, in that you do not have to provide assumptions for every asset, and you can quantify more or less confidence in different views. You can even provide views about combinations of assets.

"Wow, this works!" Litterman exclaimed to himself. In an unconstrained context, the optimizer now recommends an optimal portfolio holding some capital in the market portfolio and some in portfolios representing your views. Furthermore, if you have equilibrium as your center of gravity, you don't have to have a view on every single asset. When you do have a view on a single asset, the optimizer applies that view to an appropriate extent to every other asset correlated with it. That procedure prevents crazy portfolios. Now you can derive acceptable portfolios based on your confidence in your view and how much risk (size of positions) to allocate to your views. Now the optimizer is well-behaved! "No one trusted their optimizers," Litterman commented, "but we found out how to do that."

❖

Now it was no longer necessary to undertake the task of estimating the expected returns for each individual asset under consideration as input to the optimizer. Instead, the focus of attention shifted away from the individual assets to the portfolio as a whole. Litterman has described the new approach:

> The investor focuses on one or more views, each of which is an expectation of the return on a portfolio of his or her choosing. . . . We refer to each of these portfolios as a "view portfolio." [Then] the investor is asked to specify not only a return expectation for each of the view portfolios, but also a degree of confidence, which is a standard deviation around the expectation. . . . [Then] the optimal portfolio is a weighted combination of the market capitalization equilibrium portfolio and the view portfolios. . . . The sizes of the tilts toward the view portfolio are a function of both the magnitude and the confidence expressed in the expected returns embedded in the investor-specified views.[*7]

---

[*] The chapter that includes this paragraph provides useful examples of the Black-Litterman approach.

Black-Litterman has another interesting feature. The investor can still choose constraints to put into the optimizer. The most frequent constraint is long-only, with no short sales allowed. On the other hand, an unconstrained optimization will recommend going short on one or another of the asset classes included in the portfolios under consideration, depending on how each stacks up against the others.

Litterman looks at this remarkable combination of Black's attachment to equilibrium analysis and Goldman's attachment to active management and concludes: "This reformulation of the problem can be applied more generally . . . and has greatly facilitated the use of quantitative return forecasting models in asset management." With Black-Litterman, investors can relax constraints in the optimization process and still derive acceptable portfolios.

This approach to unshackling constraints has produced striking performance results and has led to an explosion in assets under management. Litterman takes pride in seeing the assets increase, but assets under management are not his primary objective. From his perspective, how many dollars you are creating from your strategies is a more important number than assets under management.

As a consequence of this exercise, Litterman and his associates recognized that equilibrium is not just something for academics. Indeed, the concept of equilibrium informs everything they do, even though Goldman's business is to create alpha, not beta: "If you want beta, go to Vanguard, BGI, or State Street," Litterman suggests. The introduction of Black-Litterman equilibrium into the search for alpha is simply one more view, not a step toward passive management. The Black-Litterman model's main contribution is to produce reasonable results from the optimizer without the distortions caused by overloading the optimizer with constraints.

"Now we have an alpha factory," Litterman declares, "but how do we sell the output? We used to distinguish ourselves by managing quantitatively driven low-risk stock portfolios. But the world has changed for us since the collapse of the tech bubble. The old stock pickers have come into our space." The answer was to dress their strategies in new clothes.

But how? Consider a conventional long-only portfolio with under-weights on holdings the investment manager does not like and over-weights on holdings the manager does like. Suppose this portfolio also has a 2 percent tracking error from its benchmark. If the client would accept a tracking error of 4 percent, the manager could double the weights of the favored holdings that already hold overweights. But what can the manager do about the underweights of the holdings that are out of favor? In cases where the positions are small, cutting those positions in half is meaningless. You quickly hit bottom and cannot obtain the kind of performance you seek.

The only choice is to combine the long portfolio with a portfolio of short positions. When the portfolio is structured to have a tracking error in the 4 percent to 5 percent area, Litterman found that a portfo-lio holding only 30 percent of its bets in short positions would be suffi-cient, perhaps going to 40 percent in a global context.

Another more dramatic departure from the usual long-only ap-proach comes to mind: *Eliminate the benchmark entirely, and become equally long and short.* In 2003, Goldman launched a market neutral product based on these principles. The strategy is a totally uncon-strained version of the Goldman active equity process: no beta con-cerns, and long/short. It is global, operates in all markets, and contains around 1,500 stocks. It uses leverage to achieve volatility as high as 8 percent to 10 percent with short positions as well as long positions—a combination that, without leverage, naturally produces low volatility because the investor is betting on stocks expected to go down as well as stocks expected to go up. For every $100 invested, the leverage means that Goldman buys and sells around $400 of equities.

Litterman is proud of this product. "It is unique, pure alpha, and high volatility—a great concept. It has had strong returns as well, and has grown quickly." One day in 2005, when the product had $4 billion in capital under management, Litterman was looking at a report showing the strategy both owned and had sold short about $15 billion in equities. He said to himself, "Jeez, we must be one of the biggest short-sellers in the market!" After a little checking around, he discovered that, although no individual position was particularly large, in total the firm was indeed one of the biggest short-sellers in the market.

The success of this fund leads Litterman to contrast its approach to what he sees in many other investment management firms: "One of the worst things about this industry is that people don't take risk the way they claim. They don't manage their risks. It's a crime. They don't pay attention, and they don't know what they are doing. They haven't lowered their fees, just the risks. We stay at 8 percent to 10 percent volatility by using leverage."

In expressing this impatience with what other investors do, Litterman is drawing on an important article he wrote in early 2004, "The Active Risk Puzzle: Implications for the Asset Management Industry."[8] He opens this article by setting forth what he means by the active risk puzzle. We know that active risk is uncorrelated with market risk—the market goes up or down whether or not your portfolio is doing better or worse. Trying to beat the market, in other words, adds very little to the portfolio's *overall* risk. "Then why do managers of pension fund portfolios make such small allocations to active risk?" Litterman asks. Many pension funds have an active risk allocation of between 50 and 200 basis points, which means that they will tolerate returns that differ from the benchmark returns within the low range of 0.5 percent and 2 percent. This low allocation to active risk is all the more puzzling when most pension funds have multiple managers whose returns are uncorrelated or have low coefficients of correlation. On the basis of the risk reduction provided by diversification alone, these funds could afford to have each individual manager take greater active risks.

Litterman believes this phenomenon is truly a puzzle; he speculates on what might explain it. Perhaps this narrow range of active risk must mean that the investment officers of these funds expect "only a tiny bit of positive value" from their managers. If this is the case, these officers must believe that markets are highly efficient. Even odder, they must believe that none of them has much ability to pick active managers who will outperform the averages. Most likely, the investment officers have an aversion to taking peer risk—if they take on higher-volatility positions, they run the risk of too much short-run underperformance in relation to their strategic benchmark at a time when other funds are enjoying better track records than theirs. But then why do they incur the costs of active management in the first place?

Even though the explanation for the active risk puzzle is probably a combination of behavioral motivations and agency conflicts, Litterman believes "It is unlikely to persist. . . . It is simply not optimal for all funds to take just a little bit of active risk." And he already sees signs of change, with some large endowments taking on more active risk and less market risk.

An important part of this change in attitude has developed as a result of the growing popularity of portable alpha, which allows active risk strategies without disturbing the underlying asset allocation of the policy portfolio. There are clear signs of a loosening in unnecessary restraints on active managers. In fact, the traditional stock-picking manager with a no-short constraint is gradually becoming obsolete, to be replaced either by low-risk enhanced index products or by high-risk long/short hedge funds. Unlike the traditional portfolio strategies, enhanced indexing and hedge fund strategies have improved the odds of earning alpha by identifying stocks expected to produce poor performance. The enhanced index fund can underweight such stocks and offset that underweight with stocks it likes, while the hedge funds can short-sell stocks they perceive as overvalued.

Litterman goes on to warn, however, that "the capital required to generate active risk is the ultimate constraint on alpha generation, rather than the level of active risk itself. . . . When there is a binding constraint on available capital, investment strategies should be judged on the basis of alpha per unit of capital. . . . Then borrowing to increase the availability of capital may be advantageous. . . . It is critically important to recognize [that] when the level of active risk is not an important [sic] constraint . . . optimal portfolio construction requires a completely different set of trade-offs."

The article concludes with an interesting prediction:

> The demand for alpha will drive the market toward greater efficiency. . . . As markets get more efficient, finding skill will become more difficult. And, since finding skill requires skill at the fund level and is a zero-sum game, we believe Boards and CIOs will have to heighten their focus on developing a sustainable skill advantage over their peers, or default to an indexing strategy at the lowest possible cost, thus solving the active risk puzzle. . . . The days of "investing with the pack" are numbered.

The success of the Black-Litterman approach has led to a brand new active management strategy for what Goldman calls "optimal tilt portfolios." The use of the word "tilt" usually refers to the difference in risk and return between the actual portfolios and their appropriate benchmarks, or, in a hedge fund setting, calculation of the optimal balance between long and short positions. These Black-Litterman optimal tilt portfolios are the optimizer's allocation of risk among the "view portfolios"—portfolios taking both long and short positions to express a view or a set of views about the future. They are portfolios you "intuitively like—they make sense," as Litterman describes them.

"At first," Litterman recalls, "when Fischer and I first came up with Black-Litterman, we thought in terms of economists' views, or one market versus another. But today we are more sophisticated about our views, for example, value versus growth or companies' earnings dominated by accruals versus companies with rich cash flows. We create portfolios to express those views. The optimal tilt portfolio is then an allocation of risk across all those view portfolios you would like to hold." An optimal tilt portfolio, in other words, is some combination of all the view portfolios.

But what determines the precise character of that combination? As the portfolios in question are all long/short, little or no capital is involved. The primary metric you are allocating, then, is risk, and the Sharpe Ratio is the most useful guide in that process. The Sharpe Ratio measures the ratio of return over the risk-free rate to the volatility of return.

That is the design. Execution is something else again. The optimal tilt portfolio makes money almost every month—on paper—but in the real world every portfolio has to incur costs to trade. "When you compare the paper portfolio to the returns on the actual portfolio, you come to respect how small and uncertain your realized alpha really is," Litterman pointed out.

Nevertheless, the procedure is flexible and permits the investor to generate all kinds of portfolios—high-risk or low-risk and with or without constraints. "We run an alpha factory here," Litterman describes it. "On any given day we have one set of views, represented by the optimal tilt portfolio, but lots of different optimal actual portfolios. These portfolios are all optimal, but differ for a variety of reasons—they may have different benchmarks, different constraints, different active risk levels, and even if all these characteristics are the same, they will differ because they have a different size or may have been invested for different lengths of time and transactions costs matter a lot."

◧

The devil is always in the details, and Goldman Sachs runs devilishly complex strategies. That very fact is the consequence of Goldman Sachs's simple philosophical approach to portfolio management. The competition out there is fierce. It is becoming increasingly fierce with the passage of time. Fischer Black may have admitted that, "The market appears a lot more efficient on the banks of the Charles River than it does on the banks of the Hudson" when he first joined up, but the market even in 1984 was tough to beat, and it is even closer to genuine efficiency now. Equilibrium is a powerful and pervasive force in our markets and, increasingly, in markets all around the world.

If that is the case, as Litterman believes so strongly, Capital Ideas and the notion of equilibrium compose the foundation on which investors must build their strategies. All four elements of Capital Ideas focus on risk management—mean/variance, the Capital Asset Pricing Model, the efficient market (including the work of Modigliani-Miller), and the theory of options pricing. While active portfolio managers will seek alpha as urgently as they can, they cannot control the results. The whole process of implementing investment strategies, therefore, must focus on risk management. Here is where our skills really matter.

Echoing Myron Scholes, Goldman Sachs identifies risks it can manage and avoids or hedges all other risks. The results have been impressive to observe.

PART IV
CAPITAL IDEAS
TOMORROW

16

Nothing Stands Still

W hen I was drafting the original edition of *Capital Ideas,* I wanted the book to include some practical applications to make these theories credible to the wider audience I hoped to reach. That was no simple task. Much of the theory was unpalatable to an investing world where people saw no hurdle in beating the market and were focused on making money. Risk was an incidental matter.

After a good deal of scrounging around, I could come up with only three worthwhile examples of putting theory into practice—Wells Fargo Investment Advisors and its lonely effort to develop marketable products like indexing and tactical asset allocation; Barr Rosenberg's stimulating and influential seminars on what Capital Ideas were all about; and Hayne Leland and Mark Rubinstein's "ultimate invention," portfolio insurance, an operational version of Merton's replicating portfolio for a put option on the market. There was nothing else I could find at that moment.

Risk management was at the heart of all three of these applications. But risk management has always been at the heart of the theory of finance. *Nothing more deeply divides us from the world before 1952 than the belated recognition of risk as the dominant element in portfolio management.* This delay in understanding the role of risk unquestionably explains why practical applications of Capital Ideas were so hard to find fifteen to twenty years ago.

As the years have passed, the subject matter of finance has been turned on its head. There are no new theories of finance to match Markowitz's paradigm for portfolio selection, Modigliani and Miller's insights into corporate finance, the Efficient Market Hypothesis, the Capital Asset Pricing Model, and options pricing theory. But implementation of these ideas rushes ahead at a breathtaking pace, driven and shaped by theory and, in turn, reshaping many aspects of theory.

Barclays Global Investors employs variations on the theme of indexing to provide new insights into what market efficiency is all about. David Swensen at Yale employs a radical structure of asset allocation to illuminate the immense importance of Markowitz's device of mean/variance optimization. Bill Gross and Marvin Damsma detach alpha from beta and shed entirely new light on the operational possibilities of CAPM. Goldman Sachs finds novel insights in Fischer Black's vision of equilibrium while blending it with its views of active strategies. And these are just a few examples among thousands.

Nothing stands still. New players, new institutions, and new financial instruments are leading to new strategies for risk management, new paths for seeking alpha, new markets around the world—and new variations on the structure of theory. Bold experimentation and revolutionary technologies are commonplace. That is the main theme of this book. The ideas will remain at the center, but the structure around them is dynamic and unstable, characterized by an unremitting process of Darwinian evolution. As I quoted Robert Merton earlier, "We have a whole new paradigm. No, a *richer* paradigm. The answers given by Capital Ideas are still valid—it's not like they got it wrong and now we have a revolution. My point is understanding institutions and how they make implementation of these ideas possible."

Evolution has a quality of inevitability—species will change and develop as a result of forces beyond their control. But humans are a separate set among species. Unlike the development of natural phenomena, the development of human institutions is contingent on the goals or purposes that motivated their establishment in the first place. Many institutions are not somebody's brainstorm making an instantaneous appearance on the scene. Rather, institutions are a result of trial and error, where perfection is impossible but something less than perfect can often suffice. Institutions change as a result of purposeful decisions by human beings who make use of them, but the pattern of change is in response to the forces of evolution.

I can think of no reason for this process to come to a halt. In view of how much time has passed and how much financial innovation has boomed since *Capital Ideas* appeared in 1992, the amazing vitality of the daring theoretical concepts of these ideas is there for all to see. The possibilities of their uses in implementation appear to be limitless. As every chapter of this story has demonstrated, Capital Ideas have been motivating the institutional environment, defining the structure of financial markets and investment strategies, establishing the benchmarks, and opening new economic and financial panoramas for putting markets to new uses.

These developments ramify well beyond the markets for stocks, bonds, and derivatives. They also reflect the profound difference between finance, the subject matter of these pages, and its older and more prestigious sibling, the broad field of economics. The world of economics may have been surprised when Harry Markowitz, Bill Sharpe, and Merton Miller received their Nobel Prizes in Economic Sciences in 1990 "for their pioneering work in the theory of financial economics," but in fact it was high time for finance to receive full recognition on a par with the broader field of economics.*

Economics itself has come a long way in recent years in the range and depth of the problems for which it is seeking solutions. But empirical tests of economic theory are difficult to develop and inherently controversial in nature. The available data are almost all estimates rather than hard numbers, and more recent data are subject to repeated revisions. Economists can devise ingenious policy recommendations based on economic theory, but how can they ascertain ahead of time that their ideas will work when applied in practice? The history of economic policy is checkered, to say the least. In microeconomics, too, there are problems in connecting the models to the ever-changing variety of business forms. And all too often the soft social sciences like politics and sociology intervene and curl back the hard edges of economic hypotheses.

---

*Franco Modigliani, Miller's associate in developing the theory of corporate finance, had received the Nobel Prize in Economic Sciences in 1985 for his "pioneering analyses of saving and financial markets."

Finance has the enormous advantage of a colossal data bank of real-time numbers extending back over a period of about 200 years, not subject to revision, and available in greater detail and accuracy since 1925. Those numbers reflect fortunes made and lost, along with hopes and despair, but those numbers are also critical variables in the economy as a whole. As Federal Reserve Governor Frederic Mishkin has put it, "Think of the financial system as the brain of the economy. That is, it acts as a coordinating mechanism that allocates capital, the lifeblood of economic activity, to its most productive uses by businesses and households. If capital goes to the wrong uses or does not flow at all, the economy will operate inefficiently, and ultimately economic growth will be low."[1] The data of financial markets reveal, for better or for worse, "the brain of the economy" and "the lifeblood of economic activity."

This extraordinary data bank was the key mechanism that revealed the fundamental character of financial markets as early as 1900 to Louis Bachelier, little-known but surely among the most powerful of finance theorists (see *Capital Ideas,* pp. 18–23), and later to all to the creators of Capital Ideas. Much more was to follow.[*]

Although time had to pass before practitioners could persuade themselves to accept the implications of theory, the data bank became the stepping-stone to implementation, from the first index fund at Wells Fargo Investment Advisors in 1971 to the diverse activities of today's practitioners described in this book. Once understood—and tested against real-time data—the theories of finance motivated the flood of innovations in financial practice and strategies.

※

Merton, Lo, and Shiller are employing the elements of Capital Ideas to design new institutional structures and financial instruments to improve the risk/return trade-off for individual investors. Markowitz and Sharpe are opening fresh areas of study on the nature of risk, while Scholes deploys his skills at the heart of the markets where risk transfers occur. On the firing line of active management, intense competition

---

[*] Bachelier, in his seminal work, *Theory of Speculation,* first recognized the inherently random character of changes in stock prices, a notion that led to the development of the Efficient Market Hypothesis in the 1960s.

combined with increased sophistication is leading to radical innovations in portfolio strategies, risk management, and the costs of transacting. In the unlikely possibility that the source of new ideas might dry up, the researchers in Behavioral Finance are hard at work to provide what appears to be a never-ending supply of signposts to new sources of alpha and new strategies reaching for higher returns and lower levels of risk.

These developments are by no means limited to institutional investors in the United States. The Dutch pension giant, Stichting Pensionfonds PGGM, with assets of about $100 billion, has completely revised its internal investment process toward an emphasis on alpha and beta. By this means, according to the chief investment officer, Leo Lueb, the fund "can now more effectively manage its risk budget and focus more resources on finding sustainable investment returns." ATP, the big Danish pension fund worth nearly $60 billion moved in the same direction in 2005, explicitly to improve risk management and diversification.[2]

Under these circumstances, it is easy to predict that markets and investment strategies five to ten years from now will differ in many ways from what has already taken place. Such a forecast has little value, however, because it provides us with no sense of direction. How will we get from here to there? We may not know where the road will lead, but at least we must identify its most visible signposts.

As of late 2006, two forces appear to dominate the path to future outcomes: globalization, and capital markets that are increasingly efficient and hard to beat. We shall examine each of these developments in turn.

Globalization is an overused word. But globalization in this context means more than just the flow of capital and trade between the old world and the emerging world, although no one can underestimate the importance of those developments. As Federal Reserve Governor Randall Kroszner has put it, globalization "[shrinks] the barriers between time and distance."[3] No wonder, then, that globalization is also the cutting edge in the evolution of markets.

In *Capital Ideas*, I referred to America's financial markets as "dazzling creations." Without in any way diminishing the validity of that observation, markets in other nations are catching up to us at a pace we must also call dazzling. These markets are now in hot pursuit of our depth, breadth, liquidity, and the variety of instruments traded.

These developments have been increasingly apparent since the Asian nations were able to free themselves from the financial crisis of 1997–1998. From the end of 1998 through September 2006, world stock market capitalization rose by 68 percent, as measured in dollars by Morgan Stanley Capital International (MSCI). The world market ex-United States, however, increased by 79 percent while the United States trailed at 57 percent. The difference in performance becomes even more dramatic if we exclude the ten largest markets, not just the United States Markets in the rest of the world have increased in size by 108 percent since the end of 1998.

The outperformance of foreign markets has become even more visible with the passage of time. From the end of 2002—very near the bottom after the crash of 2000—through September 2006, the United States was up 58 percent while the rest of the world scored a rise of 128 percent. Only three of fifty-four markets in this universe trailed the United States over this period. The result has been a shrinkage of the United States market share of world markets from 54 percent at the end of 2002 to only 45 percent in September 2006.*

This result reflects more than the extraordinary growth in smaller markets among the emerging economies. Yes, there were plenty of whopping triple-digit percentage increases among these markets, but even the largest markets outperformed the United States, and by a lot: The next five largest markets after the United States in 2002—the U.K., Japan, France, Switzerland, and Germany—outperformed the U.S. stock market by an average of 57 percentage points.

No one can forecast how markets abroad will perform relative to the U.S. markets in the future. Nevertheless, there is evidence to suggest that recent trends may have developed self-reinforcing characteristics favoring a further shrinkage in the U.S. share of world equity markets over the years ahead.

In the past, the U.S. equity markets have dominated the business of global public offerings.† With the rapid development shown by international markets in recent years, that is no longer the case. Twenty-seven

---

*In dollar terms, the total world equity market portfolio as of September 2006 was at the staggering sum of $26.7 trillion, of which the U.S. accounted for $12.1 trillion and the rest of the world came to $14.6 trillion.

† A global IPO is the first time shares are offered on any exchange worldwide.

of the top thirty new global public offerings in 2005 were issued in markets outside the United States The three domestic offerings came to only $5 billion out of a worldwide total of $60 billion. Twenty-four of the thirty top global offerings during the first three quarters of 2006 were issued abroad, amounting to a total of $67 billion versus $7 billion for the U.S. issues. Part of the shift to foreign issuance may be accounted for by efforts to bypass increasingly strict U.S. securities regulation, notably Sarbanes-Oxley, but that volume of business would not shift to other markets unless those markets were equipped to handle so large a share of this volume.[4]

All that was just the beginning. In late October 2006, the world's largest offering ever—$16 billion—was issued on the Hong Kong Exchange for China's biggest bank, Industrial and Commercial Bank of China. The bank simultaneously raised $6 billion on the Shanghai market.

Similar trends have been at work in the issuance of corporate debt. Through 2003, the U.S. markets consistently accounted for over 50 percent of worldwide corporate debt issuance, while Europe accounted for less than 40 percent. These relationships began to reverse in 2004. In 2005 and in 2006 (through October), Europe's share of corporate debt issuance was up over 45 percent while the U.S. share had dropped to about 43 percent.[5]

The drive toward ever-greater market efficiency has become as relentless and as powerful as globalization in its impact on markets. Steve Ross's active sharks swirl through the market waves, gobbling up every delicious shred of alpha to be found. The active managers cited in this book—Yale, Pimco, Marvin Damsma, BGI, Goldman Sachs—are responsible for huge sums of assets, and all of them are sharks at heart. They know better than most what the pressures are. They compete every day against the crowds of managers devising portable alpha strategies, wading deep in the derivatives markets, and studying the latest research reports from Behavioral Finance. Thanks to the rapid growth of the hedge fund business, and variations on the theme like 120 percent long/20 percent short, short-selling is now destined to increase market efficiency by providing more effective means of betting against what appear to be overvalued assets.

Innovative strategies are only part of the story. Technology is constantly changing the process of buying and selling in the markets, with a rising proportion of transactions bypassing traditional markets and sailing through computers directly from buyer to seller. The lower the transactions costs, the greater the variety of strategies managers can implement, and the more intense the drive toward market efficiency becomes.

Blake Grossman at BGI says, "The markets are very efficient, very dynamic, constantly reaching greater levels of efficiency that makes them more and more difficult to beat. The half-lives of our strategies [are] shrinking." David Swensen at Yale acknowledges his "huge respect for efficient markets." Bob Litterman at Goldman Sachs asserts that "I am not worried that markets are fully efficient—yet. But they are becoming more efficient all the time, and fast. The world is going quant, and there are no secrets! Alpha is in limited supply and hard to find." Myron Sholes has a similar view: "We are one group among myriad teams making markets more efficient by compressing time."

Moreover, portable alpha strategies are focused more on generating excess returns than the old-fashioned method of hoping for alpha from a manager whose primary mission is to produce a beta, or asset class, rate of return.

Carried to an extreme, this process could provide the seeds of its own destruction, or, as Steve Ross sees it, "I think of this as a sort of Heisenberg Principle of Finance: Observing an anomaly brings about its extinction."[*] Every form of alpha pursued by sharks with insatiable appetites has a short half-life. Why should the markets not reach a point where the sharks have consumed everything in sight? Then we would end up with a fully efficient market where the trade-off between risk and return is precisely aligned. We would have attained Fischer Black's nirvana of equilibrium.

---

[*] Ross is referring to the Heisenberg Uncertainty Principle: "The more precisely the position is determined, the less precisely the momentum is known in this instant, and vice versa" (Heisenberg, 1927).

There are those who believe we could actually come close to that state. On November 14, 2005, Henry Blodget, famous as well as infamous senior Internet analyst for Merrill Lynch during the dot-com bubble of the 1990s, had this to say in his Internet blog, *The Internet Outsider:*

> Here's the most interesting and, probably, annoying part—I believe the best investment strategy for most investors is not to buy and sell stocks at all, but simply to allocate assets to low-cost passive funds. I didn't use to believe this. When I worked on Wall Street, it seemed absurd to think that the massive amount of energy, brainpower, and money expended on buying 'good' stocks and selling 'bad' ones was usually wasted (or worse). In the years since leaving the business, however, I have examined the evidence, and I have been startled and disappointed to realize how conclusive it is.

Despite Blodget's high degree of conviction, and even at the extreme, this outcome has the lowest probability of all. Jack Treynor put the matter well when he observed that "As soon as you assume that everyone has the same information, you've assumed away most of the trading problems, which arise because people think they know something that other people don't know."[6]

Let us consider what would happen if the markets did one day reach full equilibrium because all alpha opportunities were exhausted by ravenous sharks and everyone drifted into index funds. As Treynor points out, no one would have any incentive to trade. Asset prices would remain unchanged. If that moment were to arrive, however, the world beyond the markets would not be sitting poised at equilibrium: The world beyond the markets is *always* in a state of change and disequilibrium.

The bizarre result of static markets in a dynamic world is obvious: If the fundamentals are shifting while asset prices are constant, thousands of trading opportunities would open up. The sharks, sensing a meal of unlimited abundance, would swarm back into the markets as fast as they could travel. The markets would instantly come back alive, and the scene would be much as it is today, except that form and function probably would have developed in new directions during that momentary spell of quiet as brand new feeding opportunities would now open up.

The miraculous vitality of markets is impossible to suppress, as even communist countries have learned. But the great theories of Capital Ideas have nurtured and guided the development of today's markets to a much greater extent than most of the participants in these markets stop to realize. In the most vivid manner, Adam Smith's Invisible Hand is always in play, while Joseph Schumpeter's "perennial gale of creative destruction" blows compellingly, to a point where, as Schumpeter also reminds us, "Profit . . . is temporary by nature: it will vanish in the subsequent process of competition and adaptation."[7]

Here is what the evolution of Capital Ideas is all about.

Notes

PREFACE

1. Kim, Morse, and Zingales (2006).
2. Burton (1998).
3. MacKenzie (2006), p. 58.
4. Samuelson (2004).
5. Von Neumann and Morgenstern (1944), p. 9.
6. MacKenzie (2006), p. 42.
7. Warsh (2006), p. 376.
8. Smithson and Simkins (2005).
9. MacKenzie (2006), p. 259.

CHAPTER 1   WHO COULD DESIGN A BRAIN . . .

1. Tversky and Kahneman (1992).
2. http://nobelprize.org/economics/laureates/2002 for Kahneman's autobiography and Nobel address.
3. Ibid.
4. Kahneman (2002).
5. Thaler and Johnson (1990).
6. Benartzi and Thaler (2001).
7. Rosenberg (2005–2006).
8. Kahneman (2003).
9. Odean and Barber (2000).
10. Goyal and Warhof (2005).
11. Kahneman, Slovic, and Tversky (1982).
12. Thaler (1991, 1992).
13. Simon (1957).
14. Fuller & Thaler, Quarterly Update for third quarter of 2006.

CHAPTER 2   THE STRANGE PARADOX OF BEHAVIORAL FINANCE

1. Black (1986).
2. Rau, Dimitrov, and Cooper (2001).
3. Malkiel (2005a).
4. Malkiel (2005b).
5. Kosowski et al. (2006), p. 2551. (Emphasis in the original.)
6. Ibid., p. 2552.
7. Harlow and Brown (2006), p. 15.
8. Ibid., p. 17.
9. Chan, Getmansky, Haas, and Lo (2005) and Lo (2005).
10. Ross (2001). See also Ross (1976) and Roll and Ross (1984).
11. Shleifer and Vishny (1997).
12. Rashes (2001).
13. Modigliani and Cohn (1979).
14. Temin and Voth (2003).
15. Brunnermeier and Nagel (2003).
16. MacKenzie (2006), p. 367.
17. Fama (1998).
18. *Pensions & Investments,* November 27, 2006.
19. Rosenberg (2005–2006).
20. Grossman (1976).

CHAPTER 3   PAUL A. SAMUELSON

1. Samuelson (1974a).
2. Shiller (2006).
3. Samuelson (1937).
4. Samuelson (2004).
5. Samuelson (1974b).
6. Markowitz (1952); see also Markowitz (1959).

CHAPTER 4   ROBERT C. MERTON

1. Kahneman et al. (2005).
2. Merton (1975).
3. Merton and Bodie (2005).
4. Ibid.
5. Hakansson (1979).
6. Plexus News (2005).
7. Merton and Bodie (2005).

8. *Oxford Analytical Daily Brief* (March 2005).
9. Barber, Lee, Liu, and Odean (2006).
10. Kahneman et al. (2005).

CHAPTER 5   ANDREW LO

1. See Farrell (2006).
2. See *Against the Gods,* p. 118 ff., for the source and for more discussion of this passage.

CHAPTER 6   ROBERT SHILLER

1. Shiller (1999).
2. Fama (1965).
3. Shiller (2001), p. 254.
4. Campbell and Shiller (1998).
5. The citation is in *Irrational Exuberance,* 2nd ed. (2001), p. 243.
6. Jung and Shiller (2005).
7. Ibid., p. 222.
8. Ibid., pp. 222–223.
9. Ibid., p. 223.
10. MacKenzie (2006), pp. 332–333.
11. Shiller (1981).
12. Shiller (2003).
13. Shiller (1989), p. 433.
14. Ibid., p. 433.

CHAPTER 7   BILL SHARPE

1. Kahneman et al. (2005).
2. Ibid.

CHAPTER 8   HARRY MARKOWITZ

1. Kahneman et al. (2005).
2. Jacobs, Levy, and Markowitz (2004).
3. Kahneman et al. (2005).
4. Markowitz (2005).
5. Clarke, de Silva, and Thorley (2006).
6. Calio (2005).
7. De Finetti (1940).

CHAPTER 9   MYRON SCHOLES

1. Grossman (1990).

CHAPTER 10   BARCLAYS GLOBAL INVESTORS

1. *Pensions & Investments,* September 20, 2006, p. 20.
2. *Alpha Magazine,* Institutional Investor, July 2006.
3. *Institutional Investor,* August 1987, p. 137.
4. Grauer (2006).
5. Grinold and Kahn (2000), p. 6.
6. Ibid., p. 6.
7. Ibid., p. 6.
8. Ibid., pp. 5–6.
9. Ibid., p. 6.
10. See Roll and Ross (1980) and Fama and French (1995).

CHAPTER 11   THE YALE ENDOWMENT FUND

1. "Investment Fund Management," Report to Yale University (July 1966), p. 75, quoted in Mehrling (2005), p. 59.
2. See Swensen (2000), p. 104.
3. TIFF, Commentary (Fall 2005), p. 2.
4. See Swensen (2005).

CHAPTER 12   CAPM II: THE GREAT ALPHA DREAM MACHINE

1. Fama and French (2004).
2. Mehta (2006).
3. Treynor (1961).
4. Perold (2004).
5. Fama and French (1995, 2005).
6. Mehta (2006).
7. Anderson and Smith (2006).
8. Campbell, Hilscher, and Szilagyi (2006).
9. Burton (1998).
10. Ineichen (2006).
11. Treynor and Black (1973).
12. Mehta (2006).
13. Schwarz, Hill, and Schneeweis (1986).
14. Damsma and Williamson (1996).
15. Anson (2005).

CHAPTER 13   MAKING ALPHA PORTABLE

1. Middleton (2004).
2. Jones (2006).
3. Dimson and Marsh (1982).

CHAPTER 14   MARTIN LEIBOWITZ

1. Leibowitz (1992).
2. Homer and Leibowitz (1972, 2004).
3. Leibowitz and Bova (2005b).
4. Leibowitz (2005).
5. Leibowitz and Bova (2005b).
6. Ibid.

CHAPTER 15   GOLDMAN SACHS ASSET MANAGEMENT

1. Black (1988). See also Mehrling (2005), pp. 274–265.
2. Mehrling (2005).
3. Black and Litterman (1992).
4. Gottlieb (2003).
5. Grantham (2006).
6. Black (1989).
7. Litterman (2003).
8. Litterman (2004).

CHAPTER 16   NOTHING STANDS STILL

1. Mishkin (2006).
2. *Pensions & Investments,* October 16, 2006, p. 2.
3. Kroszner (2006).
4. Data supplied by Dialogic.com.
5. Thomson Financial.
6. Mehta (2006).
7. Schumpeter (1942), p. 84, and Schumpeter (1939), p. 105.

Bibliography

Anderson, Jeff, and Gary Smith, 2006. "A Great Company Can Be a Great Investment," *Financial Analysts Journal,* July/August, pp. 86–94.

Anson, Mark, 2005. "Institutional Portfolio Management," *The Journal of Portfolio Management,* Summer, pp. 33–43.

Barber, Brad M., Yi-Tsung Lee, Yu-Jane Liu, and Terrance Odean, 2006. "Just How Much Do Individual Investors Lose by Trading?" American Finance Association Annual Meetings.

Benartzi, Shlomo, and Richard Thaler, 2001. "Naive Diversification Strategies in Retirement Savings Plans," *American Economic Review,* Vol. 91, No. 57, pp. 1593–1616.

Bernstein, Peter, 1992. *Capital Ideas: The Remarkable Origins of Modern Wall Street,* New York: Free Press.

Bernstein, Peter, 1996. *Against the Gods: The Remarkable Story of Risk,* New York: John Wiley & Sons.

Black, Fischer, 1986. "Noise," *Journal of Finance,* Vol. 41 (July), pp. 529–545.

Black, Fischer, 1988. "Unobservables," Fischer Black papers, Box 25.

Black, Fischer, 1989. "Universal Hedging: Optimizing Currency Risk and Reward in International Equity Portfolios," *Financial Analysts Journal,* July/August, pp. 16–22.

Black, Fischer, and Robert Litterman, 1992. "Global Portfolio Optimization," *Financial Analysts Journal,* September/October, pp. 28–43.

Brock, Horace, 2006a. "Reconceptualizing 'Market Risk' from Scratch," New York: Strategic Economic Decisions.

Brock, H. W., 2006b. "The Logical Justification for 'Active' Investment Management" in *Thoughts on the Bottom Line,* Barclay Douglas, ed., New York: John Wiley & Sons.

Brunnermeier, Markus, and Stefan Nagel, 2003. "Hedge Funds and the Technology Bubble," *Journal of Finance,* Vol. 59, No 5 (October), pp. 2013–2040.

Burton, Jonathan, 1998. "Revisiting the Capital Asset Pricing Model," *Dow Jones Asset Manager,* May/June.

Calio, Vince, 2005. "Operational Risk Back in Spotlight," *Pensions & Investments,* October 4.

Campbell, John, 2006. "Household Finance," *Journal of Finance,* Vol. 61, No. 4 (August), pp. 1553–1604.

Campbell, John, Jens Hilscher, and Jan Szilagyi, 2006. "In Search of Distress Risk," National Bureau of Economic Research, Working Paper No. 12362.

Campbell, John, and Robert Shiller, 1998. "Valuation Ratios and the Long-Run Stock Market Outlook," *The Journal of Portfolio Management,* Vol. 24, No. 2 (Winter).

Chan, Nicholas, Mila Getmansky, Shane Haas, and Andrew Lo, 2006. "Do Hedge Funds Increase Systemic Risk?" *Economic Review,* Federal Reserve Bank of Atlanta (Fourth Quarter).

Clarke, Roger, Harindra de Silva, and Steven Thorley, 2006. "Minimum-Variance Portfolios in the U.S. Equity Market," *The Journal of Portfolio Management,* Vol. 33, No. 1 (Fall), pp. 10–24.

Cohen, Jonathan, 2005. "The Vulcanization of the Human Brain: A Neural Perspective on Interactions Between Cognition and Emotion," *Journal of Economic Perspectives,* Vol. 19, No. 1 (Fall), pp. 3–24.

Damsma, Marvin, and Gregory Williamson, 1996. "Managing Risk in the Aggregate Portfolio: The Rewards of Portable Alpha," in *Alpha—The Positive Side of Risk: Daring to Be Different,* New York: Investors Press.

De Long, J. Bradford, Andrei Shleifer, Lawrence Summers, and Robert Waldmann, 1991. "The Survival of Noise Traders in Financial Markets," *Journal of Business,* Vol. 64, No. 1 (January), pp. 1–19.

De Finetti, Bruno, 1940. "Il Problema dei *«pieni»*" ["The Problem of 'Full-Risk Insurances'"], *Giornale dell'Istituto Italiano degli Attuari,* Vol. 11, No. 1, pp. 1–88.

Dimson, Elroy, and Paul Marsh, 1982. "Calculating the Cost of Capital," *Long Range Planning,* Vol. 15, No. 2, pp. 112–120.

Fama, Eugene, 1965. "The Behavior of Stock Prices," *Journal of Business,* Vol. 37, No. 1 (January), pp. 34–105.

Fama, Eugene, 1998. "Market Efficiency, Long-Term Returns, and Behavioral Finance," *Journal of Financial Economics,* Vol. 49, pp. 283–306.

Fama, Eugene, and Kenneth French, 1992. "The Cross Section of Expected Stock Returns," *Journal of Finance,* Vol. 47, No. 2 (June), pp. 427–465.

Fama, Eugene, and Kenneth French, 1995. "Size and Book to Market Factors in Earnings and Returns," *Journal of Finance,* Vol. 50, No. 1 (March), pp. 131–155.

Fama, Eugene, and Kenneth French, 2004. "The Capital Asset Pricing Model: Theory and Evidence," *Journal of Economic Perspectives,* Vol. 18, No. 3 (September), pp. 25–46.

Fama, Eugene, and Kenneth French, 2005. "The Value Premium and the CAPM," *Journal of Finance,* Vol. 61, No. 5 (October), pp. 2163–2184.

Farrell, Christopher, 2006. "Darwinian Investing," *Business Week,* February 20, p. 22.

Gabaix, Xavier, Arvind Krishnamurthy, and Olivier Vigneron, 2005. "Limits of Arbitrage: Theory and Evidence from the Mortgage-Backed Securities Market," National Bureau of Economic Research, Working Paper No. 11851.

Gottlieb, Jason, 2003. "Risk Management and Risk Budgeting at the Total Fund Level," in Bob Litterman and the Quantitative Resources Group of Goldman Sachs Asset Management, *Modern Investment Management: An Equilibrium Approach,* Hoboken, NJ: John Wiley & Sons, pp. 211–228.

Goyal, Amit, and Sumil Warhal, 2005. "The Selection and Termination of Investment Management Firms by Plan Sponsors," American Finance Association Annual Meeting, Boston.

Grantham, Jeremy, 2006. GMO Quarterly Letter (April).

Grauer, Fred, 2006. "Notes For 'Us Principals' Conference." Informal document.

Grinold, Richard, and Ronald Kahn, 2000. Active Portfolio Management: Quantitative Theory and Applications, New York: McGraw-Hill.

Grossman, Sanford, 1976. "On the Efficiency of Competitive Stock Markets Where Traders Have Informational Externalities," Journal of Finance, Vol. 32, pp. 573–585.

Grossman, Sanford, 1990. "Asset Allocation Strategies and the Risk Premium Phenomenon," in William F. Sharpe and Katrina F. Sherred, Eds., Quantifying the Market Risk Premium Phenomenon for Investment Decision Making, Charlottesville, VA: Institute of Chartered Financial Analysts.

Grossman, Sanford, and Joseph Stiglitz, 1980. "On the Impossibility of Informationally Efficient Markets," American Economic Review, Vol. 70, No. 3 (June), pp. 393–408.

Hakansson, Nils H., 1979. "The Fantastic World of Finance: Progress and the Free Lunch," Journal of Financial and Quantitative Analysis, Vol. 14, No. 4 (November), pp. 717–734.

Harlow, W. V., and Keith Brown, 2006. "The Right Answer to the Wrong Question: Identifying Superior Active Portfolio Management," Journal of Investment Management, Vol. 4, No. 4 (Fourth Quarter), pp. 15–40.

Heisenberg, Werner, 1927. "Ueber den anschaulichen Inhalt der quantentheoretischen Kinematik and Mechanik" ["On the anschaulich [intelligible or physical] content of quantum theoretical kinematics and mechanics"], Zeitschrift für Physik, Vol. 43, pp. 172–198.

Hill, Joanne, 2006. "Alpha as a Net Zero-Sum Game," The Journal of Portfolio Management, Vol. 32, No. 4 (Summer), pp. 24–32.

Homer, Sidney, and Martin Leibowitz, 1972. Inside the Yield Book: New Tools for Bond Market Strategy, Englewood Cliffs, NJ: Prentice-Hall and New York: New York Institute of Finance.

Homer, Sidney, and Martin Leibowitz, 2004. Inside the Yield Book: The Classic That Created the Science of Bond Analysis, Princeton, NJ: Bloomberg Press.

Ineichen, Alexander, 2006. Asymmetric Returns: The Future of Active Asset Management, Hoboken, NJ: John Wiley & Sons.

Jacobs, Bruce, Kenneth Levy, and Harry Markowitz, 2003. "Portfolio Optimization with Factors, Scenarios, and Realistic Short Positions," Operations Research, July/August.

Jacobs, Bruce, Kenneth Levy, and Harry Markowitz, 2004. "Financial Market Simulation," The Journal of Portfolio Management, 30th Anniversary Issue (September), pp. 142–152.

Jacobs, Bruce, Kenneth Levy, and Harry Markowitz, 2006. "Trimability and Fast Optimizations of Long-Short Portfolios," Financial Analysts Journal, March/April.

Jensen, Michael, 1965. "The Performance of Mutual Funds in the Period 1945–1964," *Journal of Finance,* Vol. 23 (December), pp. 587–616.

Jones, Bob, 2006. *Pensions & Investments,* April 3, p. 20.

Jung, Jeeman, and Robert Shiller, 2005. "Samuelson's Dictum and the Stock Market," *Economic Inquiry,* Vol. 43, No. 5, pp. 221–228.

Kahneman, Daniel, 2002. Autobiography and Nobel Address. Available at http://nobelprize.org/economics/laureates/2002.

Kahneman, Daniel, 2003. "Maps of Bounded Rationality: Psychology for Behavioral Economics," *American Economic Review,* Vol. 93, No. 5 (Fall), pp. 1449–1475.

Kahneman, Daniel, Harry Markowitz, Robert C. Merton, Myron Scholes, Bill Sharpe, and Peter Bernstein, 2005. "Most Nobel Minds," *CFA Magazine,* November-December, pp. 36–43.

Kahneman, Daniel, Paul Slovic, and Amos Tversky, 1974. "Judgment Under Uncertainty," *Science,* Vol. 185, pp. 1124–1131.

Kahneman, Daniel, Paul Slovic, and Amos Tversky, 1982. *Judgment Under Uncertainty: Heuristics and Biases,* New York: Cambridge University Press.

Kahneman, Daniel, and Tversky, Amos, 1979. "Prospect Theory," *Econometrica,* Vol. 47, No. 2 (March).

Kim, E. Han, Adair Morse, and Luigi Zingales, 2006. "What Has Mattered to Economics Since 1970?" *Journal of Economic Perspectives,* Vol. 20, No. 4 (Fall), pp. 189–202.

Kosowski, Robert, Allan Timmerman, Russ Wermers, and Hal White, 2006. "Can Mutual Fund 'Stars' Really Pick Stocks? New Evidence from a Bootstrap Analysis," *Journal of Finance,* Vol. 61, No. 6 (December).

Kritzman, Mark, and Lee Thomas, 2004. "Re-Engineering Investment Management," *The Journal of Portfolio Management,* 30th Anniversary Issue (September), pp. 70–79.

Kroszner, Randall, 2006. "The Conquest of Worldwide Inflation: Currency Competition and Its Implications for Interest Rates and the Yield Curve," Cato Monetary Policy Conference, November 16.

Kurz, Mordecai, 1994. "On the Structure and Diversity of Rational Beliefs," *Economic Theory,* Springer-Verlag, Vol. 4, pp. 877–900.

Kurz, Mordecai, ed., 1997. *Endogenous Economic Fluctuations: Studies in the Theory of Rational Beliefs,* Springer Series in Economic Theory, No. 6 (August), Springer-Verlag.

Kurz, Mordecai, M. Jin, and M. Motolese, 2005. "Determinants of Stock-Market Volatility and Risk Premia," *Annals of Finance,* Vol. I, pp. 109–147.

Lamont, Owen, and Jeremy Stein, 2006. "Investor Sentiment and Corporate Finance: Micro and Macro," *American Economic Review* (May), pp. 198–204.

Leibowitz, Martin, 1992. *Investing: The Collected Works of Martin L. Leibowitz,* Chicago: Probus Publishing Company.

Leibowitz, Martin, 2004. "The Beta-Plus Measure in Asset Allocation." *The Journal of Portfolio Management,* Vol. 30, No.3 (Spring), pp. 26–36.

Leibowitz, Martin, 2005. "Alpha Hunters and Beta Grazers," *Financial Analysts Journal,* September/October, pp. 32–39.

Leibowitz, Martin, and Anthony Bova, 2005a. "Allocation Betas," *Financial Analysts Journal,* September/October.

Leibowitz, Martin, and Anthony Bova, 2005b. "Beta-Based Asset Allocation: A Summary," Morgan Stanley, November 30.

Litterman, Bob, 2003. "Beyond Equilibrium: The Black-Litterman Approach," in Bob Litterman and the Quantitative Resources Group of Goldman Sachs Asset Management, *Modern Investment Management: An Equilibrium Approach,* Hoboken, NJ: John Wiley & Sons, pp. 76–88.

Litterman, Bob, 2004. "The Active Risk Puzzle: Implications for the Asset Management Industry," *The Journal of Portfolio Management,* September, pp. 88–93.

Lo, Andrew, 2004. "The Adaptive Market Hypothesis," *The Journal of Portfolio Management,* 30th Anniversary Issue (September), pp. 15–29.

Lo, Andrew, 2005. "Risk Management for Hedge Funds: Introduction and Overview," *Financial Analysts Journal,* November/December, pp. 16–33.

Lowenstein, Roger, 2000. *When Genius Failed: The Rise and Fall of Long-Term Capital Management,* New York: Random House.

MacKenzie, Donald, 2006. *An Engine, Not a Camera: How Financial Models Shape Markets,* Cambridge, MA: MIT Press.

MacKinlay, A. Craig, and Andrew Lo, 1999. *A Non-Random Walk Down Wall Street,* Princeton, NJ: Princeton University Press.

Malkiel, Burton, 1996. *A Random Walk Down Wall Street,* 6th Ed., New York: W. W. Norton.

Malkiel, Burton, 2005a. "Reflections on the Efficient Market Hypothesis: 30 Years Later," *Financial Review,* Vol. 40, No. 1 (February), pp. 1–9.

Malkiel, Burton, 2005b. "Market Efficiency Versus Behavioral Finance," *Journal of Applied Corporate Finance,* Vol. 17, No. 3 (Summer), p. 125.

Markowitz, Harry, 1952. "Portfolio Selection," *Journal of Finance,* Vol. 7, No. 1 (March), pp. 77–91.

Markowitz, Harry, 1959. *Portfolio Selection: Efficient Diversification of Investments,* New York: John Wiley & Sons.

Markowitz, Harry, 2005. "Market Efficiency: A Theoretical Distinction and So What?" *Financial Analysts Journal,* September/October, pp. 17–30.

Markowitz, Harry, 2006. "de Finetti Scoops Markowitz," *Journal of Investment Management,* Vol. 4, No. 3 (Third Quarter).

Markowitz, Harry, 2006. "Market Equilibrium in Non-CAPM World," A Group Presentation, October 16.

Mauboussin, Michael, 2006. "Interdisciplinary Perspectives on Risk," delivered to the Greenwich Round Table, July 28.

Mehrling, Perry, 2005. *Fischer Black and the Revolutionary Idea of Finance,* Hoboken, NJ: John Wiley & Sons.

Mehta, Nina, 2006. "Jack Treynor: The FEN One-on-One Interview," *Financial Engineering Notes.* Available at www.fenews.com/fen49/one_on_one/one_on_one.html.

Merton, Robert C., 1975. "Theory of Finance from the Perspective of Continuous Time," *Journal of Financial and Quantitative Analysis,* Vol. 10, No. 4 (November), pp. 659–674.

Merton, Robert C., and Zvi Bodie, 2005. "Design of Financial Systems: Toward a Synthesis of Form and Structure," *Journal of Investment Management,* Vol. 3, No. 1 (March), pp. 1–25.

Middleton, Timothy, 2004. *The Bond King: Investment Secrets from Pimco's Bill Gross,* Hoboken, NJ: John Wiley & Sons.

Mishkin, Frederic, 2006. "Globalization: A Force for Good?" Weissman Center Distinguished Lecture Series, Baruch College, New York, October 12.

Mitchell, Roger, 2005. "All Systems No," *CFA Magazine,* July/August, p. 24.

Modigliani, Franco, and Richard Cohn, 1979. "Inflation, Rational Valuation, and the Market," *Financial Analysts Journal,* Vol. 35 (March/April), pp. 24–44.

Odean, Terrance, and Brad Barber, 2000. "Trading Is Hazardous to Your Wealth: The Common Stock Investment Performance of Individual Investors," *Journal of Finance,* Vol. 55, No. 2 (April), pp. 773–806.

Perold, André, 2004. "The Capital Asset Pricing Model," *Journal of Economic Perspectives,* Vol. 18, No. 3 (September), pp. 3–24.

Plexus News, 2005. *Commentary 83* (March).

Prasch, Robert, 1992. "Review of *Capital Ideas,*" *Journal of Economic Issues,* Vol. XXVI, No. 4 (December), pp. 1313–1316.

Rashes, Michael, 2001. "Massively Confused Investors Making Conspicuously Ignorant Choices (MCI-MCIC)," *Journal of Finance,* Vol. 56, No. 5 (October), pp. 1911–1927.

Rau, P. Raghavendra, Orlin Dimitrov, and Michael Cooper, 2001. "A Rose.com By Any Other Name," *Journal of Finance,* Vol. 56, No. 6 (December), pp. 2372–2388.

Roll, Richard, and Stephen Ross, 1980. "An Empirical Investigation of the Arbitrage Pricing Theory," *Journal of Finance,* Vol. 35, No. 5 (December), pp. 1073–1103.

Roll, Richard, and Stephen Ross, 1984. "A Critical Reexamination of the Empirical Evidence on the Arbitrage Pricing Theory," *Journal of Finance,* Vol. 39, No. 2 (June), pp. 347–350.

Rosenberg, Barr, 2005–2006. "From Concept to Function: Converting Market Theories into Practical Investment Tools—A Discussion with Barr Rosenberg," *The Journal of Investment Consulting,* Vol. 7, No. 3 (Winter), pp. 10–20.

Ross, Stephen, 1976. "The Arbitrage Theory of Capital Asset Pricing," *Journal of Economic Theory,* Vol. 13, pp. 341–360.

Ross, Stephen, 2001. "Neoclassical Finance, Alternative Finance, and the Closed End Fund Puzzle," Keynote address, European Financial Management Association Annual Meeting.

Ross, Stephen, 2005. *Neoclassical Finance,* Princeton, NJ: Princeton University Press.

Rubinstein, Mark, 2006. "Bruno de Finetti and Mean-Variance Portfolio Selection," *Journal of Investment Management*, Vol. 4, No. 3 (September).

Samuelson, Paul A., 1937. "A Note on Measurement of Utility," *Review of Economic Studies*, Vol. 4, No. 2 (February), pp. 155–161.

Samuelson, Paul A., 1974a. "Challenge to Judgment," *The Journal of Portfolio Management*, Vol. 1, No. 1 (Fall), pp. 17–19.

Samuelson, Paul A., 1974b. "Introduction" to James Bicksler, *Investment Portfolio Decision-Making*, New York: Lexington Books/D. C. Heath & Co.

Samuelson, Paul A., 1998. "Summing up on Business Cycles: Opening Address," in Jeffrey Fuhrer and Scott Schub, *Beyond Shocks: What Causes Business Cycles*, Boston: Federal Reserve Bank of Boston.

Samuelson, Paul A., 2004. "The Backward Art of Investing Money," *The Journal of Portfolio Management*, 30th Anniversary Issue (September), pp. 30–33.

Schumpeter, Joseph, 1939. *Business Cycles*, New York: McGraw-Hill & Co.

Schumpeter, Joseph, 1942. *Capitalism, Socialism and Democracy*, New York: Harper & Row.

Schwarz, Eduardo, Joanne Hill, and Thomas Schneeweis, 1986. *Financial Futures: Fundamentals, Strategies, and Applications*, Homewood, IL: Irwin.

Sharpe, William, 1963. "A Simplified Model for Portfolio Analysis," *Management Science*, Vol. 9 (January), pp. 277–293.

Sharpe, William, 1964. "Capital Asset Prices: A Theory of Market Equilibrium under Conditions of Risk," *Journal of Finance*, Vol. 19, No. 3 (September), pp. 425–442.

Sharpe, William, 2006. *Investors and Markets: Portfolio Choices, Asset Prices and Investment Advice*, Princeton, NJ: Princeton University Press.

Shiller, Robert, 1981. "Do Stock Prices Move Too Much to Be Justified by Subsequent Changes in Dividends?" *American Economic Review*, Vol. 71, No. 3 (June), pp. 421–436.

Shiller, Robert, 1989. *Market Volatility*, Cambridge, MA: MIT Press.

Shiller, Robert, 1993. *Macro Markets: Creating Institutions for Managing Society's Largest Economic Risks*, New York: Oxford University Press.

Shiller, Robert, 1999. "Human Behavior and the Efficiency of the Financial System," in John B. Taylor and Michael Woodford, eds., *Handbook of Macroeconomics*, Elsevier Science Ltd.

Shiller, Robert, 2001. *Irrational Exuberance*, New York: Broadway Books. (Second Edition, Princeton, NJ: Princeton University Press.)

Shiller, Robert, 2003. "From Efficient Markets Theory to Behavioral Finance," *Journal of Economic Perspectives*, Vol. 17, No. 1 (Winter), pp. 83–104.

Shiller Robert, 2003. *The New Financial Order: Risk in the 21st Century*, Princeton, NJ: Princeton University Press.

Shiller, Robert, 2006. "Tools for Financial Innovation: Neoclassical versus Behavioral Finance," *Financial Review*, Vol. 41, No. 1 (February), pp. 1–8.

Shleifer, Andrei, and Robert Vishny, 1997. "The Limits of Arbitrage," *Journal of Finance*, Vol. 52, No. 1 (March), pp. 35–55.

Simon, Herbert, ed., 1957. "A Behavioral Model of Rational Choice," in *Models of Man: Social and Rational: Mathematical Essays on Rational Human Behavior in a Social Setting,* London: John Wiley & Sons.

Simon, Herbert, 1969. *The Sciences of the Artificial,* Cambridge, MA: MIT Press.

Smithson, Charles, and Betty Simkins, 2005. "Does Risk Management Add Value? A Survey of the Evidence," *Journal of Applied Corporate Finance,* Vol. 17, No. 3 (June), pp. 8–17.

Swensen, David, 2000. *Pioneering Investment Management: An Unconventional Approach to Institutional Investment,* New York: Free Press.

Swensen, David, 2005. *Unconventional Success: A Fundamental Approach to Personal Investment,* New York: Free Press.

Thaler, Richard, 1991. *Quasi Rational Economics,* New York: Russell Sage Foundation.

Thaler, Richard, 1992. *The Winner's Curse: Paradoxes and Homilies of Economic Life,* Princeton, NJ: Princeton University Press.

Thaler, Richard, and Eric Johnson, 1990. "Gambling with the House Money and Trying to Break Even: The Effects of Prior Outcomes on Risky Choice," *Management Science,* Vol. 36, No. 6 (June), pp. 643–660.

Thaler, Richard, Daniel Kahneman, and J. L. Knetsch, 1992. "The Endowment Effect, Loss Aversion and Status Quo Bias," in Richard Thaler, *The Winner's Curse,* Princeton, NJ: Princeton University Press.

Temin, Peter, and Hans-Joachim Voth, 2003. "Riding the South Sea Bubble," MIT Economics Department Working Paper No. 04-02 (December).

Treynor, Jack, 1961. "Toward a Theory of Market Value of Risky Assets." Unpublished manuscript.

Treynor, Jack, and Fischer Black, 1973. "How to Use Security Analysis to Improve Portfolio Selection," *Journal of Business,* Vol. 46, pp. 66–73.

Tversky, Amos, and Daniel Kahneman, 1992. "Advances in Prospect Theory: Cumulative Representation of Uncertainty," *Journal of Risk and Uncertainty,* Vol. 5, No. 4, pp. 297–323.

Von Neumann, John, and Oskar Morgenstern, 1944. *Theory of Games and Economic Behavior,* Princeton, NJ: Princeton University Press.

Warsh, David, 2006. *Knowledge and the Wealth of Nations: A Story of Economic Discovery,* New York: W. W. Norton.

Acknowledgments

The help of others makes every project of this kind a richer task and surely more fun than it would have been without such assistance. My gratitude is boundless for all whose names I mention here.

My first expression of thanks must go to the men whose ideas and whose accomplishments this book describes. They are the true protagonists of this story. In every case, they made themselves available to me for extended interviews and correspondence; they took the time to read and comment on what I had to say about them; and then they were available for questions that often reached beyond what our focus had been in earlier exchanges. Their generosity made the whole project possible.

I list them in alphabetical order, because it would be difficult to assign any kind of priority to their contributions: Marvin Damsma, Russ Fuller, Fred Grauer, Bill Gross, Blake Grossman, Jeff Hord, Ron Kahn, Daniel Kahneman, Martin Leibowitz, Bob Litterman, Andrew Lo, Harry Markowitz, Robert C. Merton, Steve Ross, Paul A. Samuelson, Myron Scholes, Bill Sharpe, Robert Shiller, Larry Siegel, David Swensen, Richard Thaler, and Jack Treynor.

Barbara Bernstein, my wife and business partner, was once again my essential colleague in the process of planning and writing this book. Long before I embarked on the task, she was rooting for it and explaining why I had to undertake it. It was her serendipitous idea to make this a whole new book rather than just an add-on to *Capital Ideas*. Throughout, her suggestions and criticisms have carried weight and have improved on my own efforts. If the story moves along, without interminable sentences or wasted words, she gets all the credit. In short, the whole thing never would have happened without her.

Over the years, many people have urged me to write a sequel to *Capital Ideas,* but something else more interesting always seemed to get in the way. Nari Yamaguchi, who had translated *Capital Ideas* into Japanese, was the catalyst who finally prodded me to pursue this project and turn it into a reality. His timing was perfect, his arguments irresistible.

André Perold read most of the manuscript in an early stage, while Ron Kahn read the entire manuscript at a later stage. André and Ron were a perfect combination for me. Their wise comments and criticisms were critically important throughout the process. Ron was also gracious about helping me to fill in gaps in the chapter about Barclays Global Investors.

Many others provided essential assistance along the way, including Rob Arnott, Anthony Bova, Jonathan Burton, Sabrina Callan, Jonathan Clements, Ember Dahlvig, Lara della Rocca, Gene Fama, Gifford Fong, Ken French, Will Goetzmann, Bruce Grundy, Joanne Hill, Alexander Ineichen, Paul Kaplan, Dwight Keating, Mark Kritzman, Burt Malkiel, Terri Mullan, Raghu Rau, Brian Singer, Rodney Sullivan, Tom Taggart, Timothy Weber, Mihir Woran, and Jason Zweig.

This book is the fifth occasion on which Peter Dougherty has worked with me as editor. In addition to our maiden voyage on *Capital Ideas,* we have joined to explore risk, gold, and the Erie Canal. This fifth expedition has been as exciting and rewarding as the first four. Although Peter recently became Director of the Princeton University Press, he was just as committed, enthusiastic, and rewarding a companion as ever. I doubt whether I could have reached the final destination without his unerring sense of direction and expansive view of the entire project.

I am happy that John Wiley continues as my publisher. Joan O'Neil, Vice President and Publisher at John Wiley, has been great to work with all the way through. Her expert knowledge and generous assistance helped us to get over many of the bumps the publishing process inevitably puts in the way of impatient authors. In addition, Mary Daniello's skilled assistance made a big difference in the final stages of the project.

P. L. B.

Index